MONSTER AND HORROR MOVIES

MONSTER AND HORROR MOVIES

Thomas G. Aylesworth

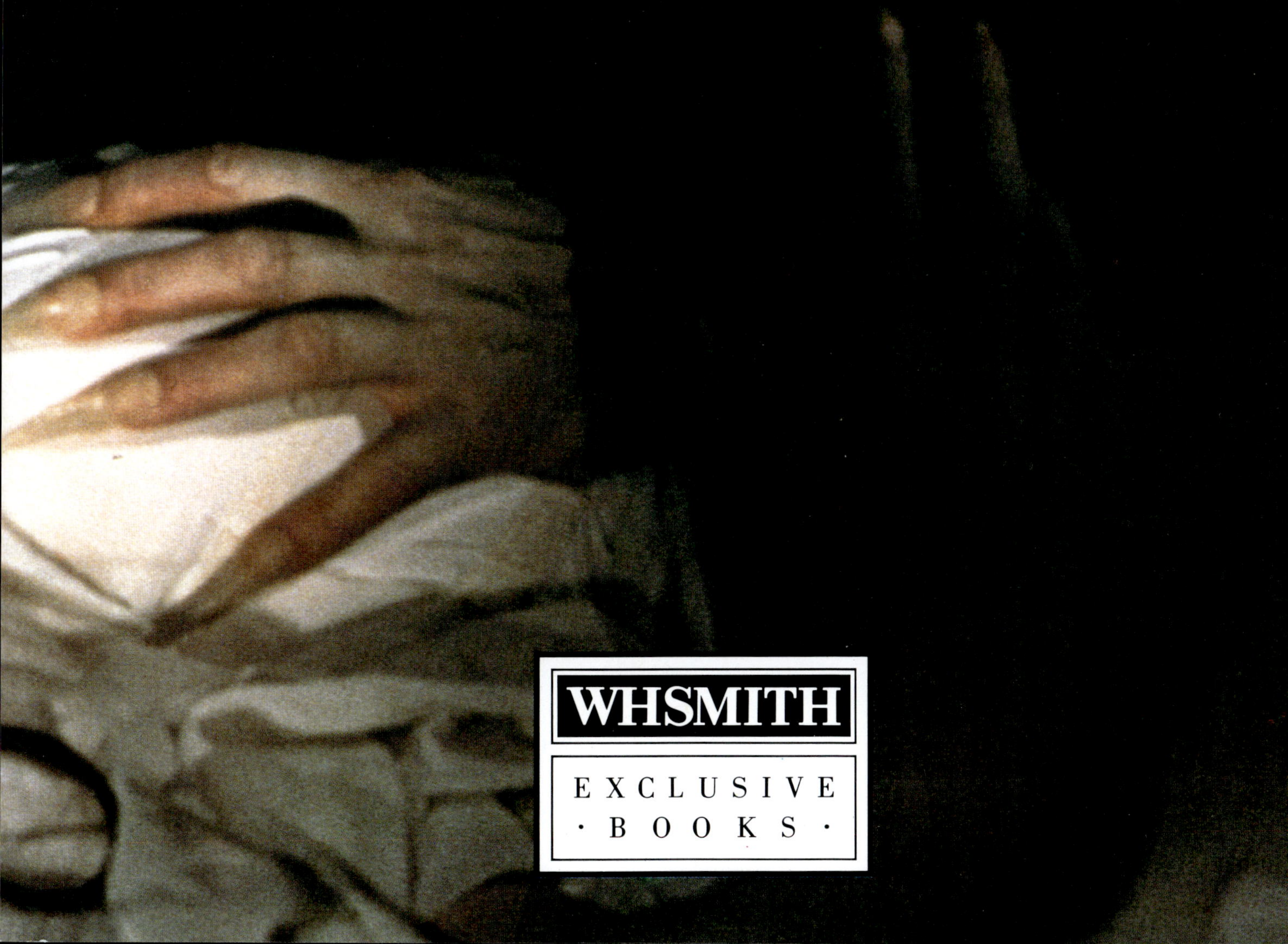

WHSMITH
EXCLUSIVE
· BOOKS ·

This edition produced exclusively for
W. H. Smith & Son Limited
Greenbridge Road
Swindon SN3 3LD

Produced by
Bison Books Ltd
176 Old Brompton Road
London SW5

ISBN 0 86124 285 8

Printed in Hong Kong

Contents

LEFT ABOVE: Peter Cushing as Dr Frankenstein.

LEFT: Peter Lorre and Valerie Hobson in *Mad Love* (1935).

OPPOSITE TOP: Tom Tyler as the Mummy.

OPPOSITE BOTTOM: Jack Nicholson as the crazed novelist in *The Shining* (1980).

PREVIOUS SPREAD: Klaus Kinski in *Nosferatu, the Vampire* (1979).

PAGE 1: Boris Karloff (left) and Bela Lugosi in *The Black Cat* (1934).

For Robin Langley Sommer, without whose help this book never would have happened.

COME WITH ME TO THE THEATER

ST. LOUIS
SUPER SHOCKERS OF THE CENTURY
KENSTEIN'' WITH BORIS KARLOFF
CULA'' STARRING BELA LUGSI
RANKENSTEIN
NOW 2 FIRST RUN FEATURES
BELA LUGOSI
DRACULA
HELEN CHANDLER
25
35
AFTER
DRACULA

Few people would argue with the statement that the movie, seen in the movie theater, is the best medium of all for conveying the horror of the supernatural. When the lights go out, the theater becomes dark and a little spooky – something like being at a séance, waiting for the spiritualist to summon the ghosts of our dear, and not so dear, departeds. There is the darkness, there is concentration, and there is expectancy, plus a sense of being alone. We are ready to yield to an image on the screen that is visible, yet not quite believable.

Horror films show us the world we know and recognize, but they do it in such a way as to throw us off balance. We know what is waiting for us in the gloomy dark at the top of the stairs, but we are not more confident because we have our hand on a shaky banister.

There are many methods of frightening us: sudden shocks, grotesque makeup, huge rampaging monsters. But sometimes the unseen is more frightening than the seen. A slowly opening door is often more chilling than an open door through which we can see a monster. When the camera lingers on a scene for a bit too long, we can be terrified, even though we are merely looking at a deserted alley. Sometimes the anticipation of the fearful happening, or the wait for the appearance of the horrible monster, is more frightening than the event itself. We are more frightened by the empty, foreboding scene than we are by the scene when the climax comes or the monster appears. Indeed, when the fiend or the horrible creation of the makeup and special-effects teams appears too early in the film, we lose interest. One reason for the popularity of *King Kong* (1933 and 1976) is that the great beast does not appear until the film is half over. By that time, the audience is ready for anything. And *The Phantom of the Opera* (1925, 1943 and 1962) is not unmasked until the last reel.

Sometimes it is best not to see the monster at all. Director Val Lewton knew this, and in his *Cat People* (1942), the killer panther is never seen. In *Monster of Horror* (1965), Boris Karloff's wife is slowly being destroyed by radiation poisoning, but is never fully seen because she is hidden behind the net curtains surrounding her bed.

ABOVE: Claude Rains behind his mask when he played *The Phantom of the Opera* (1943).

OPPOSITE: Lon Chaney, who designed his own makeup, in his memorable version of *The Phantom of the Opera* (1925), undoubtedly his most famous role.

LEFT: A poster advertising Val Lewton's *Cat People*– a most unusual monster picture in that the monster (a killer leopard), was never seen. But the terror was there.

PREVIOUS SPREAD: A double 'Creature Feature' in St Louis (coincidentally Vincent Price's home town). It would seem that Missourians didn't know how to spell Bela Lugosi's name. Note the number of people lined up in the 1930s to pay their 35 cents for admission.

RIGHT: Vincent Price about to commit his dastardly deed in *The Pit and the Pendulum* (1961). In this Roger Corman epic, based loosely on the Edgar Allan Poe short story, Price thinks he is his late father, the most vicious torturer of the Spanish Inquisition. Here he sets his sharp pendulum in motion. At each stroke it will get closer and closer to the poor victim on the table.

OPPOSITE: Bela Lugosi in *Dracula* (1931), coming down the cobwebbed stairs of his Transylvanian castle to greet his guest. This was Lugosi's greatest role, and audiences believed him when he said in his Middle-European accent, 'I Am—Dracula!'

Of course there are some kinds of horror that movies cannot handle. For example, there have been very few good versions of stories by two of our most talented masters of terror – Edgar Allen Poe and M R James. Both these writers communicate an almost untranslatable feeling of the supernatural that emerges from our inner feelings, and films cannot do this effectively.

For the most part, Poe's tales are concerned with suffocation, which means that they include isolation and a great feeling of weight upon our chests. 'The Tell-Tale Heart' has a victim beneath the floorboards. 'The Cask of Amontillado' tells of a man being walled up alive. 'Berenice' and 'A Descent into the Maelstrom' are stories about drowning. How can anyone translate these physical feelings into film?

The stories of M R James usually deal with flesh coming into contact with something ghoulish. A wallpaper pattern turns into human hair and creeps over the narrator in 'The Diary of Mr Poynter.' A giant spider drops onto the face of the hero in 'The Tractate Middoth.' A bed sheet with an intense horrible face of linen starts creeping up on the sleeper in 'Oh Whistle, and I'll Come to You, My Lad.' On film the sound of the sheet would have had to substitute for the feel of it. It wouldn't have worked.

It is true that horror films on television do not give us the same thrill that they do in a darkened theater. *King Kong* and *Dracula* seen on a small screen in a well-lighted room are not nearly as frightening. But it is also true that, for horror film buffs, television is where the action is.

The television industry discovered the wonderful world of horror early in the game. In the 1950s, Alfred Hitchcock was the host of a popular network anthology show, 'Alfred Hitchcock Presents,' and once in a while an old film like *White Zombie* (1932) could be seen. Then, in 1957, came 'Shock Theater.' This program consisted of many of the old Universal horror films that had just been released for television, and a whole new generation could shudder at the original *Frankenstein* (1931), *Dracula* (1931) and *The Mummy* (1932). From then on, television viewers were inundated. Rod Serling's 'Twilight Zone' was a tremendous success (it was reincarnated in 1985), as was his later series, 'Night Gallery.' Both of these series can still be seen in reruns. 'Dark Shadows,' an afternoon soap opera starring Jonathan Frid as a vampire, was popular for a few years. We were treated to two comedy shows starring monsters – 'The Addams Family' and 'The Munsters' – both of them still in reruns. And there were regular weekly showings of horror films, often called 'Creature Features' or 'Jeepers Creepers,' that became staples of our television diets.

We could look upon the typical film of terror as a sort of ladder. On the top rung is the evil one – the monster, the devil, the mad scientist – the one with the power. Next we come to the second rung down, where we find the normal people – the citizens of Frankenstein's village, the people on the boat heading toward King Kong's island, and so on. These people might be frightened, but they probably will not suffer.

On the third rung are the people who make up the comic relief – the silly, chattering servants in the castle, the ineffective detectives, the gravediggers. They are put into the picture to offer us a few minutes of relaxation between the moments of terror. Finally, on the bottom rung, we find the real sufferers. These are the hero and heroine, the hapless ones who are cut off from all aid (we think), the helpless maiden and the unarmed youth. Most of the time they are not as helpless, hapless or unarmed as expected, but they find their power only in the last reel.

To sum it all up, the ladder is a hierarchy of power. There are vast, indefinable strengths at the top and some apparent weaknesses at the bottom. And the confrontation is usually between a single cruel force and one or perhaps two victims.

The main fascination that these movies have for us is probably the immense power that the villains possess. To be sure, we want the bad guy to be conquered in the final reel, but we also want to get several good looks at his evil doings before he exits. The power that the evil one has is something like a thunderstorm – violent and complete with lightning – that terrifies us and yet holds us spellbound.

The power has three characteristics. First of all, it must be mysterious. There is nothing mysterious in the power of an armed movie gangster, but Dracula's ability to change normal living people into the undead is mysterious. Next, the power must be tremendous. It must be so great, as in *Godzilla* or *King Kong*, that it seems unconquerable. Finally, it must be fascinating: one cannot help looking at it. Take away one or two of these characteristics and we end up with a common, everyday cops-and-robbers film, but add them all up and we have a horror movie.

The father of the monster movie and the horror film was undoubtedly Georges Méliès. This film pioneer, born in 1861, was a popular magician and the owner and manager of the Théâtre Robert-Houdin in Paris. The theater was, of course, named for the internationally famous French magician whose name was copied by Erich Weiss of Appleton, Wisconsin, when he assumed the stage name of Harry Houdini.

In the beginning, Méliès thought he might use the movies that had been developed by Edison in America and Louis Lumière in France as a useful addition to, and extension of, his magic acts. He was more interested in optical illusions than he was in making films, but he bought a movie camera and started experimenting. At first he photographed everything that moved. Then came a lucky accident. He was standing in front of the Paris Opéra, taking movies of

credited as the first motion picture director. People called him 'The King of Phantasmagoria,' 'The Jules Verne of the Cinema' and 'The Magician of the Screen.'

At the same time, the Lumière brothers were showing films that had more reality – trains coming at the audience head-on and similar effects. The theater audience would cringe back from the frightening thing coming at them full steam. But while the Lumières were frightening their audiences with motion, Méliès was frightening them with ghostly techniques.

Méliès had happened on almost all the tricks that modern cameramen use today. He developed the double exposure to give the impression of ghostly presences. In 1896 he made a woman disappear from the screen merely by stopping the camera and having her step out of range, then starting the camera again – this was the stop-motion photography that was later to be used so successfully in such movies as *King Kong* (1933).

Méliès also developed the technique of making underwater scenes by photographing a submerged object through the walls of a fish tank. He discovered fast- and slow-motion effects (for which Charlie

RIGHT: An interior view of the submarine in Georges Méliès' *The Impossible Voyage/Le Voyage a Travess l'Impossible* (1904).

ABOVE: In Georges Méliès' *A Trip to the Moon/Le Voyage dans la Lune* (1902), the rocket ship lands in the right eye of the Man in the Moon. The scene was shot with a painting of the moon's surface that served as a mask for an actor when holes were cut for his mouth, nose and eyes.

OPPOSITE: The master at work – Georges Méliès preparing the Man in the Moon scene.

a bus going along the street, when his camera jammed. By the time he had straightened out the trouble, the bus had disappeared, and a hearse was coming down the same street. He continued taking pictures of the hearse. When the film was developed, he had a reel in which a bus turned into a hearse right in front of the viewer's eyes. Méliès decided to go into the movie business.

In the Parisian suburb of Montreuil, Méliès built the world's first movie studio. Its walls and ceiling were made of glass to let in the light, and it had trapdoors in the floor and translucent curtains that were used to get silhouette shots. Méliès wrote his own scripts, produced his own films and directed his own actors. Sometimes he appeared in the films himself. He can be

Chaplin and Sam Peckinpah must have been grateful), and often used animation in his movies. He discovered how to use the fade, which is the gradual appearance or disappearance of a scene, and the dissolve, which is a slow transition from one image to another. He experimented continually.

Méliès was the first person to make a film with a real story. It was in 1900, and the tale was *Cinderella*. This was the first movie in history that had a story with a beginning, a middle and an end. He used many of his tricks in it, too. The pumpkin seems actually to turn into a coach; Cinderella's dress, as if by magic, becomes a beautiful gown; and the dancers at the ball are shown in dream-like slow motion.

Méliès was proud of himself. He decided to give up

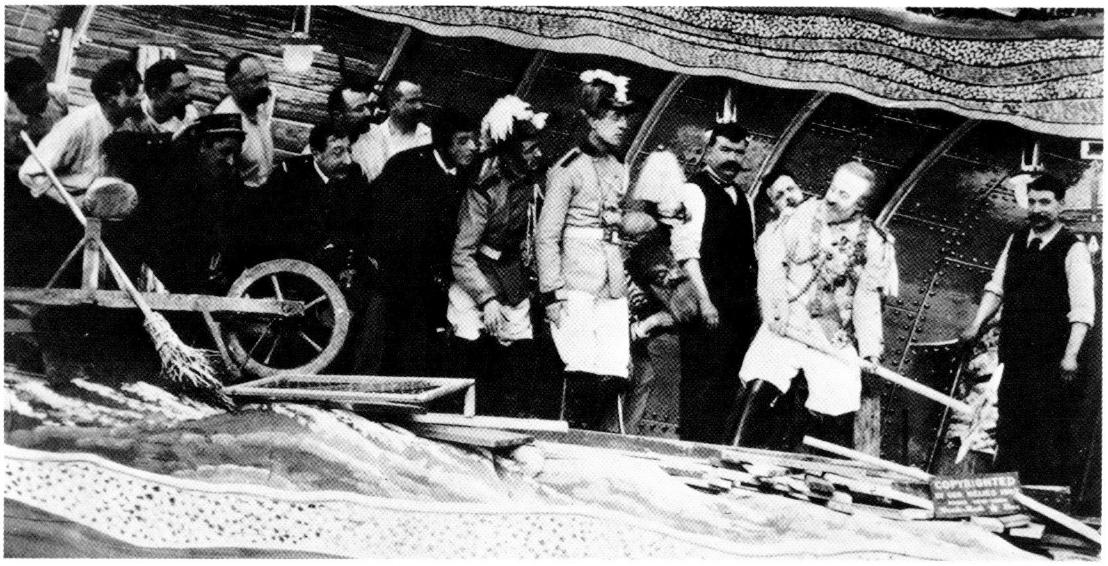

LEFT: Workers watch the king give a couple of symbolic swipes with his pickaxe in *Tunneling the English Channel* (1907), another Méliès triumph.

LEFT BELOW: Méliès created the Abominable Giant of the Snows for his *The Conquest of the Pole* (1912).

OPPOSITE: George Méliès, 'the King of Phantasmagoria,' tending his shop in Paris in 1929.

magic and go completely into the movie business. He advertised that he was going to make movies involving 'transformations, tricks, fairy tales, apotheoses, artistic and fantastic scenes, comic subjects, war pictures, fantasies and illusions.'

His masterpiece was *A Trip to the Moon* in 1902, and the script was borrowed from two novels – Jules Verne's *From Earth to the Moon*, and H G Wells's *The First Men in the Moon*. The film lasted 30 minutes and told the story, naturally enough, of a trip to the moon. A rocket is fired from a cannon and eventually lands right in the eye of 'The Man in the Moon,' whose face shows a great deal of pain. All sorts of things then happen on the moon. An umbrella takes root and starts to grow. Girls in Grecian costumes seem to fly through the air. The astronauts descend into the center of the moon and find beautiful women and gorgeous vegetation. Why they ever came back from this paradise is a mystery.

Then came *The Impossible Voyage*, about a trip to the sun, in 1904, followed by *Tunnelling the English Channel* in 1907. Méliès went on to make *The Conquest of the Pole* in 1912. The hero of this picture was the Abominable Giant of the Snows, a full-sized monster animated by chains and pulleys who had the unpleasant habit of gobbling up the members of a polar expedition. But Méliès was no businessman. Instead of renting out films to theaters, he sold them outright. His career as a producer was over by 1914, and he even lost his theater in 1925. Méliès was so upset that he destroyed all of the irreplaceable films in his possession and disappeared from sight.

He was not heard of again until 1929, when he was found working as a newsboy in the Paris streets. A friend bought him a little candy stand, and he worked there until he was too old and infirm to continue. 'The Father of the Movies' spent the last days of his life at the old actors' home in Orly and died in 1938, probably never knowing what a debt was owed to him by the makers of modern horror films.

But before we go on with the show, it must be decided just what sort of movies will appear in this book. Of course, there will be various kinds of monsters, human fiends, devils and psychokinetic wonders, but what should be left out?

First of all, there are no films about out-and-out nut cases – these villains do not have a supernatural sickness, after all. We see their likes in newspaper headlines every day. And eliminating them can be a blessing, insofar as we can also eliminate most of the slash-and-burn, snuff-and-decapitate films that have proliferated in the past few years.

These films seem to try only two ways to scare us. One is by springing a surprise on us, as, for example, when an assailant jumps out of the dark. Many times the directors play coy and touch off false alarms, and the jumper turns out to be nothing more than an alley cat. The other tactic is to bombard us visually with blood, guts, hacked limbs and mutilated bodies.

The shock of surprise is a cheap way of making an audience jump. The same instant the surprise is sprung, the shock is over. It's the kind of scene where we breathe a sigh of relief because, this time at least, it was only a shutter in the wind, or a cat – not the monster. The blood-and-gore terror is more common, more popular and more vicious. Audiences eventually become inured to it, so it is also more dangerous. And, as audiences become desensitized, the directors try harder still, and the bloodletting becomes more copious.

So, alas, *Psycho* (1960), with the madman Norman Bates, does not belong in this book. But, happily, neither do *Friday the 13th* (1980), *Halloween* (1978) and their numerous offspring and reincarnations.

There will also be no films of the science fiction genre – no outer-space futurism. There just isn't room. True, this eliminates some of the real white-knucklers, like *The Thing* (1951) and *The War of the Worlds* (1953), whose monsters were truly thrilling. But they came from outer space, after all, and are more sci-fi than horror.

There will be no natural monsters here, either. They are just normal creatures that turned out to be a bit hyperactive. So no *Jaws* (1975) or *Piranha* (1978) and their sequels.

Finally, and regrettably, there is no room for the horror and monster comedies. No *Canterville Ghost* (1943), *The Ghost Goes West* (1936), or *Young Frankenstein* (1974). On the other hand, to look at the bright side, none of the various run-ins that Abbott and Costello had with Frankenstein, Dracula, the Wolf Man, the Mummy, and others.

So come with me to the theater. It's time for the lights to dim.

JUST PLAIN MONSTERS

It seems as though there has always been some sort of monster hanging around, throwing fear into the hearts and minds of unsophisticated peasants. Over four thousand years ago, there was Ea, the fish god worshipped by the Babylonians. He was a helpful monster, however, half man and half fish, who had come out of the sea to teach the alphabet to the people. Sea serpents and mermaids have always been with us, and now we have our Loch Ness Monster.

One of the first films that gave audiences a look-see at prehistoric monsters was the 1925 movie *The Lost World*. This had been adapted from a story by Sir Arthur Conan Doyle, the creator of Sherlock Holmes. It was the tale of a scientific expedition to the jungles of the Amazon River. The party discovers a long-forgotten plateau, and after members of the group climb to the tableland, they find gigantic ancient lizards. There is also an ape man living there, whom they think might be the missing link that will explain man's evolution.

Although Wallace Beery and Lewis Stone (later to become kindly Judge Hardy opposite Mickey Rooney) were given top billing, the real stars of the film were the dinosaurs. These beasts had been created by a man who was to make his mark in horror films and become the dean of special-effects men for many years – Willis H O'Brien. He had made a picture in 1917, called *The Dinosaur and the Missing Link*, which the Edison Company bought for five thousand dollars and released. It lasted for only five minutes on the screen, but it had taken two months to make. O'Brien had created the animals out of modeling clay and had used stop-motion photography to give them animation.

O'Brien made 10 films for Edison over the next few years, but for *The Lost World*, produced by First National-Watterson R Rothacker, he gave up the clay technique and shifted to rubber models that could be made to move. Then human characters were photographed against a backdrop of the dinosaur antics. *The Lost World* may have been the first film to tell the story of a strange beast who goes to the city. In the movie, a brontosaurus runs through the streets of London, doing what King Kong did to New York and what Godzilla did to Tokyo.

In 1960, when O'Brien was 70 years old, his work was still on display in the remake of *The Lost World*, which substituted real lizards for puppets. The film starred Claude Rains, Michael Rennie, David Hedison, Fernando Lamas and Jill St John. Strangely enough, the living animals did not have the personality of the rubber replicas. But the cost of photographing the models, one frame at a time, would have been exorbitant. Of course, the technique was simple, but time-consuming. When the model was in position, one frame of film was exposed. Then the model was moved a tiny bit, and another frame was exposed, and so on. Sometimes it took a whole crew 10 hours to shoot 30 seconds' worth of film. Salaries had gone up between 1925 and 1960, and the producers just didn't have the money to spend on such an activity.

ABOVE: A pair of Willis O'Brien's prehistoric monsters fight it out to the death in *The Lost World* (1925). O'Brien made the beasts of modeling clay and used stop-motion photography to make them appear to move.

RIGHT: *The Lost World* was made again in 1960. Fernando Lamas is at far left and Jill St John at far right. At the center, Richard Haydn (left) and David Hedison help their fellow travelers scale the wall.

OPPOSITE: Wallace Beery, Lloyd Hughes, Bessie Love and Lewis Stone starred in the original *The Lost World* (1925).

PAGE 17: The face of the great ape, Kong, in Dino De Laurentiis' *King Kong* (1976), the disappointing remake of the 1933 classic.

KING KONG
FAY WRAY
ROB'T ARMSTRONG
BRUCE CABOT
A PERSONALLY DIRECTED
MERIAN C.
COOPER

Perhaps the greatest monster movie of all time opened at Radio City Music Hall in New York City in 1933. It was *King Kong*, the brainchild of several fine film minds. Merian C Cooper had been in Africa shooting a documentary and had become interested in gorillas. He was the one who thought up the idea of a huge gorilla – quite intelligent – who escapes into the streets of New York City. He also dreamed up a setting in which the gorilla would be surrounded by prehistoric monsters with which it would fight. Cooper thought that he could film live gorillas and lizards, using trick photography.

In 1931 David O Selznick (who was later to be responsible for *Gone With the Wind* and many other fine pictures) was a vice-president in charge of production at RKO. He brought Cooper in to do *King Kong*. In the meantime, Cooper had become familiar with the work of Willis O'Brien and had changed his mind about the special effects, deciding to film the movie in the studio, using models.

Cooper, with his co-director, Ernest B Schoedsack, and with O'Brien as the special-effects man, started the film in 1932. The filming took a whole year and cost $650,000. But it was worth it.

OPPOSITE: Kong, holding Fay Wray, fends off the Air Force planes.

BELOW: Kong puts Fay Wray in a tree for safety's sake. Fay continued to scream.

Twenty-seven different models of the giant gorilla were made, ranging in size from a few centimeters in height to the torso that was large enough to fit a man into the mouth. It took 40 bearskins to provide enough fur to cover the life-sized bust of Kong that was created. Sometimes, when the heroine, Fay Wray, was being held in the giant hand of the beast, she would kick so hard that the hand would open and she would be dangling 10 feet above the ground, holding onto the thumb for dear life.

King Kong's roar was a recording of a lion's roar run backward at slow speed. The wall separating the native village from Kong's domain was the same one that had been used in C B DeMille's Biblical film *King of Kings* (1927) – only the door was new. And Hollywood, ever mindful of saving a dollar here and there, reused the wall again in 1939. It met its end by burning in the fall-of-Atlanta scenes in *Gone With the Wind*.

Kong was, oddly enough, both human and sympathetic. He met a horrible death while protecting the woman he loved. Yet he was probably the most terrifying of all the giant monsters.

The story is a simple one. A producer of movies, Carl Denham (Robert Armstrong), hears of a far-off island inhabited by prehistoric monsters. He discovers a beautiful, down-and-out girl (these were Depression times), Fay Wray, who is so hungry that she consents

LEFT: In *King Kong* (1933), Kong has a battle with a Tyrannosaurus rex while Fay Wray watches apprehensively from her tree refuge.

OPPOSITE TOP: It has been said that Fay Wray sometimes skipped lunch to practice screaming for her role in *King Kong* (1933).

OPPOSITE BOTTOM: The climax of *King Kong* (1933). Kong, atop the Empire State Building, has just destroyed an Air Force fighter plane. Note that he has put Fay Wray on a ledge for safety. But the rest of the air armada is coming in for the kill.

BELOW: Kong saves Wray from the clutches of a pterodactyl on the front porch of his cave.

bottom of the chasm.

Finally, the desperate hero finds Fay, brings her back to the village and prepares to fight off King Kong, who is following. Denham is able to use gas bombs on Kong, bring him back to New York and exhibit him in a theater. As newspaper photographers are taking pictures of Fay, Kong thinks that the flashbulbs are doing her harm: he breaks free from his chains and escapes.

Kong finds Fay in her hotel room, reaches in through an open window and carries her to the top of the Empire State Building. The Army Air Force is called out, and airmen fly around Kong, shooting him with hundreds of bullets. The gorilla, mortally wounded, tenderly puts Fay down in a safe place and falls to the street below – stone dead. Denham confides to a passing policeman, 'It was Beauty killed the beast.'

One footnote – the pilots in the particular plane that finally shot down Kong are visible in one brief flash. They are co-directors Merian C Cooper and Ernest B Schoedsack.

The only carping about *King Kong* that was heard at the time was a comparison of this film with the earlier *Lost World.* Kong was superior in every way except one. *The Lost World* had had families of dinosaurs rather than the lone members of each species that came in to fight Kong like a series of variety acts.

to star in a film whose supporting characters are huge monsters. Every other actress in town turned Denham down, and who can blame them?

The movie crew sails to Skull Island, only to find that it is inhabited by a tribe of natives restricted to a small peninsula on the island's end, because they have built an enormous wall across the neck of the peninsula to keep out the monsters – one of them being the tremendous gorilla, Kong. The natives have never seen a white girl before, and poor Fay seems quite unusual to them. They seize her, tie her up outside the wall and declare that she is the bride of Kong.

Of course, King Kong comes to claim her, but instead of killing her, he falls in love with her. Needless to say, because of their relative sizes, the marriage is never consummated. At any rate, he picks her up and starts back to his cave with her, while she screams all the way. En route, he must defend her from various prehistoric creatures like a tyrannosaurus and a pterodactyl. In the meantime, a crew of sailors led by Fay's sweetheart, the ship's mate, Jack Driscoll, give chase. Bruce Cabot played Driscoll after Joel McCrea turned down the part.

Originally, there was a scene in *King Kong* in which the giant ape, finding the pursuing sailors trying to cross a chasm by means of a fallen log, picks up the log and throws it into the abyss. It was at this point that the scene was cut: the missing footage showed the approach of a giant spider, which proceeds to consume these nautical Miss Muffets. For some reason, it was thought that the spider scene was too grisly. The only thing that remained was the sailors falling through the air and bouncing on the

ABOVE: Kong gives Jessica Lange a bath under a waterfall in *King Kong* (1976).

The death of Kong after his fall from the World Trade Center building – *King Kong* (1976).

Some wags at the time joked that King Kong was not killed at all; he had been lured from the Empire State Building to the Chrysler Building, where the United States Marines had placed a giant banana. At any rate, *King Kong* appeared again in a 1976 remake by the Italian producer Dino de Laurentiis. It turned out to be a semi-spoof remake with added sexual overtones, lacking both the charm and the technical resources of its predecessor. This time the ship was sailing to an island in search of a new supply of oil (this was during the OPEC oil crunch). Charles Grodin was the leader, Jeff Bridges was a stowaway scholar and Jessica Lange was Dwan, the survivor of a shipwreck. The rest was similar to the original, but the producers didn't have time for the fights with the prehistoric monsters and had to make do with a snake. The big problem in the film was that Kong seemed rather stupid, and who could feel sympathy with an animal who could not even frighten the heroine?

However, a lot of money was spent on this venture. The first King Kong had cost $650,000; this one cost $24 million – $2 million just for the mechanical model of Kong. Seven sound stages were used, and location shooting occurred in Kauai, Hawaii; New York City; on board a research ship owned by American University; and on board a supertanker. A new wall was built – 45 feet high and 500 feet wide – that could hold 300 extras on its top. The building of the wall required 5500 pound of nails, 8157 eucalyptus poles, 372,000 feet of grapevines to hold the poles together and 6420 quarts of vinyl paint. Construction alone cost about $800,000.

Kong was played by a man in a gorilla suit –it was quite a believable performance – plus two models, each about 40 feet in height. The styrofoam model was used on the ship and in the New York streets, and the moveable model was used in the rest of the scenes. This last model weighed 6.5 tons and contained 3050 feet of electrical wiring. Its chest was 20 feet wide and its armspread was 40 feet. The arms could move into 16 different positions, and the model could walk, turn from the waist and move its eyes and mouth. It was covered with almost 4000 pounds of horsehair, and it took six men to operate the control panel.

But back to the 1930s. Schoedsack, O'Brien and Armstrong had been so successful with *King Kong* that they teamed up again that same year – 1933 – with an atrocity called *Son of Kong*. Carl Denham (Armstrong) goes back to Skull Island and finds a huge white gorilla – allegedly the son of Kong. (His mother's identity is never explained.) Kong's son is a gentle animal who befriends Denham after the producer bandages the ape's sore finger. At the end of the film, the island is sinking, and the poor simpering gorilla is holding Denham in his upraised hand as the water gradually rises over his head. Denham is rescued by a boat, the island is no more and gone is the great white gorilla.

The whole huge-ape idea returned in 1949, with the release of *Mighty Joe Young*, another venture by Ernest B Schoedsack and Willis O'Brien. O'Brien won an Academy Award for his special effects for this one. Joe Young is a ten-foot-high gorilla who is the household pet of a sweet little orphan girl (Terry Moore) who lives in Africa. The girl is persuaded to take her pet to the United States and show him off. Joe defeats the world's 10 strongest men in a tug of war, and he and the girl end up in a night club where he holds a grand piano over his head on which the girl plays 'Beautiful Dreamer.' Of course, à la King Kong, Joe thinks that all the people in the audience are there to hurt his mistress, and he goes berserk while the spectators flee in terror. Joe is forgiven when he rescues some helpless children from a burning orphanage, and he and Miss Moore go back to Africa, presumably to live happily ever after. It's hard to believe that this bit of frippery took three years to complete.

Beginning in the early 1950s, a new kind of monster began to emerge – both prehistoric creatures and normal animals that had been either freed from be-

RIGHT: A poster for *Mighty Joe Young* (1949). Joe holds Terry Moore aloft during her night club act. Joe Young went back to Africa and Moore went on to marry Howard Hughes, and, in her 50s, to pose nude for *Playboy* magazine.

OPPOSITE: The giant white gorilla protects his friends from a prehistoric monster on Skull Island in *Son of Kong* (1933). On the ledge are Helen Mack and Robert Armstrong, who again played movie maker Carl Denham.

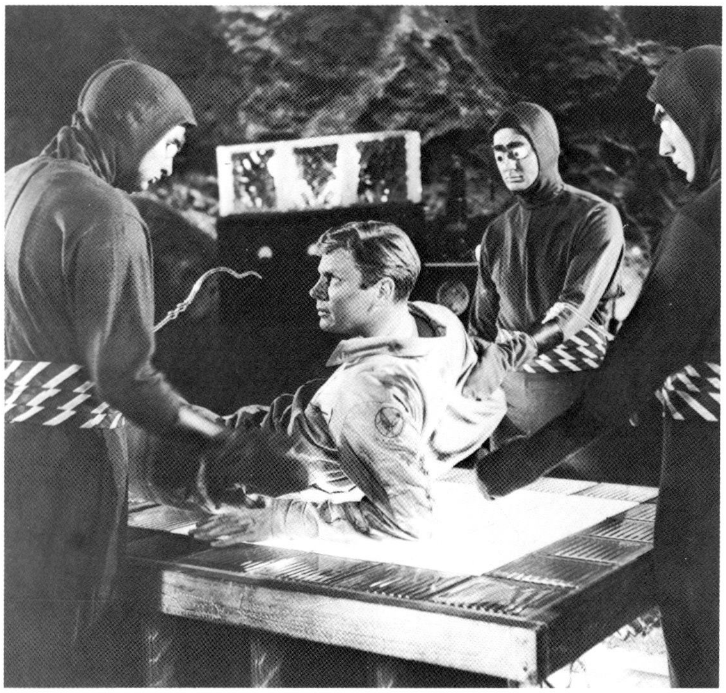

LEFT: Peter Graves (on table) was captured by alien space invaders who want vital information in *Killer from Space* (1954).

LEFT CENTER: The United States Army prepares to face *The Beast from 20,000 Fathoms* (1953) in a Coney Island amusement park. Kenneth Tobey (in the trench coat) knew a thing or two about monsters – he had handled *The Thing* in 1951.

BELOW LEFT: James Whitmore (right) questions a little girl about the giant ants in *Them!* (1954).

RIGHT: The *Beast from 20,000 Fathoms* (1953) tries to destroy New York.

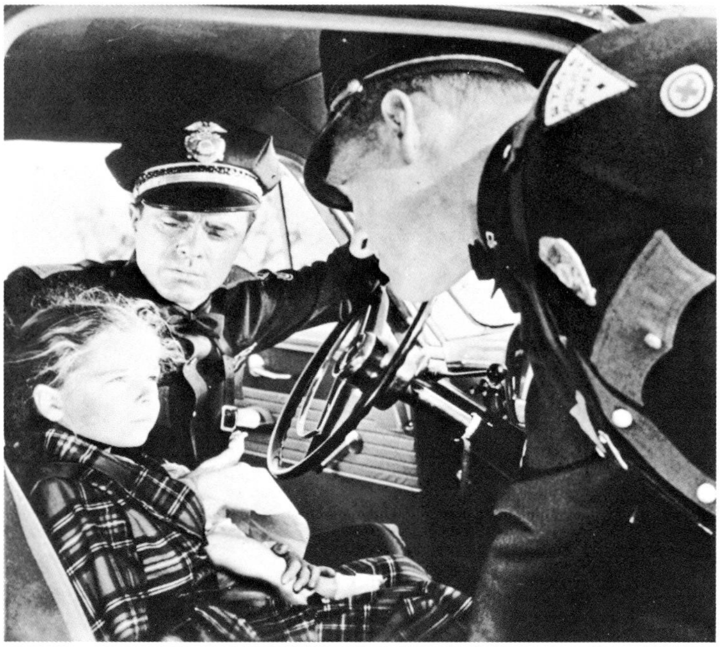

neath the sea by an explosion or changed into a horrible mutant by atomic testing.

One of the first was *The Beast from 20,000 Fathoms* (1953), whose most distinguishing feature was the work of Ray Harryhausen, the American trick-film specialist and model maker. It concerned a dinosaur – a rhedosaurus, part brontosaurus and part tyrannosaurus – which is awakened from its sleep by atomic testing. It comes out of the sea to answer a mating call, but it turns out that its mate is a lighthouse, whose

call is a foghorn (the producers were serious). The creature is naturally miffed, destroys the lighthouse and runs to a Coney Island amusement park, which it also destroys. Finally, the beast is killed by a radioactive bullet fired by Lee van Cleef.

Also in 1953, *Killers from Space* was released. It had a terrible story line about giant locusts and other monsters and starred Peter Graves, who would later get better scripts on the 'Mission Impossible' television series.

The Magnetic Monster (1953) was one of the few movies to feature a non-living creature. Richard Carlson and King Donovan run a shop called the Office of Scientific Investigation and discover a monster – a new radioactive element – that has been created by a mad scientist. The element grows and (using pirated footage from a German film of 1934, *Gold*) is finally destroyed by giving it an undigestible meal – 900,000,000 volts of electricity.

A couple of ant pictures came out in 1954. One was

Them!, which featured giant ants mutated by atom tests on the desert. The desert sequences were eerie and the ending, set in the Los Angeles sewer system, was scary. It starred Edmund Gwenn, James Whitmore and James Arness. Director Gordon Douglas said about it: 'I asked the [film] editor: "How does it look?" And he said: "Fine." I said: "Does it look honest?" He said: "As honest as twelve foot ants can look."'

In *The Naked Jungle* (1954), soldier ants pursued Charlton Heston and Eleanor Parker. Directed by George Pal, the Academy-Award-winning trick photographer, the movie was based on Carl Stephenson's thrilling short story 'Leiningen and the Ants,' set in South America.

The Snow Creature (1954) told of a Yeti who kidnaps a botanist's wife in the Himalayas. The Abominable Snowman is captured and brought to Los Angeles, which it wrecks.

The Creature from the Black Lagoon (1954) told the story of scientists who encounter a fearful fanged creature who is half man, half fish. The rest of the film was called by one critic 'Unpersuasive and unsuspenseful horror hokum from the bottom drawer of imagination.' But the underwater photography was splendid. Director Jack Arnold had come up with the idea of setting the film in an Amazonian swamp, after watching some Frankenstein and Mummy movies. He got the idea for the monster's rubber suit when he saw a picture of the Academy Awards' Oscar statuette and visualized it with added gills, fins and flippers. The picture starred Richard Carlson, Julie Adams, Richard Denning and, in the rubber suit as the creature, Ricou Browning, the diver and stunt man who would become a specialist in underwater direction for Ivan Tors, producer of the 'Flipper' television series.

The poor creature came back in *The Revenge of the Creature* (1955). Again, he was portrayed as a jealous madman chasing the heroine through the swamps. But in the third picture of the series, *The Creature Walks Among Us* (1956), the monster has an unsuccessful romance and finds out about the pains of unrequited love.

It Came from Beneath the Sea was released in 1955. In the film, a giant octopus – mutated by atomic radiation – lays waste to San Francisco. It starred Kenneth Tobey and Faith Domergue.

The Abominable Snowman reappeared in *Half-Human* (1955). This was a low-budget horror yarn starring John Carradine, and the prehistoric zombie-like monster was laughable.

RIGHT: *The Creature from the Black Lagoon* (1954) comes up out of the slime without a trace of seaweed on his skin.

OPPOSITE: Charlton Heston being set upon by soldier ants in *The Naked Jungle* (1954).

BELOW: *The Creature Walks Among Us* (1956) marked the third appearance of the Creature from the Black Lagoon. It is Rex Reason gazing on him with the curious expression.

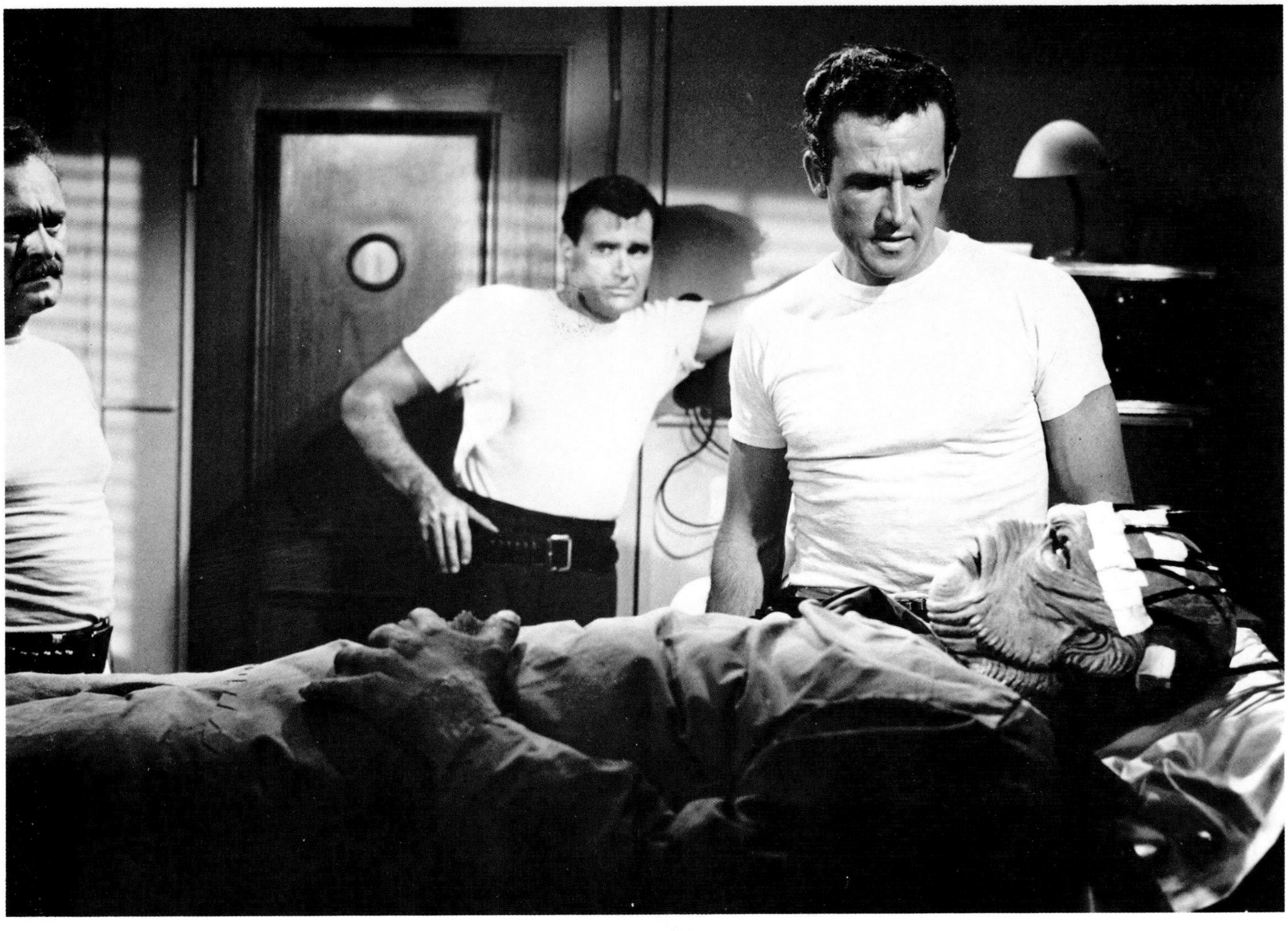

In the British film *The Quatermass Experiment* (1955), retitled *The Creeping Unknown* for the American market, an infected spaceman becomes a monster on his return to earth from a space probe. Professor Quatermass (Brian Donlevy, the obligatory American for US film sales) is forced to electrocute him – in Westminster Abbey. Richard Wordsworth was the spaceman. The movie came from the theme of a British Broadcasting Company series, for which the English film company Hammer had obtained screen rights.

Leo G Carroll starred in *Tarantula* (1955). In this film, a spider treated by Carroll with a serum grows to a weight of 50 tons and eats entire cities, until the Air Force bombs it with napalm. The title creature was the result of effective matté photography. Also in the cast were John Agar (the former husband of Shirley Temple) and Mara Corday.

Not to be outdone by these American and British monsters, the Japanese film company Toho produced *Godzilla, King of the Monsters (Gojira)* in 1955. This creature looked a lot like a fat tyrannosaurus, except that he had a long tail and plates that stuck up along his spine. He had atomic breath, the better to destroy whole cities – that is, when he was not merely mashing them with his feet. Godzilla came up from the depths of the sea to destroy Tokyo and was finally eliminated by atomic energy. But no, that's a lie – he had to be put back together for the sequels. In the US-market version, the American actor Raymond Burr was the star (long before 'Perry Mason' and 'Ironsides' on television). But that was an afterthought. The Japanese had filmed the movie, and it was so popular at home that they thought they could make even more money overseas. So they stuck in shots of Burr looking out his window at the devastation and describing it over the telephone. He was never in the original shooting.

Godzilla (or Gojira, an amalgam of Japanese *gorira*, or gorilla, and *Kujira*, whale) returned time and time again. For three decades this outsized, outdated lizard in dire ned of a good orthodontist, with a vocabulary limited to a grating 'Aaarrgh,' lived on in films as one of Japan's most enduring celebrities. He was the star of 15 feature films and the idol of an estimated 200,000 followers, who banded together in several hundred fan clubs. Some of the sequels were laughable, including *King Kong Versus Godzilla* (1963), in which the two monsters had it out (King Kong had blue eyes, probably accounted for by Japanese reservations about anyone who doesn't have brown eyes), and *Counterattack of Meka Godzilla* (1975). But along the way, Godzilla turned from a fierce monster into a good guy, saving the world from such hideous creatures as Megaro and Mothra. And audiences, especially in Japan, began to stay away in droves.

OPPOSITE: Richard Wordsworth was the afflicted spaceman in *The Creeping Unknown* (1955).

TOP RIGHT: The 50-ton spider from *Tarantula* (1955).

CENTER RIGHT: *Godzilla, King of the Monsters* (1955).

BOTTOM RIGHT: Godzilla fights Kong in *King Kong Versus Godzilla* (1963).

Then came the stunning news – Godzilla Number 16 was to hit the screens in 1985, and it would be the old Godzilla, ravaging the Ginza and smashing the skyscrapers that dominate Tokyo's historic Shinjuku section – an act that many traditionalists might regard as a form of urban renewal. The film, called in the United States *Godzilla 1985*, cost about $6 million, small by American standards, but three to five times the cost of the usual Japanese film. A computerized robot more than eight feet tall was built to represent Godzilla's upper half; it offered a broader range of subtle emotions than the rubber dolls used in earlier films. And the monster had grown – from a supposed 160 feet to 260 feet – reflecting the growth of Tokyo architecture; in the mid-1950s no Tokyo building was more than seven stories high.

In the film, Godzilla runs amok, smashing into high-rise buildings and gobbling up Japan's 'Bullet Train' as though it were a strand of spaghetti. But, alas, the eagerly awaited return after nine years turned out to be a dud. The special effects would not have fooled a five-year-old. Godzilla walked as if he had had too many martinis, and the movie was heavily laden with antinuclear messages, bad dubbing and worse dialogue. Sleepwalking through the film was Raymond Burr, reprising his role as reporter Steve Martin.

The monsters kept coming in 1956. There were *The Mole People*, found by explorers John Agar, Nestor Pavia and Hugh Beaumont (before he became the Beaver's father) inside the mountains of Asia – dominated by a tribe of long-lost albino Sumerians living in a preserved city under the earth. There was *The Beast of Hollow Mountain*, written by the old special-effects man Willis O'Brien – pleasant enough, but who ever heard of a cowboy movie in which the villain was a dinosaur?

There are those who would argue that one of the greatest monster roles of all time was not really a monster movie at all. But *The Incredible Shrinking Man* (1957) did have as its star a grotesque mutant – Scott Cary (Grant Williams), who was hit by radioactive fallout. This was one of the best 'effects of radiation' films of all time. Cary gradually dwindles in size,

OPPOSITE: The fake-looking rubber monster from *The Beast of Hollow Mountain* (1956), not one of Willis O'Brien's better creations.

LEFT AND BELOW: Grant Williams as *The Incredible Shrinking Man* (1957) is almost drowned and nearly stepped on when he shrinks to one inch high.

and the terror of his changing circumstances is maintained throughout: the man shrunk to a third of normal size sitting in an enormous armchair; his grappling with a giant telephone; his panic-stricken flight into a doll house to escape a clawing cat; his fight with a spider; his desperate efforts to obtain cheese from a mousetrap for food. It was an epic story of the struggle for survival, and the ending, when Cary shrinks to the size of an invisible atom, was uncompromising.

Giant mutants continued to infest the screen in 1957. In *The Black Scorpion*, huge scorpions from the Triassic Period appeared in Mexico. At the end of the picture, the last scorpion fights off helicopters and the militia in the Mexico City bullring. It starred Richard Denning and Mara Corday, and featured special effects by the old master, Willis O'Brien. The Japanese came up with *Rodan*, a pterodactyl who leveled Tokyo again. In *The Beginning of the End*, we had grasshoppers 15 feet long, who looked as if they were the real things crawling over fake miniature buildings as they attacked Chicago. *The Attack of the Crab Monsters* was a film by Roger Corman, who started as a messenger boy at 20th Century-Fox and directed an infinite number of Z-grade films before making a mark with his adaptations of Edgar Allen Poe – films starring Vincent Price, Peter Lorre and Boris Karloff. Scientists marooned on a South Pacific island are attacked by mutant crabs eight feet high and 25 feet across. Using all that sand saved Corman the cost of building sets. Richard Garland and Pamela Duncan led the scientists, whose numbers dwindled as the crabs bit off their heads and absorbed their minds. They then sent out telepathic messages to the survivors to lure then to destruction.

The Monster That Challenged the World, another 1957 film, was a giant caterpillar created by atomic experiments and loosed from the sea by an earthquake. What a caterpillar was doing at the bottom of the sea was never explained. Another 'what was he doing there?' of 1957 was *The Deadly Mantis*, 100 feet

ABOVE: Those are not supposed to be toy cars. The picture was *The Deadly Mantis* (1957) and the giant insect was said to be 100 feet in length.

LEFT: A poor scientist meets his end in *The Attack of the Crab Monsters* (1957). The mutant hunk of seafood was supposed to be eight feet in height and 25 feet across.

long and 40 feet wide, who thaws out of his hibernation in the Arctic. Craig Stevens (later to become 'Peter Gunn' on television) chases it across America. The beast then settles on the Washington Monument, where it knocks airplanes out of the sky (perhaps they were thinking how easy a mark King Kong was). The creature is finally destroyed in a tunnel under New York's Hudson River by poisonous gas and land mines.

In *From Hell It Came* (1957), a corpse comes back as a tree. One critic commented, 'To hell send it back.' And in *The Land Unknown* (1957), Jock Mahoney, Shawn Smith and William Reynolds crash in a lost valley in the Antarctic. There they find prehistoric beasts – most of them looking like men in animal suits – and carnivorous plants. Somehow the men find a spare part for their helicopter and escape to safety.

Arthur Franz was a science professor in *Monster on the Campus* (1958). He had the misfortune to be accidentally cut by a coelocanth's tooth, which turned him into an ape-like monster. Among the other goings-on were combats with a dragonfly who was turned into a giant prehistoric creature and a dog who was changed into a wolf.

The year 1959 brought us *The Hideous Sun Demon*, in which Robert Clarke was a scientist changed by radiation into a scaly lizard-like creature, and *The Killer Shrews*, in which those tiny animals were turned into monsters the size of large dogs. When they are full grown, they start eating humans. Finally, the humans escape and the shrews turn on each other.

The decade of the 1950s ended with *The Tingler* (1959). It starred Vincent Price, and was a ridiculous shocker with a certain amount of effrontery. The plot concerned a large insect-like creature who kills people by pinching the nerves at the base of their spines. The problem was that the parasite could be dislodged by the screams of the victim, so the ideal prey for the beast was a mute. A system for wiring the theater seats had been developed so that at the proper times, members of the audience would be given tiny shocks.

ABOVE: *Reptilicus* (1962) about to make an illegal turn at a street corner in Copenhagen.

RIGHT: Actress Mary Ann Miles tries to fight off *The Horror of Party Beach* (1963), Del Tenny's wretched monster film.

But few houses would risk the expense of the wiring, so the film went on unelectrified.

Coleen Gray, Grant Williams and Gloria Talbott starred in *The Leech Woman* (1960), about a woman who finds a youth-giving formula, which, unfortunately, makes her not only young – but a young leech. *Gorgo* (1960) was a monster with a maternal instinct. When her baby monster is put into a sideshow in London, she rescues it, destroying most of the city.

Ray Harryhausen was back with *Mysterious Island* in 1961. It starred Michael Craig, Joan Greenwood, Michael Callan and Gary Merrill, and concerned itself with the story of Confederate officers who escape the enemy by sailing in a balloon to a small island. There they meet not only some shipwrecked English ladies, but also a menagerie of monsters – giant birds, huge bees, monster crabs and an enormous octopus. Finally, they are saved by Captain Nemo, no less.

The Japanese came back with another monster in 1961. He was *Varan, the Unbelievable* (Japanese title:

ABOVE: Tenny came back in 1963 with *The Curse of the Living Corpse.*

Daikaiju Baran). Starring the American actor Myron Healey (inserted for the same reason as had been Raymond Burr in *Godzilla*), it told the story of a scaly, spiny monster who eats ships and aircraft. He is killed by explosives, but naturally not before he destroys most of Tokyo.

In 1962 it was Copenhagen's turn to be knocked down by a monster. The perpetrator was *Reptilicus*, a dragon/dinosaur who grew from the frozen tail of a prehistoric creature. He is taken to Copenhagen to be studied and placed in a freezer. Of course, the freezer door is left open by accident, and Reptilicus thaws and escapes to do his dirty work. Finally, he is killed by Professor Martens (Asbjorn Andersen) and General Mark Grayson (Carl Ottosen), who fire poisoned rockets into his mouth. The publicity department at the studio went wild: 'SEE: missiles and atom bombs powerless! SEE: civilization rioting with fear! SEE: a mighty city trampled to destruction!'

Director Del Tenny came out with one of the worst films of the decade – *The Horror of Party Beach* (1963) – certainly the worst picture ever filmed in Stamford, Connecticut. It featured the hit song 'The Zombie Stomp,' and sea monsters who crawl out of the ocean to kill some teenagers who are having a beach party. Some critics suggested that the monsters just wanted to stop all the loud music. Tenny, probably thinking that he was on a roll, followed up this atrocity with *The Curse of the Living Corpse* (1963), a film notable only for the movie debut of Roy Scheider.

Peter Cushing and Christopher Lee were the stars of *The Gorgon* (1964), the story of Megaera, the Gorgon of ancient myth, who can turn people into stone by looking at them and can also take on human form. She lives in a ruinous castle near a German village, which added atmosphere but not much credibility.

In *The Reptile* (1966), Jacqueline Pearce played the part of Anna Franklin, the daughter of the local doctor in a Cornish village, who periodically turns into a deadly snake and kills some of the villagers. The publicity blurb read: 'Forked tongue flashing awful intent . . . blood-red eyes holding grim hypnotic sway . . . repellant scales . . . lizard-like paws.' The ads were more exciting than the movie. And the makeup was so bad that you could smell the papier-mâché.

Petrie's Island was the place in question in *Island of Terror* (1966). In the film, a scientist makes monsters called the silicates – tentacled giant jellies capable of sucking the bones from humans and other animals.

ABOVE: Jacqueline Pearce periodically changed her form in *The Reptile* (1966).

LEFT: *Trog* (1970), the troglodyte monster.

OPPOSITE: Megaera, *The Gorgon* (1964), gets hers through her serpent-tressed scalp.

One of the better scenes was when Peter Cushing was grabbed on the arm by one of them, and his arm had to be chopped off with an axe by his fellow scientist, Edward Judd. Finally, the men inject cattle with strontium-90 and feed them to the creatures.

In *Trog* (1970), Joe Cornelius played the part of a man-ape – a huge-headed underground troglodyte – discovered by Joan Crawford, who tries to tame him. But villain Michael Gough works his evil on the creature, who, à la King Kong, abducts Chlöe Franks to his lair. The film was so ridiculous that it degraded Joan Crawford.

Ray Milland was the villain in *Frogs* (1972), destroying the environment of the island on which he lives, and being cruel to the animals there. The frogs in the vicinity organize an uprising among the fauna. The frogs had plenty of co-stars: scorpions, spiders, snakes, lizards, salamanders, toads, alligators, a giant vulture and leeches. Finally, Milland and his wife are eaten by a giant turtle.

Rabbits came into their own in *Night of the Lepus* (1972). Janet Leigh and Stuart Whitman were stars in

ABOVE: Ralph Meeker is confronted by a giant rat in *The Food of the Gods* (1976).

LEFT: The giant reptile in *Alligator* (1980) occasionally came up out of the sewer.

this tale of a serum gone haywire. The formula is designed to thin out the rabbit population in the Arizona desert, but instead turns the rabbits into four-foot-tall monsters.

The Giant Spider Invasion (1975), featured, of course, giant spiders who came from the center of the earth and had to be destroyed by a neutron bomb. Barbara Hale and Steve Brodie starred.

Marjo Gortner and Ida Lupino were the stars of *The Food of the Gods* (1976). Based on a story by H G wells, it told of a strange white substance that oozes out of the ground and turns common animals into monsters – giant roosters and tiger-sized rats, for example. As might be expected, they immediately start eating people.

Giant ants menace a stretch of the Florida coast as a result of radioactivity in *Empire of the Ants* (1977). The film was nowhere nearly as well done as *Them!* but at least it had a good cast – Joan Collins, Robert Lansing and Albert Salmi.

A sewer system was the setting in *Alligator* (1980). The giant reptile was on the loose underground in this fairly humorous horror spoof that starred Jack Carter, Bart Braverman and Dean Jagger.

The lead monster in the film *Q* (1982) was Quetzalcoatl, a gigantic prehistoric bird who decides to wreak glorious pandemonium on New York City. Again, a fine actor was wasted – this time Michael Moriarity.

Baby . . . Secret of the Lost Legend (1985) was a Disney movie that missed the mark by a mile. George Loomis (William Katt) and his wife Susan (Sean Young) discover living dinosaurs in Africa – a daddy and a mommy brontosaurus and their baby. Along the way, they try to save the animals from predatory hunters. Unfortunately, the big problem was the innate unlovability of the brontosaurus, especially

TOP: George (William Katt) and his wife (Sean Young) make friends with the tiny brontosaurus in *Baby . . . Secret of the Lost Legend* (1985).

BOTTOM: The stone-faced children in *Village of the Damned* (1960).

when the daddy and mommy looked like they were made of cement and baby's skin appeared to be stitched together from old footballs.

One of the most frightening types of movie monster was a child – in this case, a group of children. In *The Village of the Damned* (1960), which was based on the novel *The Midwich Cuckoos* by John Wyndham, the expectant mothers of a small English village bear children from another realm who have strange futuristic powers and are prepared to take over the world. The film, which was modestly made but absorbing and logical, starred George Sanders and Barbara Shelley. A sequel, *Children of the Damned* (1964), was not as successful.

Perhaps we had best leave our monsters there. The possibility exists that these last were the most horrifying of all – small children with beautiful faces, but without the slightest touch of humanity.

MAN-MADE MONSTERS

Probably the first successful fictional account of a man-made monster appeared in 1818 and was written by an 18-year-old girl, Mary Shelley. She had been born Mary Wollstonecraft in 1797 and married Percy Bysshe Shelley in Scotland in 1816. It was then that she began her book *Frankenstein, or The Modern Prometheus*. As she described the creature: 'His yellow skin scarcely covered the work of muscles and arteries beneath; his hair was of a lustrous black, and flowing; his teeth of a pearly whiteness; but these luxuriances only formed a more horrible contrast with his watery eyes, that seemed almost of the same colour as the dun white sockets in which they were set, his shrivelled complexion and straight black lips.'

The Shelleys were on a summer holiday in Switzerland and found that they were neighbors of another famous British poet, George Gordon, Lord Byron. It seems that it was a miserable summer – rainy and gloomy – and people were staying indoors, amusing themselves as best they could. One of their chief recreations was the reading of ghost stories. Then came an interesting suggestion from Byron, as recorded by Mary Shelley:

> "We will each write a ghost story," said Lord Byron; and his proposition was acceded to. There were four of us. The noble author began a tale, a fragment of which he printed at the end of his poem "Mazeppa." Shelley, more apt to embody ideas and sentiments in the radiance of brilliant imagery, and in the music of the most melodious verse that adorns our language, than to invent the machinery of a story, commenced one founded on the experiences of his early life. Poor Polidori [Dr John Polidori, a companion of Byron's] had some terrible idea about a skull-headed lady, who was so punished for peeping through a keyhole – what to see I forget – something very shocking and wrong of course; but when she was reduced to a worse condition than the renowned Tom of Coventry, he did not know what to do with her, and was obliged to despatch her to the tomb of the Capulets, the only place for which she was fitted. The illustrious poets also, annoyed by the platitude of prose, speedily relinquished their uncongenial task.

But Mary Shelley did not give up, and for that we can thank her.

There are few people alive today who have seen the original screen version of *Frankenstein*. A movie of that name was made in 1910 in the Edison Studios (that's right, Thomas Alva Edison), and all of the prints have since disappeared. In this film, the monster is created, according to the press release, in a 'cauldron of blazing chemical.' That method is closer to the original book than the creation of life by electricity with which we are familiar in later productions. At any rate, this monster was not burned up, drowned, buried in boiling mud, or subjected to any of our other favorite methods of creature disposal. He was defeated by the power of love, and he vanished into thin air. Dr Frankenstein and his lovely wife

The EDISON KINETOGRAM

VOL. 1. LONDON, APRIL 15, 1910 No. 1

SCENE FROM FRANKENSTEIN FILM No. 6604

EDISON FILMS TO BE RELEASED FROM MAY 11 TO 18 INCLUSIVE

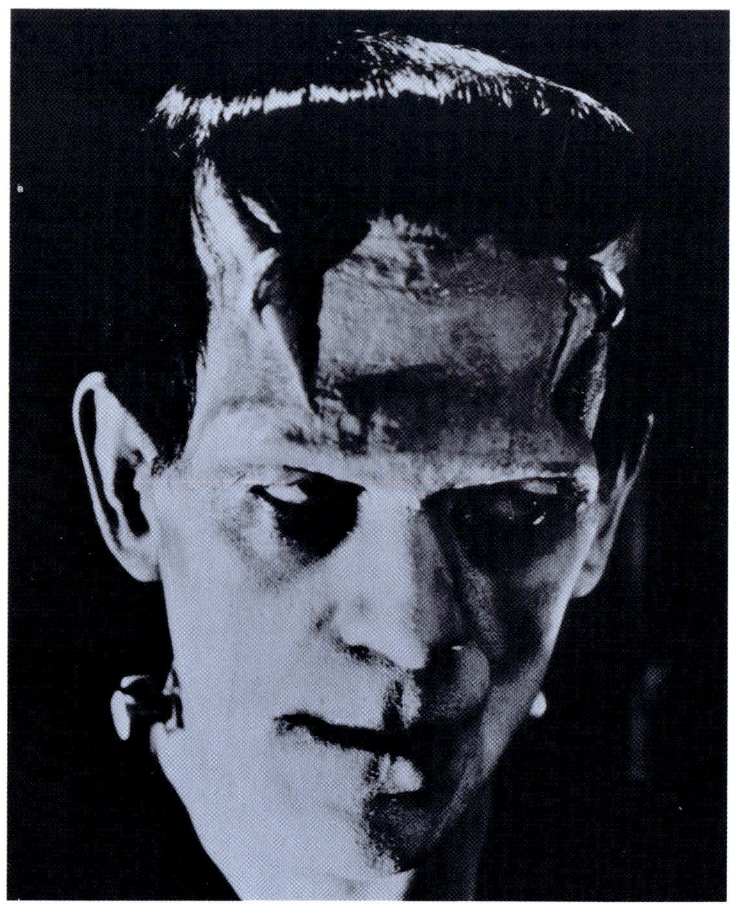

were free to live happily ever after.

The monster in this film (probably played by Charles Ogle, a member of the Edison Company acting team, although he is given no screen credit) had a pasty face, no neck to speak of and a wild mane of hair. The film was not a success, because it was too weird for movie audiences of the time.

The second production of the Frankenstein story was probably the silent film *Life Without Soul* (1915). In this, the monster was made more human, 'awe-inspiring but never grotesque,' according to the press release. He was played by Percy Darrell Standing in this production by the Ocean Film Corporation of New York. Apparently, the producers did not want the film to suffer the same fate as Edison's picture, so they ended it with a cop-out that has since become far too common – it turned out that the whole terrible thing had been the hero's dream.

Then came the greatest man-made-monster film of all time – the *Frankenstein* produced by Carl Laemmle for Universal Studios in 1931. The story of the filming of the movie has it that a French film director, Robert Florey, had written a screenplay based on Mary Shelley's book, borrowing heavily from other legends as well; the plot was about a scientist who wants to create an artificial man. Unfortunately, the scientist's assis-

RIGHT: A theater poster for *Frankenstein* (1931) – obviously printed after the picture's premiere, since Boris Karloff is given overdue credit.

OPPOSITE TOP: The cover of a promotional magazine for Edison Films showing Charles Ogle as the monster in Edison's production of *Frankenstein* (1910).

OPPOSITE BOTTOM: Boris Karloff as the monster in *Frankenstein* (1931).

PAGE 45: Karloff wearing Jack Pierce's triumph of makeup in *Frankenstein* (1931).

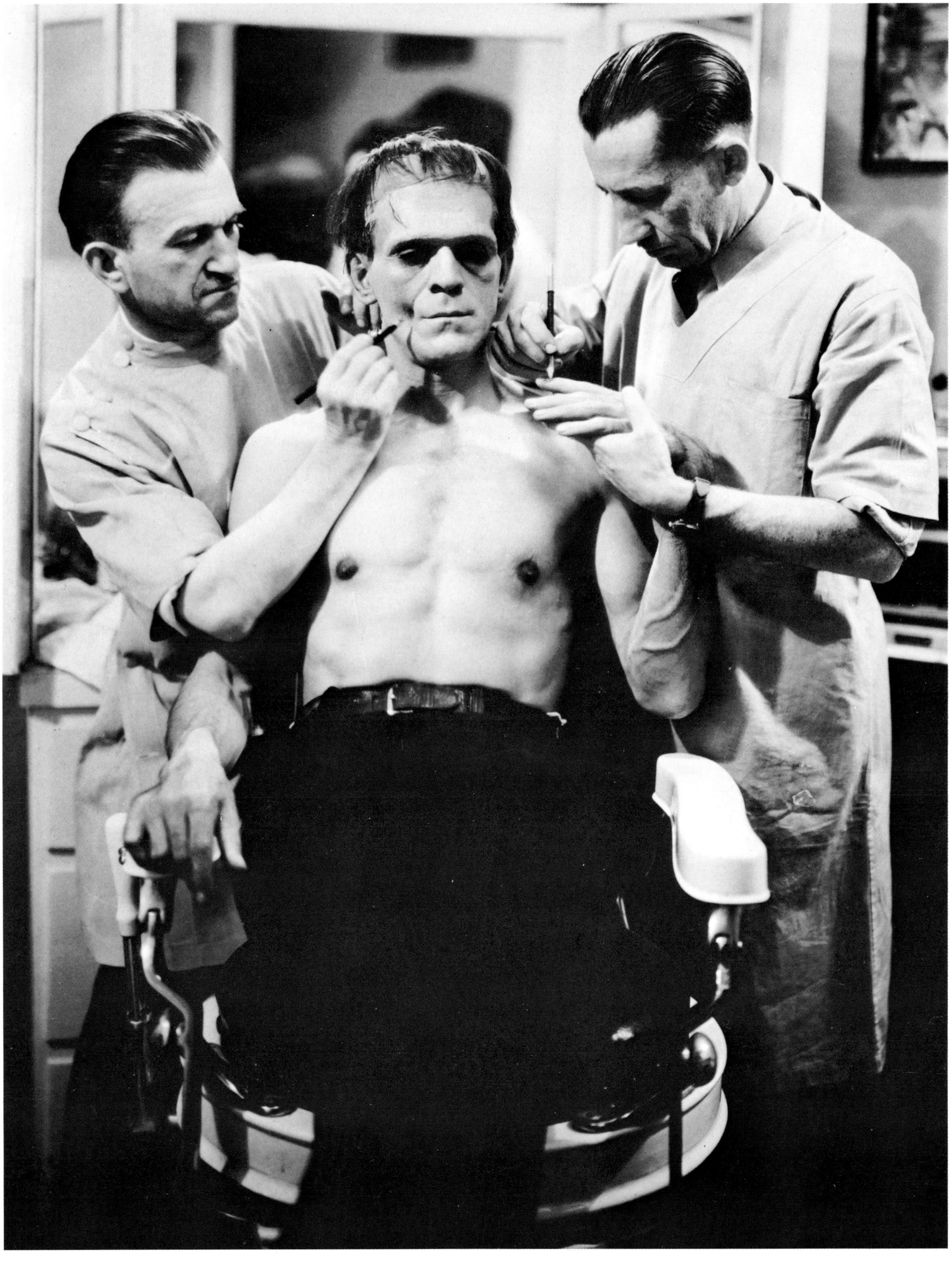

tant, while picking up spare parts with which to make the creature's body, makes a mistake and steals the brain of a dead criminal. Naturally, when the monster is given life, it creates all kinds of problems and is eventually killed off by the angry townspeople.

Florey hoped that he would be the director of the film and asked Bela Lugosi, the Hungarian actor, if he would like to play the monster. The story goes that Lugosi said anyone could play the part under such a heavy load of makeup. It was also rumored that Lugosi was a bit too conceited to want a part in which he would not be recognized and would not get a chance to speak. Meanwhile, James Whale, an English director, saw the screen tests of Lugosi's portrayal, got quite interested in the film, and suddenly became the director, replacing Florey. Whale signed Colin Clive, a British actor, to play the good Dr Frankenstein. But who would play the monster?

There is a story – perhaps apochryphal – to the effect that Whale ran into an old acquaintance in the studio commissary – an actor born in Dulwich, England in 1887 as William Henry Pratt, who was using the stage-and-screen name of Boris Karloff. Whale asked Karloff if he were interested in the role of the monster. Although he didn't think much of the idea of playing the monster, Karloff was too hungry to turn down a salary of $125 per week. So Karloff and the great makeup man of Universal Studios, Jack Pierce, worked to create the monster's appearance.

Pierce turned Karloff into a green-skinned monstrosity. He added struts to the creature's trousers to stiffen Karloff's movements, gave him a steel spine to

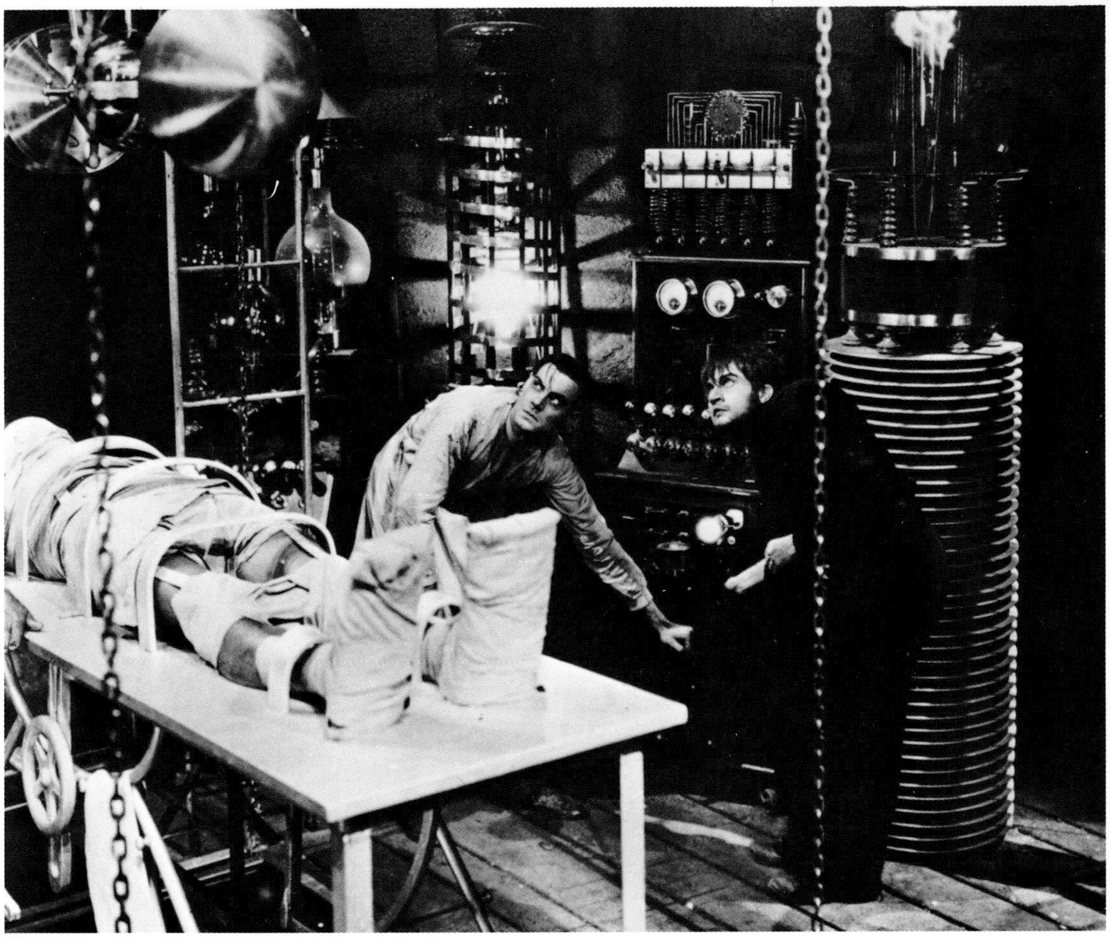

ABOVE: Boris Karloff looked menacing in the original sound version of *Frankenstein* (1931).

LEFT: With the monster on the table, Dr Frankenstein (Colin Clive, left) and his hunchbacked assistant (Dwight Frye) prepare to start the machinery. When Mel Brooks made his *Young Frenkenstein* in 1974, he was able to find this very set of machinery to use in the film.

OPPOSITE: Boris Karloff, sitting in a barber chair in the makeup room at Universal Studios, undergoing his daily three-and-one-half hour session to become the monster in *Frankenstein* (1931).

make his body rigid and had him wear quilting under his black suit to flesh out his form. He added huge boots of the type worn by hot-asphalt spreaders in those days. The makeup took three and one-half hours to put on every day, and Karloff had to sit through this, put on his 48-pound uniform and lumber to the set to work under a hot August sun shining on California. All of this probably helped him interpret the role of the suffering monster. The makeup was so frightening that Pierce had to lead Karloff around the studio because he wore a cloth covering his face.

The rest is history, except for the story that Karloff was not even invited to the grand Hollywood opening of the picture. It wasn't that the studio bosses were being cruel: it was part of a big publicity stunt. The name of the actor who played the monster was not revealed until the picture was released. This was supposed to make the public curious enough to come to the theaters in droves – which it did. The film cost $750,000 to make and has made over $14 million.

Karloff did finally get credit, of course – so much credit that most people have forgotten that John Boles and Mae Clark – Hollywood names to be reckoned

with in those days – made up the romantic interest. What romantic interest? All most people remember is Karloff's portrayal and Colin Clive's statement 'That body is not dead; it has never lived.'

Karloff brushed off his success: 'After 20 years of acting, for once I'll know where my next breakfast is coming from. [But] when you get right down to it, it was Jack Pierce who really created the Frankenstein monster. I was merely the animation in the costume,' *The Motion Picture Herald* was not so modest when it said: '[*Frankenstein*] establishes Boris Karloff as the one important candidate who has arisen for the mantle of the late Lon Chaney as a delineator of weird and grotesque roles. Because of his restraint, his intelligent simplicity of gesture, carriage, voice and makeup, Karloff has truly created a Frankenstein monster.'

A couple of scenes were cut from the original version of the film before it was seen by the public. One of them shows the monster roaming through the countryside when he comes upon a little girl who is throwing flowers into a stream. The girl is too young to be afraid of the monster, and he, obviously seeking human affection, sits down beside her and joins her in her game. But he cannot tell the difference between a flower and human life. At this point comes the cut made by the censors in the prints shown in the United States. Without knowing that he is doing anything wrong (flowers are pretty, and you throw them into the stream; the girl is pretty and you throw her into the stream), the monster tosses the girl into the water, where she drowns. After the cut, American audiences saw only the child's father carrying her dead body through the streets of the town.

RIGHT: Colin Clive (right) and Dwight Frye discuss the creation of the monster in *Frankenstein* (1931).

ABOVE: Boris Karloff stops to play with the young girl who is throwing flowers into the water – *Frankenstein* (1931). He is later, in all innocence, to drown her.

OPPOSITE TOP: Clive and Frye rob graveyards in search of parts for the new monster in *Frankenstein* (1931).

OPPOSITE BOTTOM: Boris Karloff, as the monster, confronts Mae Clark, the woman whom his creator is going to marry, in *Frankenstein* (1931).

RIGHT: Colin Clive, as Dr Frankenstein, searches for a pulse in his monster's wrist while Dwight Frye, as his assistant, looks on, in *Frankenstein* (1931).

OPPOSITE: Dwight Frye cringes in fear of the approaching monster.

BELOW: The monster is discovered after he has disposed of Dwight Frye, who was constantly tormenting him in *Frankenstein* (1931). This scene drew the wrath of the British censors, who deleted it in the version seen in England.

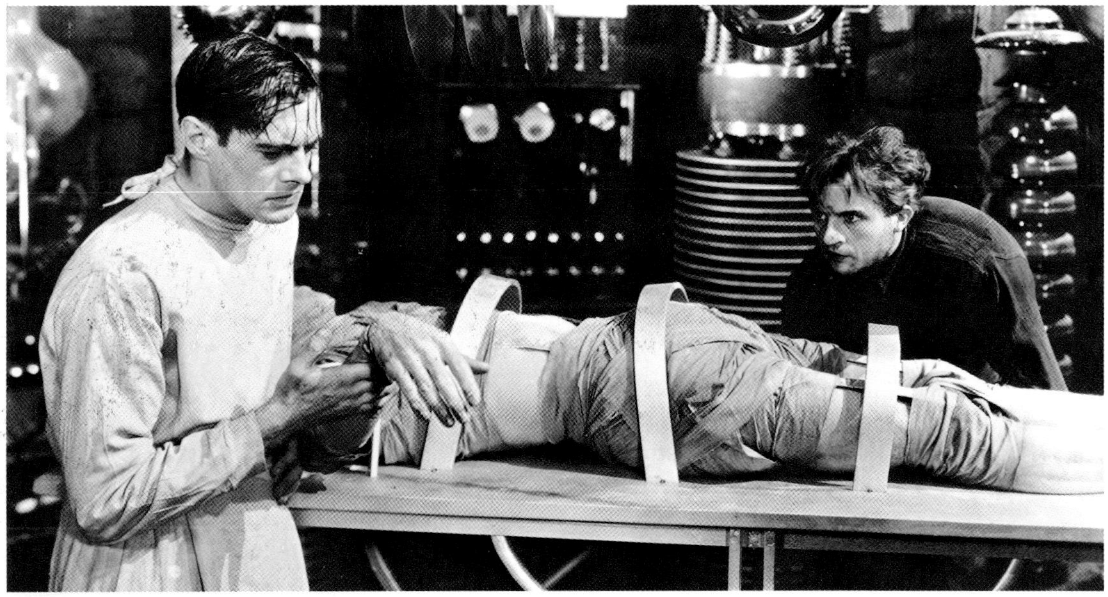

The other cut was made by the British censors. The prints of the film that were shown in England did not include the scene in which the monster, after being constantly taunted by Dr Frankenstein's cruel, hunchbacked servant Fritz (played by Dwight Frye), turns on him and hangs him.

Because of the macabre nature of the settings, it is probably a good thing that *Frankenstein* was shot in black and white, rather than in color (a not-bad three-color Technicolor process was available at the time). A color print would have destroyed some of the eerie atmosphere. But a few prints were made of the film using a green tint over the whole screen, and it is said that this coloring made the film even more horrifying. Green is the symbolic color for horror, and the tint seemed to make the monster's lips and the shadows on his face turn black – the better to frighten us.

A *Frankenstein* this well done could never have been done four years before – then it would have been a silent. Sound brought not only dialogue, but mood-inspiring musical scores and sound effects (the weird laboratory machinery, the howling wind, the barely heard tread of footsteps) to enhance the already considerable horror-manufacturing arsenal of special photographic effects and makeup.

One of the most important things to be found in this picture is the idea, unusual for the time, that a horror film must be basically logical, that every strange event must have some sort of rational explanation. Take Boris Karloff's makeup as the monster. He has a square skull – the result of the basic cut used on cadavers in primitive dissections. He has electrodes on his neck to be hooked up to wires that carry the electrical life force. The logic in *Frankenstein* worked beautifully, but many films of today suffer from the imagined need for rational explanation. We seldom see a film that requires us really to believe in monsters, ghosts or other supernatural beings: these horrors are usually explained away as the products of man's mind. Ghosts turn out to be curtains blowing in the wind, magicians are revealed as tricksters and haunted houses are shown to be figments of the imaginations of terrified heroines.

In *Frankenstein*, however, director James Whale was able to concoct an atmosphere of real sin, in the sense of a crime against a Divine Being. Dr Frankenstein, the film tells us, was really trying to usurp God's power. Add to that the great acting job turned in by Karloff – a portrayal, not of a horrible, cruel beast, rather of a victim who didn't ask for life, but who was the product of another's sin – and we begin to realize just how important this movie was.

In the book, the good doctor's first name was Victor, and why Hollywood decided to change it to Henry is anybody's guess. Also, who knows why they never gave the monster a name in the movie? Perhaps it was

the fact that he had no name in the picture that caused whole generations of movie-goers to call the monster 'Frankenstein' and forget that this was the scientist's name – the film fan didn't know what else to call the creature. In the book he was called Adam, which underlined the idea of a sin against God: Frankenstein had had the gall to name his creature after the first man as identified in the Bible.

Hollywood learned a lesson from *Frankenstein*. Monsters can be profitable. And who would blame them for bringing out more and more pictures starring the monster of Frankenstein?

The first sequel was quite good – in fact, some film critics have said that it was better than the original. Whale and Karloff, along with Colin Clive, had struck again with *The Bride of Frankenstein* in 1935. The publicity release said 'The Monster Demands a Mate.' In the film, as was the case in the book, the monster wanted companionship. He had supposedly been burned to death in a mill, but it turned out that he had crashed through the floor into a pool beneath the building. So there he was, still alive – showing the burn scars he had gotten in the fire. It's back to the

RIGHT: Basil Rathbone (left) played Dr Wolfgang von Frankenstein in *The Son of Frankenstein* (1939). Boris Karloff played the monster for the third and last time, and Bela Lugosi was Igor, the misshapen mad shepherd who was a friend of the creature.
OPPOSITE TOP: One of the tender moments in *The Bride of Frankenstein* (1935). The female monster (Elsa Lanchester) returns the monster's (Boris Karloff) gesture of friendship with a look of fear.
OPPOSITE BOTTOM: The first meeting between the monster and his 'bride' in *The Bride of Frankenstein* (1935). Colin Clive (left) again played Dr Frankenstein, while Ernest Thesiger played Dr Pretorius.
BELOW: Igor (Bela Lugosi) comes on the monster (Boris Karloff) by accident in *The Son of Frankenstein.*

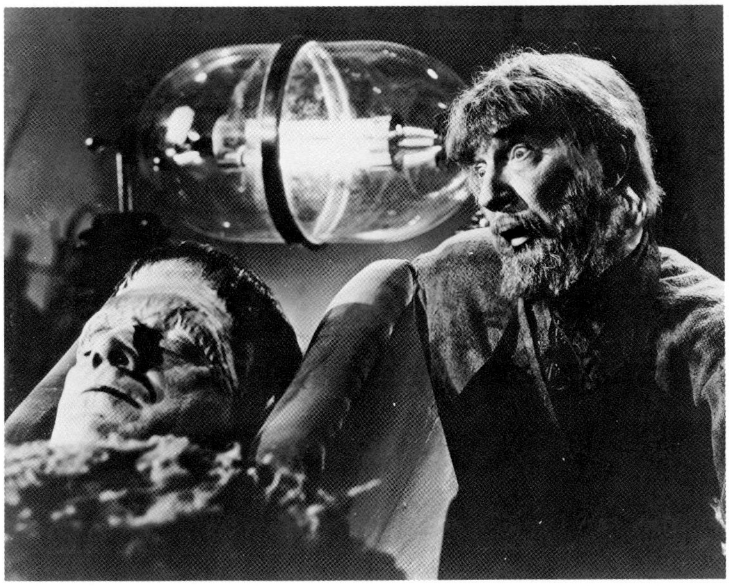

laboratory for Dr Frankenstein. At the end of the picture, he has created an artificial female (played by Elsa Lanchester, who also played Mary Shelley in the prologue), who takes one look at her intended husband and will have nothing to do with him.

One of the most touching examples of the innate humanity of the monster occurs at this point. While his lady is screaming in horror, he reaches out to pat her hand, trying to show her that he needs somebody to love. This doesn't work, however, and, shedding a tear, he directs the doctor and his wife to leave the laboratory. After they leave, the monster blows up his intended bride, and, incidentally, himself.

The makeup for Elsa Lanchester was based on the famous ancient representation of the head of the Egyptian Queen Nefertiti. By the way, in this film Dr Frankenstein's scientist friend, Dr Pretorius (delightfully portrayed by Ernest Thesiger), has been playing around with the creation of tiny people whom he keeps in bottles and dresses as kings, dancers, and other whimsical figures.

In 1939 along came *The Son of Frankenstein*. In this film, Basil Rathbone payed Wolfgang von Frankenstein, who attempted to carry on the family tradition by bringing the monster back to life. It really wasn't a bad film, although it was nowhere nearly as well done as the first two had been. It had been intended to shoot the picture in color, but the makeup department couldn't come up with a face for Karloff that looked real, so the producers went to black and white.

One area of production in *The Son of Frankenstein* deserves comment. In the first two films, the settings for the rooms of the castle were spooky enough, but in this sequel, the viewer really gets the horror treatment. Frankenstein's son is traveling back to his ancestral castle on a train. As he looks out the window, he sees the countryside gradually changing from a happy, bright landscape to one that is becoming bare and misty – just the right type of country for creating a monster. Indeed, Basil Rathbone is entering a new world, and the people in the theater are going right along with him.

Of course, Karloff played the monster in the film, and another master of screen horror joined him. It was our old friend, Bela Lugosi, who played the monster's loyal friend, Igor, a mad shepherd who had a hideously broken neck. It seems that he had been the victim of an unsuccessful hanging, and it was he who influenced the monster to kidnap Rathbone's son. In this picture, the monster ended up in a pit of boiling sulphur.

After the first three Frankenstein films in which Karloff appeared, the monster seemed to go downhill. In 1942 came *The Ghost of Frankenstein*, without the great Karloff, who had apparently had enough. In this film, lo and behold, the movie makers had found out that Dr Frankenstein had had another son! In addition to Wolfgang, who had washed his hands of the monster-making business, Henry had fathered Ludwig (played by Sir Cedric Hardwicke).

But who would play the monster now? The studio chose Lon Chaney Jr (formerly known as Creighton Chaney), the son of the famous horror-film star of the silent screen. Picking up Igor, the misshapen shepherd of *The Son of Frankenstein*, he slogged onto the screen in those 18-pound boots.

Beginning with *The Ghost of Frankenstein*, the monster was a mere shadow of his former self. He lost his powers of communication, limited though they were, as well as his ability to make us feel sympathetic

RIGHT: *Frankenstein Meets the Wolf Man* (1943).

BELOW: Lon Chaney Jr in *The Ghost of Frankenstein*.

In *Frankenstein Meets the Wolf Man* (1943), Bela Lugosi got the role of the monster that he had turned down 12 years before.

toward the artificial creature who does not understand the rules of the game of life. We can't blame all of this on Chaney's acting, either. He had already been successful playing the character Lawrence Talbot in *The Wolf Man*, and had done a fine job in *Of Mice and Men* (1939). Later he would turn in a really remarkable performance in *High Noon* (1952). We must blame the script writers: they were beginning to make a parody of Frankenstein films. In *The Ghost of Frankenstein* we have a scientist who is even more careless than his father and brother before him. He hopes to reform the monster by removing his brain and putting in a better model. But whose brain does he mistakenly use? That's right – Igor's. Who could turn in a convincing performance in a film with a plot like that?

The next entry came in the following year – 1943. Somebody decided that the monster needed some help, so out came *Frankenstein Meets the Wolf Man*. When Universal cast the picture, they realized that Chaney must go back to his werewolf role, which had been so successful two years before in *The Wolf Man*. Finally, after 12 years, Lugosi got another chance to play the monster. He wasn't as good as Karloff (nobody could have been), and his makeup left something to be desired. But he was playing the part of a monster that had been blinded in *The Ghost of Frankenstein*, and naturally he was clumsy.

In 1944 there was *House of Frankenstein*, a sort of monster party of the day. If, as in *Frankenstein Meets the Wolf Man*, two monsters appealed to movie audiences, how about making a film with three monsters? So they added Dracula, the other major movie monster of the era. Chaney stayed in as the Wolf Man,

John Carradine played Dracula, and the studio picked Glenn Strange to play the Frankenstein monster. Strange had previously been most famous for playing the bad guy in cowboy movies; he would end his career playing Miss Kitty's bartender in the Long Branch Saloon on the 'Gunsmoke' television series.

The mad Dr Niemann (Boris Karloff) thaws out the Wolf Man, who had been frozen in the previous film, and removes the stake from the skeletal remains of Dracula, which were being displayed in a traveling chamber of horrors presided over by Professor Lampini (George Zucco). Along the way, a gypsy girl shoots the Wolf Man with a silver bullet, the monster kills a psychopathic hunchback (J Carrol Naish), the monster and Niemann are chased by peasants into a pit of quicksand and Dracula is killed by the sun's rays.

However, the Frankenstein film had not hit rock bottom yet. In 1957 *I Was a Teen-age Frankenstein* was released. The monster in this picture was created from parts of teenagers. And the film even made the mistake that generations of movie audiences had been making – Frankenstein in this movie was the monster, not the doctor. The film featured several so-called jokes, one of them being the doctor's words to his monster: 'Speak to me! I know you can. I put your tongue in there myself.' It was a prime example of tastelessness and inanity in action.

In the 1950s the British began to take over. Hammer Studios released *The Curse of Frankenstein* in 1957. It starred Peter Cushing as Frankenstein and Christopher Lee as the monster. Lee's makeup was quite different from Karloff's, since Universal still owned the copyright on the original. In *The Curse of Frankenstein* Lee looked as though he had been created out of scar tissue and greasepaint, and he had to restrict his diet to mashed potatoes and drink through a straw for fear of spoiling his makeup.

It was probably *The Curse of Frankenstein* that started the rage of 'road accident cinema,' later to become 'splatter films,' in which red blood gushed from severed limbs and open wounds. Before the film went into production, Hammer's Terence Fisher was asked if he wanted to see the original movie. He said 'Certainly not. If one is going to make this film, I think that one has got to start from a personal concept and what you yourself think.'

The picture was made in six weeks, cost a mere $250,000 and made 30 times that amount for the studio. In its way, it was a believable, logical movie. Lee's makeup looked as if it were the result of real surgery. Cushing behaved as a creditable man of science, and his laboratory was a believable Victorian science room. It took three quarters of the movie to build the monster, and the ending was true to life, too – the monster was a thing of hell, and Frankenstein went to his death on the guillotine to pay for the crimes of its creation.

With this film, a new day had dawned in the world of horror films. Hammer spent little time in developing characterizations, sympathy, or even suspense. The movie seemed to concentrate on blood and guts, with a

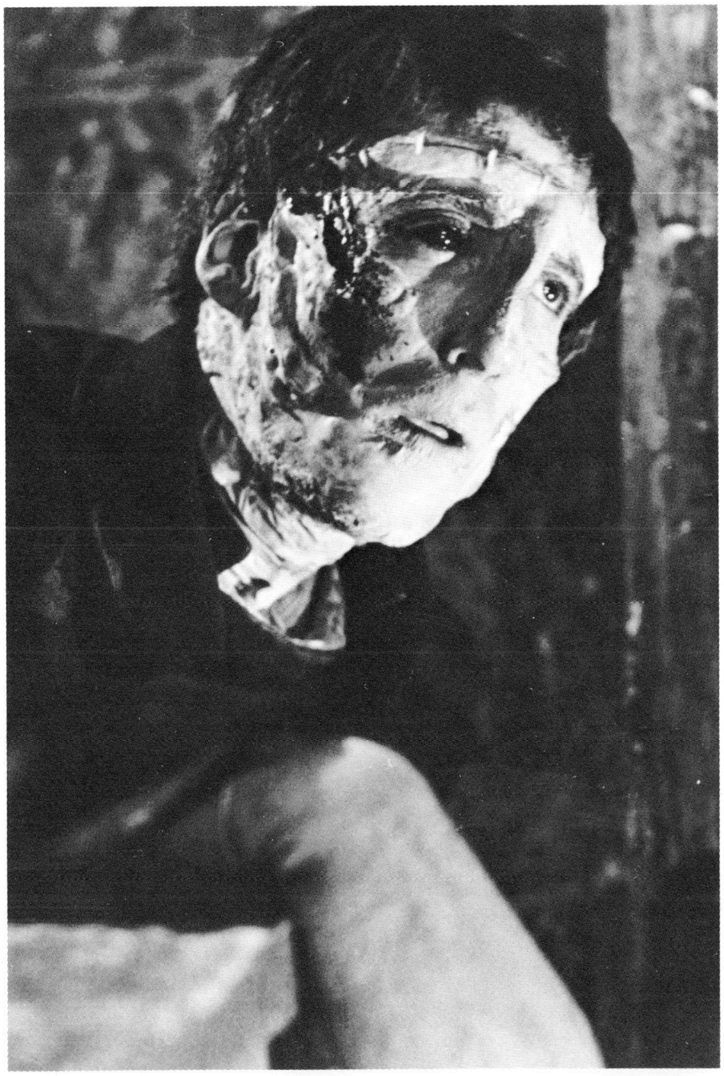

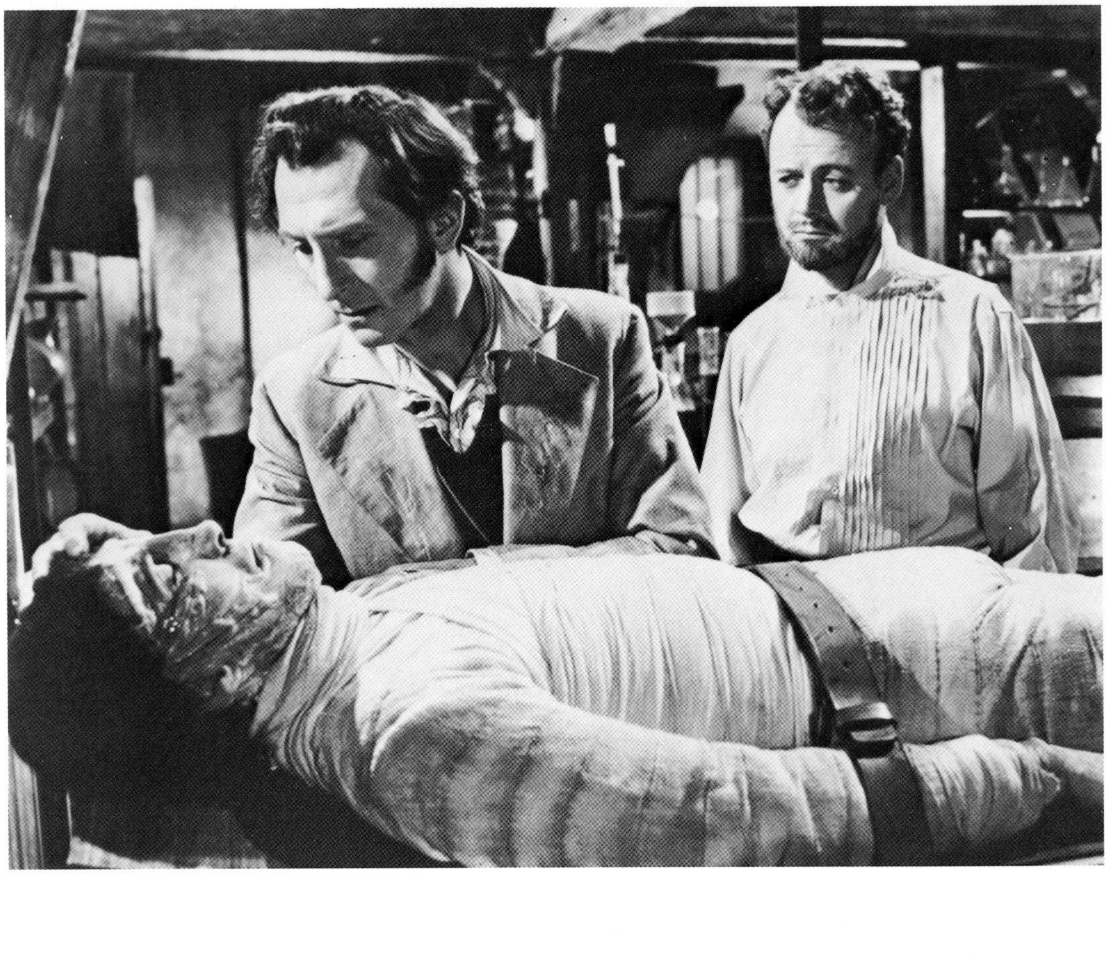

ABOVE RIGHT: A completely new concept in makeup for the monster – Christopher Lee in Hammer's *The Curse of Frankenstein* (1957).

RIGHT: Peter Cushing (center) looks upon his monster creation in *The Curse of Frankenstein* (1957), while his friend, Robert Urquhart, observes.

OPPOSITE TOP: The psychopathic assistant (J Carroll Naish) in a traveling horror show and a Gypsy girl (Elena Verdugo) are accosted by the mad Dr Niemann (Boris Karloff) in *House of Frankenstein* (1944).

OPPOSITE BOTTOM: Glenn Strange played the monster in *House of Frankenstein* (1944).

little sex thrown in. Three different versions of the picture were shot and released in different countries – a mild one, with a few shocking scenes; a medium one, with a few extra buckets of blood; and a no-holds-barred zinger with the blood flowing like wine.

Hammer followed *The Curse of Frankenstein* with *The Revenge of Frankenstein* (1958). Frankenstein's alleged death on the guillotine was explained away by saying that he had been saved by a priest. Frankenstein (Peter Cushing) takes on the new name Dr Stein and makes a new monster (Michael Gwynn) containing the brain of a homicidal dwarf. At first the monster looked like a real human being, but he was injured, became deformed and turned to cannibalism. When the monster is destroyed, Dr Stein has his own brain switched to another body and turns up in London's Harley Street as Dr Frank.

That same year, 1958, *Frankenstein 1970* was released. Boris Karloff was the star – as the doctor, not the monster. In this modern version, Karloff was an English scientist who needs a new atomic reactor for his laboratory. To get the money, he permits an American film crew to use his castle as a location for their movie. Unfortunately, his blind monster starts killing off the film crew. The whole thing ended when the reactor erupted and killed both Frankenstein and his monster.

An even worse film was *Frankenstein's Daughter*

ABOVE: The girl holds the head of her friend in *Frankenstein Created Woman* (1967).

ABOVE LEFT: The dwarf (Oscar Quitak) views the new body which Dr Frankenstein (Peter Cushing) has created for him in *The Revenge of Frankenstein* (1958).

LEFT: Peter Cushing, once more playing the good doctor, tries to reason with his monster (Kiwi Kingston) in *The Evil of Frankenstein* (1965).

OPPOSITE: Peter Cushing back in his laboratory in *Frankenstein Must Be Destroyed* (1969).

(1958). Produced in Britain by Astor Studios, it starred Donald Murphy and Sandra Knight.

One of the worst of the lot was *Jesse James Meets Frankenstein's Daughter* (1965), in which Jesse was John Lupton and the daughter was Narda Onyx. She has been in Mexico practicing brain transplants with her brother Rudolph (Stephen Geray) and creates a monster (Cal Bolder). Another girl, Estelita, shoots the monster, Jesse is taken away by the marshal, and Frankenstein's daughter resolves to wait for him to get out of prison.

Cushing came back as Frankenstein in *The Evil of Frankenstein* (1965), and this time he found his monster in a glacier. It was a terrible picture in which the monster was played by a New Zealand wrestler, Kiwi Kingston, and Peter Woodthorpe was a hypnotist who uses the monster to rob and murder for him.

Cushing never gave up. In *Frankenstein Created Woman* (1967), he revived the body of the drowned Susan Denberg, giving her the brain of her lover, who had been wrongly executed for murder. That means that she has to begin killing the perjurers who lied at his trial – after which she commits suicide by jumping off a cliff.

The 1960s ended with Cushing starring in *Frankenstein Must Be Destroyed* (1969). With him was Freddie Jones as the monster, and both of them were burned to death.

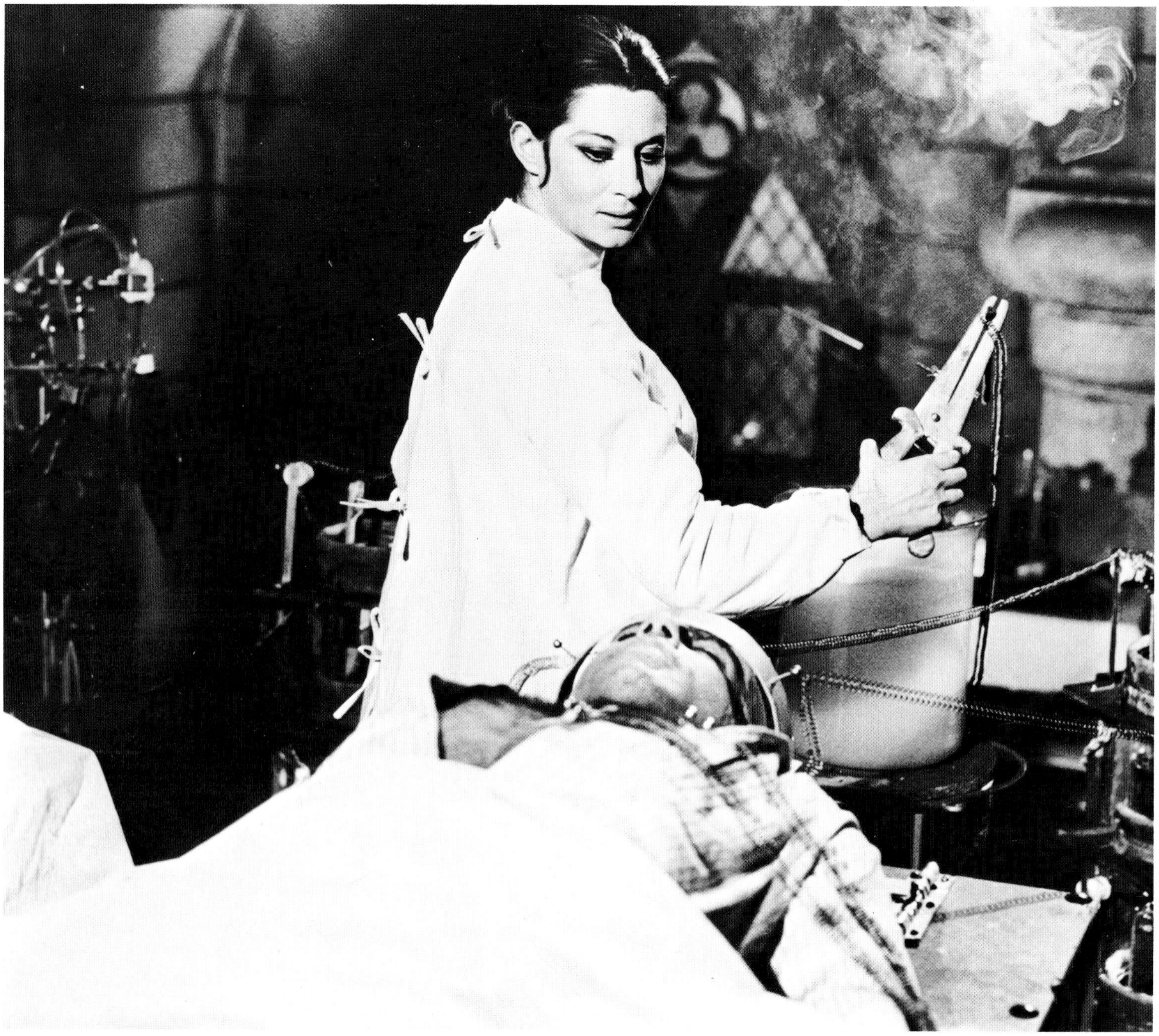

Dave Prowse played the monster and Ralph Bates was the scientist in *The Horror of Frankenstein* (1970). Bates was a new kind of Frankenstein – he arranged the murder of his father, cheated on his wife and killed his best friend, while creating his laughable monster.

Two monsters for the price of one was the grabber in *Lady Frankenstein* (1971). Made in Italy as *La Figlia di Frankenstein*, it starred Joseph Cotten as Frankenstein and Sara Bay as his daughter. Frankenstein creates a monster who immediately starts marauding the countryside. So he makes another monster to run down the first. Finally, both father and daughter are killed by the first monster.

Hollywood tried again with the bride of Frankenstein theme in 1985, this time calling it merely *The Bride*. It began in traditional form – with a storm. Frankenstein (Sting) creates a lady friend for his male creature, and the girl turns out to be Jennifer Beals. She is, of course, pretty, and rejects the monster (this time named Victor, in honor of the original Dr Frankenstein, and played by Clancy Brown), who takes off and runs into a four-foot-tall circus performer named Rinaldo (David Rappaport). The two become fast friends, and their relationship in the film is so good that it makes the rest of the movie look sleazy.

Meanwhile, the doctor has eyes for his female monster, Eva, and attempts to rape her, all the time playing Professor Higgins to her Eliza Doolittle. The film keeps shifting from one subplot to the other, with the two misfit men winning hands down. One critic said that when Beals was given the task of erupting into a feminine outburst, it was 'like watching Woody Allen play King Lear.'

But not since the 1931 film have Frankenstein and his friend really been treated properly. They have been laughed at, made to look like madmen, and turned into cartoon characters on cereal boxes.

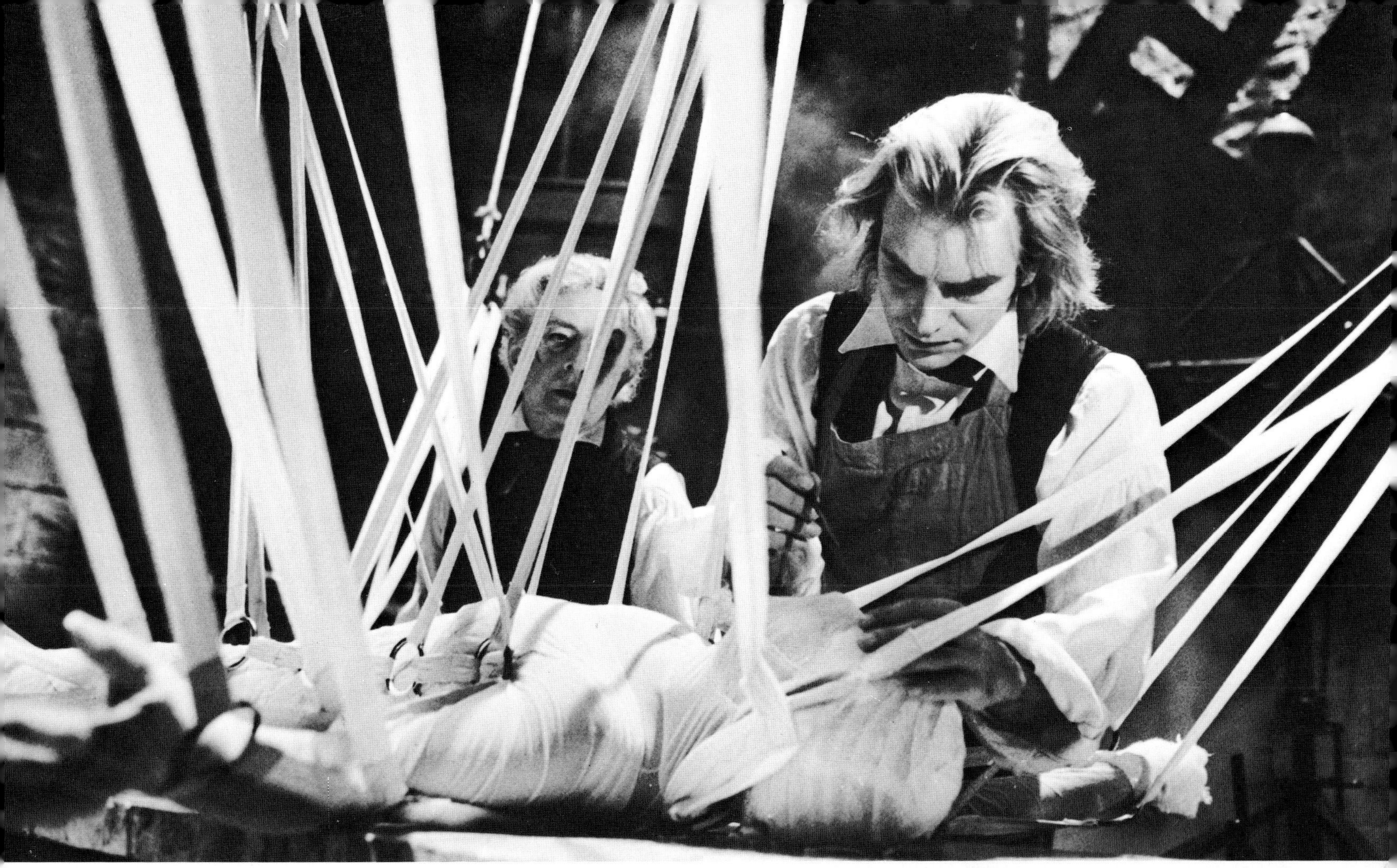

ABOVE: Quentin Crisp (left) assists Dr Charles Frankenstein (Sting) as he gives life to the perfect woman in *The Bride* (1985).

RIGHT: Sting as Frankenstein with his creation – Jennifer Beals – in *The Bride* (1985).

OPPOSITE: Sara Bay is up to no good in *Lady Frankenstein/La Figlia di Frankenstein* (1971).

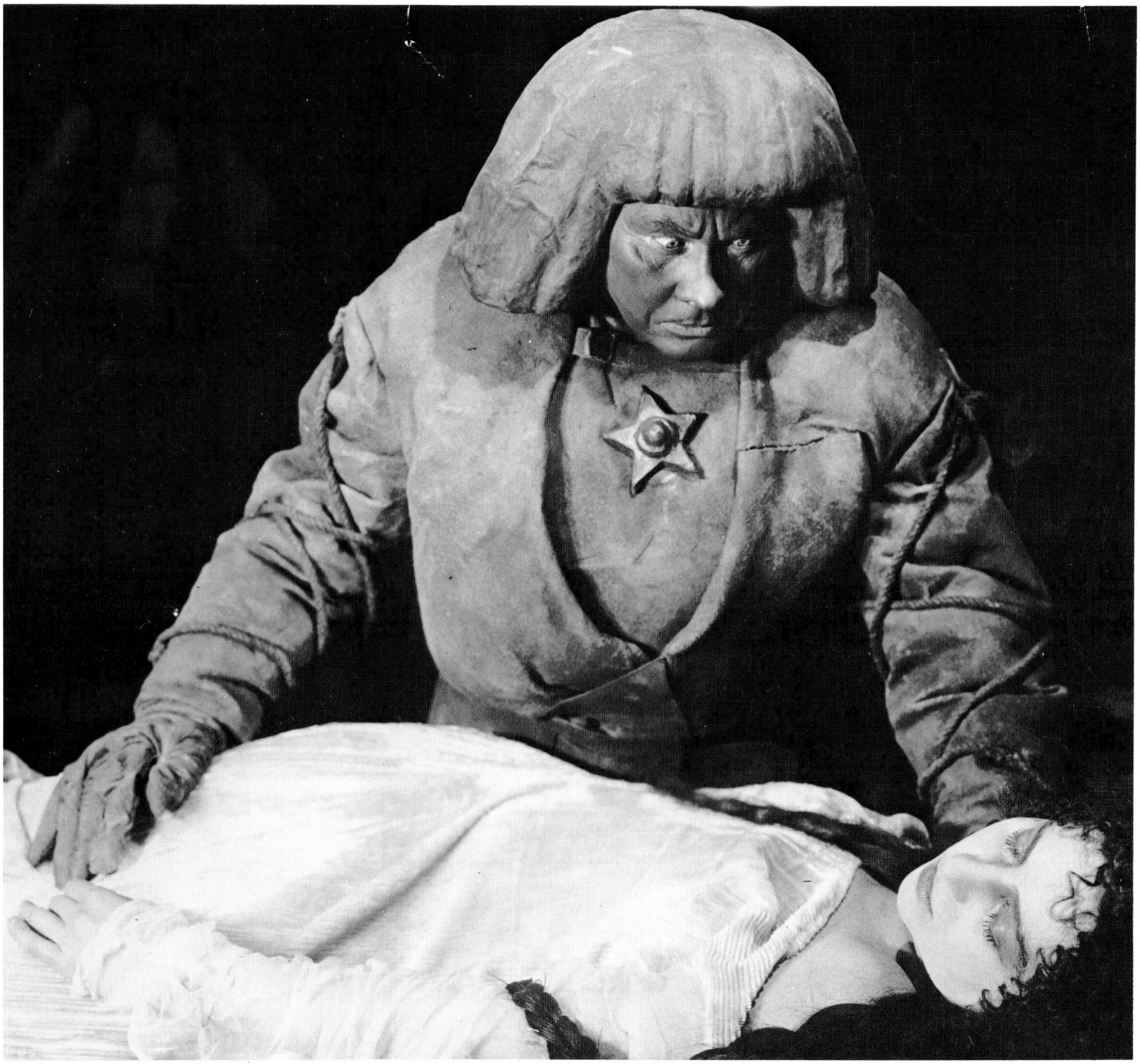

Another weird man-made monster from out of the past is the golem. This is an artificial man, according to folklore, made of clay or mud, which is brought to life when the name of God is pronounced over it. Some stories say that it is then able to understand orders and is just great for doing housework. Others say that it can be used as a frightening type of bodyguard. On its forehead is written the Hebrew word *emeth*, which means 'truth.' Every day the golem becomes bigger and bigger, heavier and heavier, until it becomes a nuisance, if not a downright danger, to have around the house. So the first letter of the word on its forehead must be rubbed out, so that the inscription now reads *meth*, which means 'he is dead.' The golem will collapse and turn into clay again.

The first golem film was a German production, *Der Golem*, made in 1915. The star in the title role was an actor named Paul Wegener, who also coscripted and codirected it with Henrik Galeen, a Dutch writer who went on to write such chillers as *Nosferatu* (1922). Wegener had been in Prague two years previously and learned about the legend of the medieval Rabbi Judah Low Ben Bezalel, who made a golem from clay to protect the Jews in the ghetto from a pogrom. The golem saves them, but then turns bad and ravages the ghetto. Wegener was so impressed with the film possibilities of the subject that he made the movie.

It concerned the discovery of a clay statue which is found during building excavations and sold to an antique dealer. The merchant brings it to life, but the golem falls in love with the daughter of the house (Lyda Salmonova). When he realizes that she is terrified of him, he tries to destroy the city, but is put out of his misery by a terrible fall from a high tower. The

RIGHT: Harry Bauer played the title role in *The Golem* (1966). Here he is with Charles Dorat.

OPPOSITE: Paul Wegener was the greatest golem of all time. Here he is with Lyda Salmonova in *The Golem* (1915), retitled *The Monster of Fate* in the United States.

BELOW: A moment of tenderness in *The Golem* (1915).

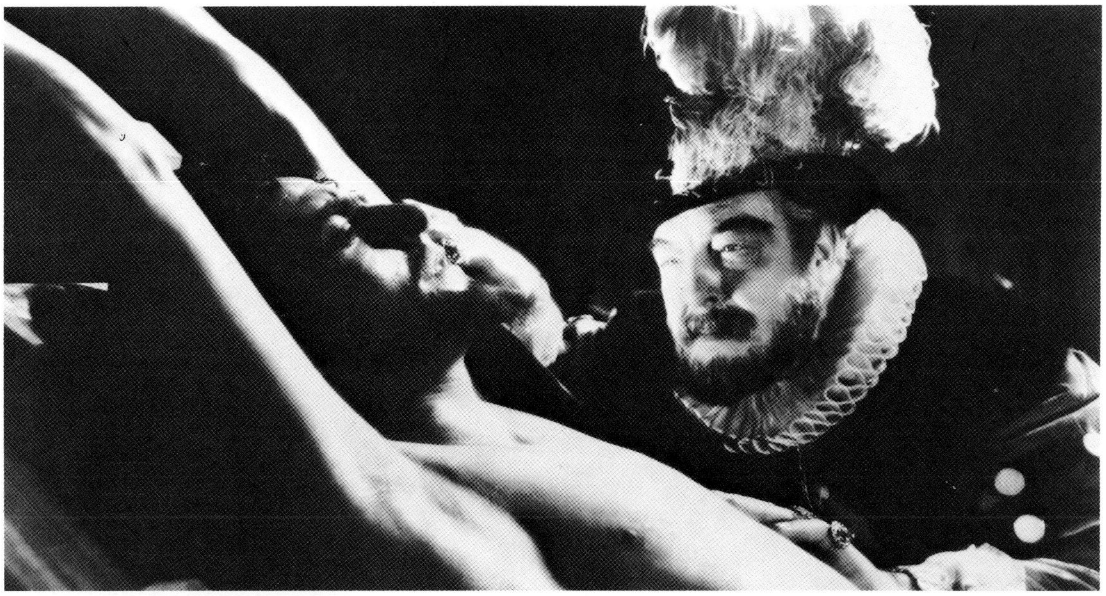

golem in this movie was a creature who had many human qualities. It seems certain that this film was a forerunner of the 1931 Frankenstein, with its sympathetic monster.

Der Golem was, unfortunately, released in the United States (retitled *The Monster of Fate*) during the week in which diplomatic relations were broken off with Germany prior to the American entry into World War I. Needless to say, the public did not react favorably to this German import. Certainly the publicists tried to sell the film: 'If you're tired of the humdrum in Photoplay Stories . . . If you're yearning for Something New in Motion Picture ideas . . . You will be interested in *The Monster of Fate*. A real mystery story. A novel idea splendidly handled. A big problem worked out. Interesting to the last flash on the screen. *The Monster of Fate* is relish for the palate of a jaded motion picture public.'

Wegener, of all people, made a takeoff film of *Der Golem* called *Der Golem und Die Tänzerin (The Golem and the Dancer)* in 1917. In it, Wegener dresses as the golem to frighten the dancer (Salmonova again). It was played for laughs, but it must have been as embarrassing as *Abbot and Costello Meet Frankenstein* (1948).

In 1920 Wegener made amends by remaking *Der Golem*. This time he used the original legend, with Rabbi Low creating the clay man. The photographer was Karl Freund, the genius who went on to photograph *The Mummy* (1932) with Boris Karloff. The special effects were exceptional – double and triple exposures with the film speeded up to triple speed at times.

Le Golem was a French film of 1936. In this case, the monster was given life by the wife of a condemned rabbi. The golem then went on to break up the execution. The French remade the film in 1966.

But the golem went the way of the Frankenstein monster, reappearing in London in 1966 in a film entitled *It!* Roddy McDowall plays a museum employee who discovers a golem (Allen Sellers) in a warehouse. He brings the monster to life and orders him off to kidnap his (McDowall's) girl friend (played by Jill Haworth, who went on to the starring role of Sally Bowles in *Cabaret* on Broadway). On the way, the golem destroys Hammersmith Bridge in London. At the end, the golem walks into the water and disappears à la Godzilla, and Roddy McDowall is killed by an atom bomb – rather like shooting a cannon at a fly.

So the man-made monsters lie quiescent in their graves. But we all know that they will be back.

BACK FROM THE DEAD

The legend of the vampire goes back at least to the ancient Greek *lamia* and *empusa*, and all through history, poets and novelists have kept the stories coming. Goethe, Lord Byron and Southey all wrote poems about the blood drinkers. Alexandre Dumas wrote a vampire play in the 1850s, and in 1853 a pulp-magazine type of book called *Varney the Vampire* was enormously successful. Then, in 1897, along came the granddaddy of all vampire books – the novel *Dracula*, by Bram Stoker, which became the basis for so many movies. Here is what the archfiend looked like, according to Stoker:

> His face was a strong – a very strong – aquiline, with high bridge of the thin nose and peculiarly arched nostrils; with lofty domed forehead, and hair growing scantily around the temples but profusely elsewhere. His eye-brows were very massive, almost meeting over the nose, and with bushy hair that seemed to curl in its own profusion. The mouth, so far as I could see it under the heavy moustache, was fixed and rather cruel-looking, with peculiarly sharp white teeth; these protruded over the lips, whose remarkable ruddiness showed astonishing vitality in a man of his years. For the rest, his ears were pale, and at top extremely pointed; the chin was broad and strong, and the cheeks firm though thin. The general effect was one of extraordinary pallor. Hitherto I had noticed the backs of his hands . . . and they had seemed rather white and fine; but seeing them now close to me, I could not but notice that they were rather coarse – broad, with squat fingers. There were hairs in the center of the palm. The nails were long and fine, and cut to a sharp point.

Movies over the years have stuck pretty close to that description when they told the story of one vampire or the other.

Vampire films are the most censor-obsessed of all the horror-film genres. In them, three of our greatest taboos – sex, violence and irreligion – compete for attention. Beyond doubt, the first of all the screen vampires appeared in *The Devil's Castle*, made by Georges Méliès in France in 1896. This beauty ends as a gentleman holds up a crucifix and the fiend gives up and disappears.

This was followed in America by a couple of long-forgotten films in which vampires had small roles – *The Legend of a Ghost* (1908) and *A Village Vampire* (1916). And *Dracula* had been filmed in Hungary by Karoly Lathjay.

But the first big breakthrough in vampire films was *Nosferatu, Eine Symphonie des Grauens*, a German production released in Europe in 1922 and in the United States in 1929. It was directed by Friedrich Wilhelm Murnau.

The Bram Stoker novel *Dracula* had been published only 25 years before *Nosferatu* was made, and the copyright was still in effect. So, in order to avoid paying the Stoker estate, some changes were made. The main action of the film occurs in Bremen, Germany – not in London. The time of the story was switched from the 1890s back to the 1830s. The names of the characters were changed – Count Dracula became Count Orlock, the Harkers became the Hutters, Renfield became Knock and Van Helsing became Butler. Finally, the film was renamed *Nosferatu*, which means '*The Undead*.' None of this worked. Stoker's widow gained a court order that called for the destruction of all prints of the film, but fortunately some were saved.

Essentially, the story was the same. A young clerk is sent to Transylvania in order to settle some business with a nobleman. He arrives at a spooky old castle and is greeted by the count, who turns out to be a vampire. The clerk spends the night and the next day finds his host laid out in a coffin in a secret room of the castle. But he also finds out that he is the count's prisoner. Presumably, the count has drained the Transylvania peasants of most of their blood, so he leaves for Bremen, taking the black plague with him, as if vampirism weren't enough.

In the book, as Dracula is committing his crimes in London, a great many people are involved in tracking him down, among them a wise Dutch scientist, Professor Van Helsing, who eventually is able to trace the

RIGHT: Max Schreck, as the evil vampire in *Nosferatu* (1922, released in the US in 1929), climbs from below decks as his ghostly unmanned ship arrives in Bremen, Germany.

BELOW RIGHT: The sun rises and Count Orlock begins to disappear in *Nosferatu* (1922).

OPPOSITE: The cover of a penny dreadful of 1853. The English public ate it up.

BELOW: The ghastly Count Orlock in all his glory – *Nosferatu* (1922).

PREVIOUS SPREAD: Christopher Lee about to get his in *The Horror of Dracula* (1958).

vampire to his coffin and kill him with a stake through his heart. But in *Nosferatu*, the wife of the clerk handles the whole thing by herself in Bremen, Her shortcut is to entice Orlock to her room and let him feast on her blood. Then she holds him there until the cock crows in the morning. He dies with the sunrise but alas, she dies with him.

The star of the film was a German actor billed as Max Schreck, but who would believe that? '*Schreck*' means 'terror' in German, and there are those who believe that the actor was really a music-hall performer named Alfred Abel. At any rate, Orlock was a terrifying figure – tall, thin, with incredibly long fingernails, sharp teeth, and a bald rat-like head.

The performances were crude, but no one who has

seen it will ever forget the final disappearance scene, the scene in which the boat sails itself into Bremen harbor with the dead captain lashed to the wheel, the scene where Orlock's shadow seems to rise and cover the houses near the pier, or the scenes of long lines of coffins that invariably followed in Orlock's wake, along with rats by the hundreds. Orlock was the very personification of pestilence and corruption, disease and death.

In *London After Midnight*, a 1927 silent film, the stars were Lon Chaney Sr playing a dual role as inspector Burke of Scotland Yard and a vampire, Polly Moran as the heroine and Edna Tichenor as Luna, the white-draped bat-girl. The movie was directed by the master of the horror film, Tod Browning, and Chaney played the vampire (who turned out to be a hoax) as a nut case – not the sophisticated nobleman we all know and love. He had an insane look about him – wide, staring eyes with circles around them, teeth filed to fine points, white, unkempt hair – and he wandered around in a black coat, white tie and top hat.

Chaney suffered in his makeup in this picture. He used circles of thin wires under his eyelids to make his eyes bulge and wore a set of false animal teeth that he could put up with for only a very short time before the pain would get the better of him.

The first vampire who talked was played by Bela Lugosi in the 1931 Universal picture *Dracula*. Although it was an American picture, about the only prominent American involved was Tod Browning, who had made many films starring the old master Lon Chaney Sr. The story selection was made by a German story editor, the movie was photographed by a German cameraman, and it starred the Hungarian Lugosi, who was forever after to be identified with the role of Count Dracula.

The story of the filming of this movie began in 1924. The English actor/producer Hamilton Deane had seen *Nosferatu* and realized that he wanted to adapt *Dracula* for the stage. He was aware that Stoker had known his novel had theatrical possibilities – even going so far as to preserve a dramatic copyright by giving a reading of the novel at London's Lyceum Theatre on 18 May 1897. Deane also knew about the court ruling against Murnau in the *Nosferatu* affair, so he took care to pay for the rights to do his stage adaptation, which was first presented in 1924 in Derby, England. Edmund Blake was Dracula and Deane was Van Helsing. The play was so successful that a second touring company was formed; it opened on Valentine's Day, 1924, in London's Little Theatre with Deane as Van Helsing and Raymond Huntley as Dracula.

American producer Horace Liveright had journalist John L Balderston Americanize the play, and it opened in 1927 on Broadway at the Fulton Theater. Bela Lugosi played the count and Edward Van Sloan was Van Helsing. It ran for 261 performances in New York and then went on tour, with Lugosi remaining on hand as Dracula.

In 1930 Universal Studios paid $40,000 for screen rights to the play, intending to have Browning and Chaney team up again, but Chaney died of cancer before shooting could begin. The studio then approached first Victor Jory, then William Courtney, then Ian Keith to take on the role. All refused, and Lugosi was given the part.

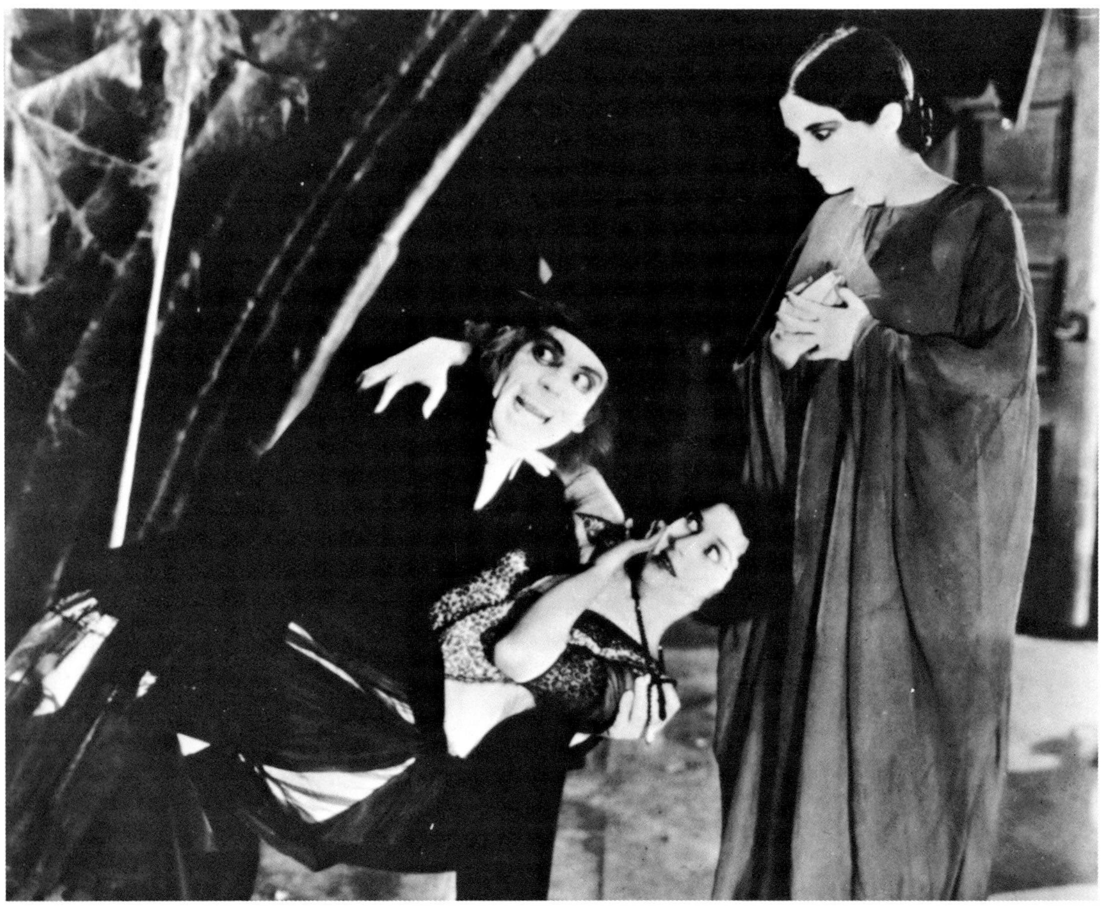

LEFT: Lon Chaney, pretending to be a vampire, frightens two sweet young things in *London After Midnight* (1927).

OPPOSITE: Chaney, as usual, created his own makeup (a painful job) for the part of the vampire in *London After Midnight* (1927).

Lugosi, born Béla Lugosi Blasko in 1882 in Lugos, Hungary, was just great. He gave the role an aura of sexuality and dominated every scene he was in. He seemed to believe that he was a vampire from the first moment when he announced to the horrified hero of the film, 'I am – Dracula.' Not that the script writer didn't give Dracula a sense of humor. At dinner he announces to the guests, 'I never drink – wine.' And when he hears the wolves he says, 'Children of the night – what music they make.' The film was Lugosi's moment of triumph. After it, he went downhill rapidly and never had another decent part except for the role as Raznin, one of the three Russian commissars sent to bring Greta Garbo back from Paris in the comedy *Ninotchka* (1939). But in this picture he was an immediate hit; two years later he was given the unique honor of having a caricature of himself appear in a Walt Disney Mickey Mouse cartoon.

A Spanish-language version of the film was made at the same time, with Dracula played by Carlos Villarias. It was directed by George Melford and used the props and scenery of the American version.

There are those who say that *Dracula* was stagey, perhaps because Browning followed the theatrical version too closely. Also, the special effects budget was pretty skimpy: witness the bat that flies like a yo-yo, and the scenes of the ship *Vesta* borrowed from an earlier film, *Head Winds*. Also, the death of Dracula was nothing more than an unconvincing offscreen groan. But the public loved it, and believed the publicity department's line, 'The strangest love a man has ever known.'

In the film *Dracula* we see a young man named Renfield riding in a carriage on his way to Castle Dracula. It is an eerie place, a ruin filled with cobwebs. It has huge staircases and cold fireplaces. Renfield meets Dracula and soon discovers that he is a vampire. Of course Dracula turns him into a vampire, too, and Renfield ends up eating flies and cackling to him-

self. The evil count has trouble getting a meal, since he has run out of people in the neighborhood to bite. So he packs up and takes a ship to England. He terrorizes a few people, turning a young girl named Lucy into a vampire, for example, but is finally killed by Dr Van Helsing (Edward Van Sloan repeating his stage role), the vampire expert.

There were a few good touches in the second part of the movie. One of them was the scene in which the normal people realize that Dracula does not cast a reflection in a silver box. But most of the horrible things that happen – Dracula's arrival in the form of a mist, his death by a stake through the heart – happen offscreen. After the excellent first section of the film, with all its mysterious scenery and creepy characters, like the weird coachman and the pasty-faced vampire girls living in the castle, the second part seems drab.

The next year, 1932, another Dracula-type film was released. This was *Vampyr*, made in France by the Danish director Carl Dreyer. Although the script by Sheridan Le Fanu was more poetic than the Browning version, it was slower paced.

A young man, David Gray, comes to spend the night at an inn in the mountains. A stranger enters his room in the night and gives him a package, with instructions to open it if he, the stranger, should die. The next day Gray visits a chateau and meets a doctor, a pleasant old lady and the owner of the house, who turns out to be the man of the package. He has two daughters, one of whom is dying. Then the owner of

RIGHT: Dr Van Helsing (Edward Van Sloan), the vampire expert, confronts Count Dracula (Bela Lugosi) with proof that his image cannot be seen in a mirror in *Dracula* (1931).
OPPOSITE LEFT: The Spanish-language version of *Dracula* (1931) starred Carlos Villarias as the count, with Carmen Guerrero as one of his victims.
OPPOSITE RIGHT: An early theater poster for *Dracula* (1931). Note that the author is listed as *Abraham* Stoker.
BELOW: The Count (Bela Lugosi) calls on his slave, Renfield (Dwight Frye), in *Dracula* (1931).

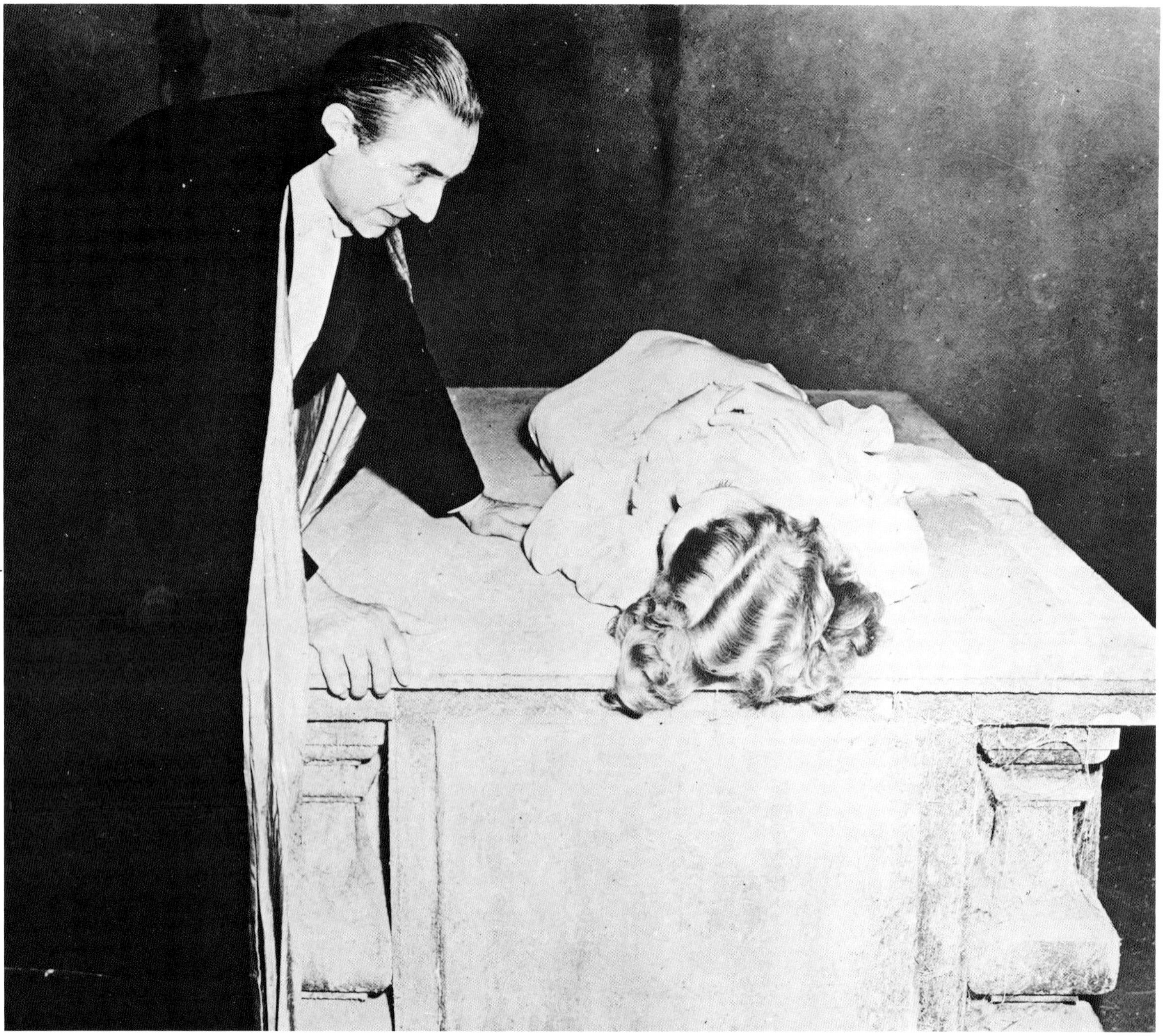

the house himself is shot dead, and Gray opens the package. In it is a book telling about vampires and how to destroy them. The old lady is a vampire who, with the help of the doctor, is killing the sick daughter. Gray offers his blood for a transfusion, but dreams that this will turn him into a vampire. When he awakens, he kills the old woman with a stake and the sick daughter dies. Gray goes off with the healthy daughter.

The acting was pretty horrible. With the exception of the dying daughter, all the actors were amateurs and showed it with a great deal of hamming and lack of discipline. But Dreyer wanted atmosphere and he got it. He told his cameraman: 'Imagine we are sitting in an ordinary room. Suddenly we are told that there is a corpse behind the door. In an instant the room we are sitting in is completely altered: everything in it has taken on another level; the light, the atmosphere have changed, though they are physically the same. This is because *we* have changed, and the objects *are* as we conceive them. This is the effect I want to get.'

Whenever the action in this movie was involved with supernatural happenings, a fine gauze filter was placed several feet in front of the camera lens. This gave a weird glow to objects and made the actors appear indistinct, as though they were moving about in a constant twilight.

Lugosi and Browning came back together in 1935 with *The Mark of the Vampire*, in which there was also a female vampire. In spite of the great cinematography by Oscar-winning James Wong Howe and the fine cast – Bela Lugosi, Lionel Barrymore, Elizabeth Allen, Lionel Atwill – Browning made a mistake. He had the vampirism and ghostly happenings end up to be an elaborate plot carried out by vaudeville performers to unmask a killer. It was basically a remake of *London After Midnight*, splitting the detective role (Atwill) and the vampire role (Lugosi).

The action took place in the village of Visoka, where the people are terrified by the vampires Count Mora (Lugosi) and his daughter Luna (Carol Borland). Lugosi had almost no lines as the vaudevillian/vampire. At the end, he turns to his daughter and says, 'This vampire business has given me a great idea for a new act, Luna. In this new act I will be the vampire. Did you watch me? I gave all of me, I was greater than any real vampire!' But he wasn't, and this film was the beginning of the skids for him.

Dracula was never known to have married, and even when he seemed attracted to a woman, it was purely for biting purposes. So it probably would have been a surprise to him to hear about the next two films.

Dracula's Daughter, billed as 'more sensational than her unforgettable father,' came along in 1936, and was based on Bram Stoker's story 'Dracula's Guest.' Van Helsing was played again by Edward Van Sloan, who is arrested for murder after he has staked Dracula. Gloria Holden, as the daughter, Countess Marya Zaleska, turns up to claim her father's body and burns it in a funeral pyre. In the end, she invites her lover, Otto Kruger, to her castle in Transylvania. When her slave tries to kill Kruger with a wooden arrow, the countess steps in front of him and takes the shaft through her heart.

Lon Chaney Jr turned up as the *Son of Dracula* in 1943. There is not much to say about the artistic merits of this film: Chaney was not the suave gentleman that Lugosi was, despite his operating under the

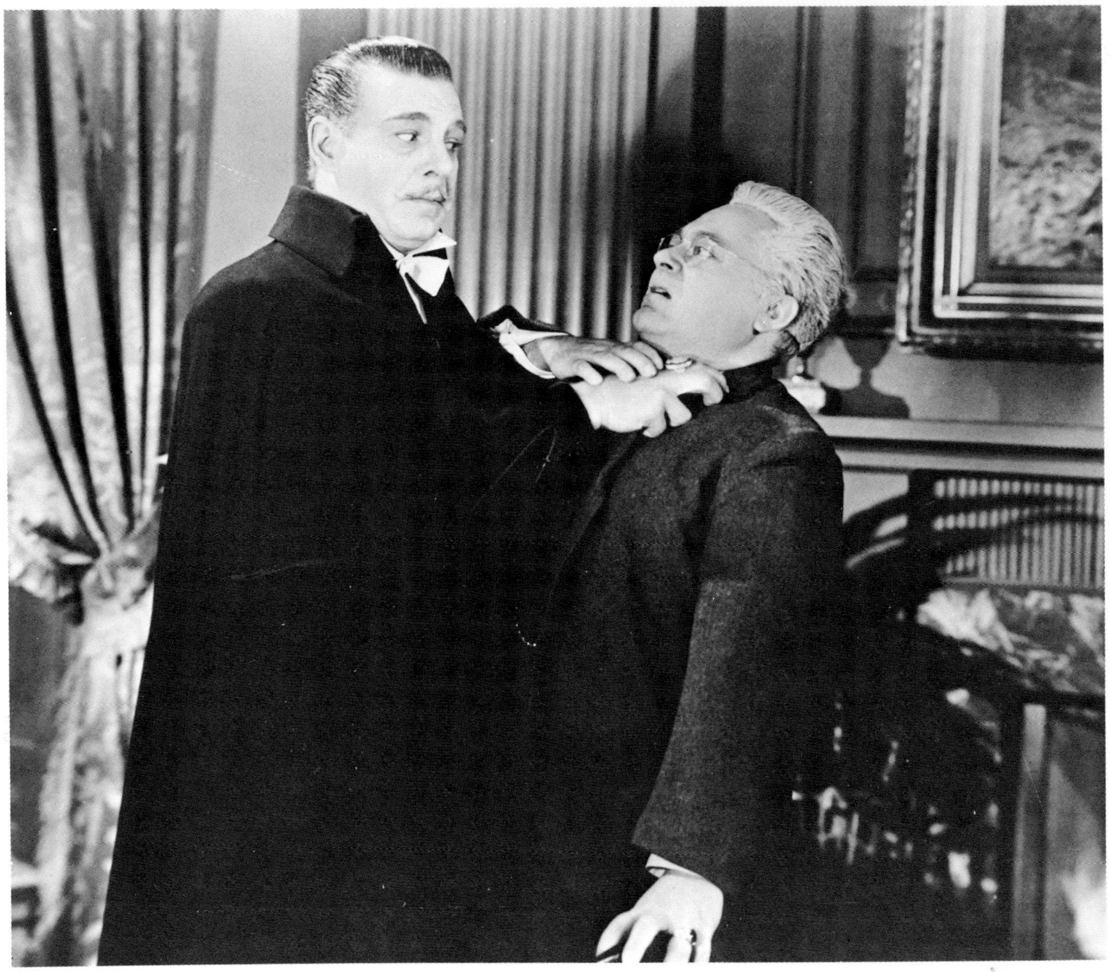

RIGHT: Lon Chaney Jr, as Mr Alucard in *Son of Dracula* (1943). Here he tries to throttle J Edward Bromberg.

ABOVE RIGHT: Otto Kruger comforts his dying lover, Marya Zaleska (Gloria Holden), in *Dracula's Daughter* (1936).

OPPOSITE: Bela Lugosi approaches Elizabeth Allen in *The Mark of the Vampire* (1935).

clever alias of Anthony Alucard (spell his last name backward), and one wonders how he could be so fat on a diet of blood alone. But Chaney had had so much practice at changing into a wolf that this time the producers let him change into a bat. His coffin is found and burned and Alucard cannot find a place to lay his weary head, so he is killed by the sunrise.

Lugosi was back in *The Return of the Vampire* (1944). This time he was Armand Tesla, a vampire who is able to change other people into werewolves. His grave is uncovered in London after the bombings of World War II, and air-raid wardens remove the stake from his heart. In this film Tesla was the first vampire to meet the Wolf Man (Matt Willis), who was his former slave, and Tesla brings him under his mystic spell again.

Boris Karloff, as a general in the Greek Army, had problems with vampires too, in *Isle of the Dead* (1945). It was an eerie tale of assorted refugees stranded on a Greek island during a quarantine and involved a special kind of Greek vampire known as the *vorvalaka*. Katherine Emery impales Karloff with a trident as he is trying to attack Ellen Drew, but the real vampire turns out to be Helene Thimig. At the end, Jason Robards Sr is left alone on the island.

After Hollywood's triumph (?) in *House of Frankenstein* (1944), along came *House of Dracula* (1945). In this one, Glenn Strange as Frankenstein's monster is revived by a Dr Edelmann (Onslow Stevens), and John Carradine as Dracula asks the doctor for a cure for vampirism. Edelmann can't come up with one, and so is turned into a vampire too. The film was so trashy that it used old film clips in which not only Karloff and Lugosi appeared as the monster, but also Lon Chaney Jr.

John Beal played a small-town vampire in *The Vampire* (1957). He was a doctor who was transformed by taking a dead scientist's drug, after which he carries off Colleen Gray. The moral, apparently, was don't take too many pills. And in the same year there was the first teenage vampire film, *Blood of Dracula*, in which a young girl is hypnotized into the life of a vampire. Sandra Harrison starred. In 1958 Francis Lederer was called Bellac in *The Return of Dracula*.

BELOW: Bela Lugosi attacks Nina Foch in *The Return of the Vampire*.

OPPOSITE: Francis Lederer was Bellac in *The Return of Dracula* (1958).

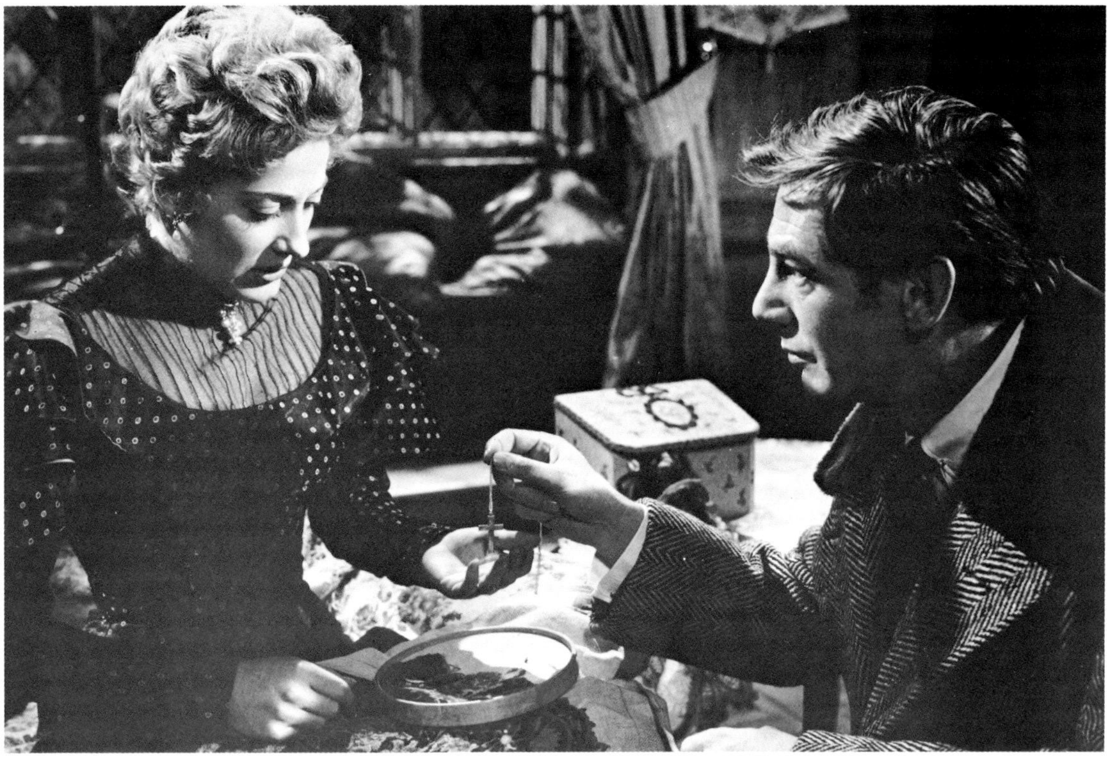

LEFT: Getting the lowdown on how to ward off vampires in *The Horror of Dracula* (1958).

OPPOSITE TOP: Christopher Lee played the Count in *Dracula, Prince of Darkness* (1966).

OPPOSITE BOTTOM: Some of the ghoulish characters, including Alfie Bass, center, in *The Fearless Vampire Killers* (1967).

BELOW: Literally, a vampire kiss from *Kiss of the Vampire* (1962).

As in the case of the Frankenstein pictures, Hammer Studios in England took over at this point. In 1958 Terence Fisher directed *Dracula*, released in the United States as *The Horror of Dracula*, starring Christopher Lee as the everlasting count and Peter Cushing as Van Helsing, who got him with a crucifix and turned him into dust. This was the first Dracula film to express the underlying sexual motif of the novel: Dracula was turned into a vampire in an erotic scene where he was bitten by a vampire woman – Valerie Gaunt. Lee made the most of the sexuality of Dracula and even made evil seem quite attractive, but there was too much blood, and shooting it in color was a disadvantage. Another vampire film from England starred Sir Donald Wolfit. It was *Blood of the Vampire* (1958), and Wolfit ended up being eaten by his own guard dogs.

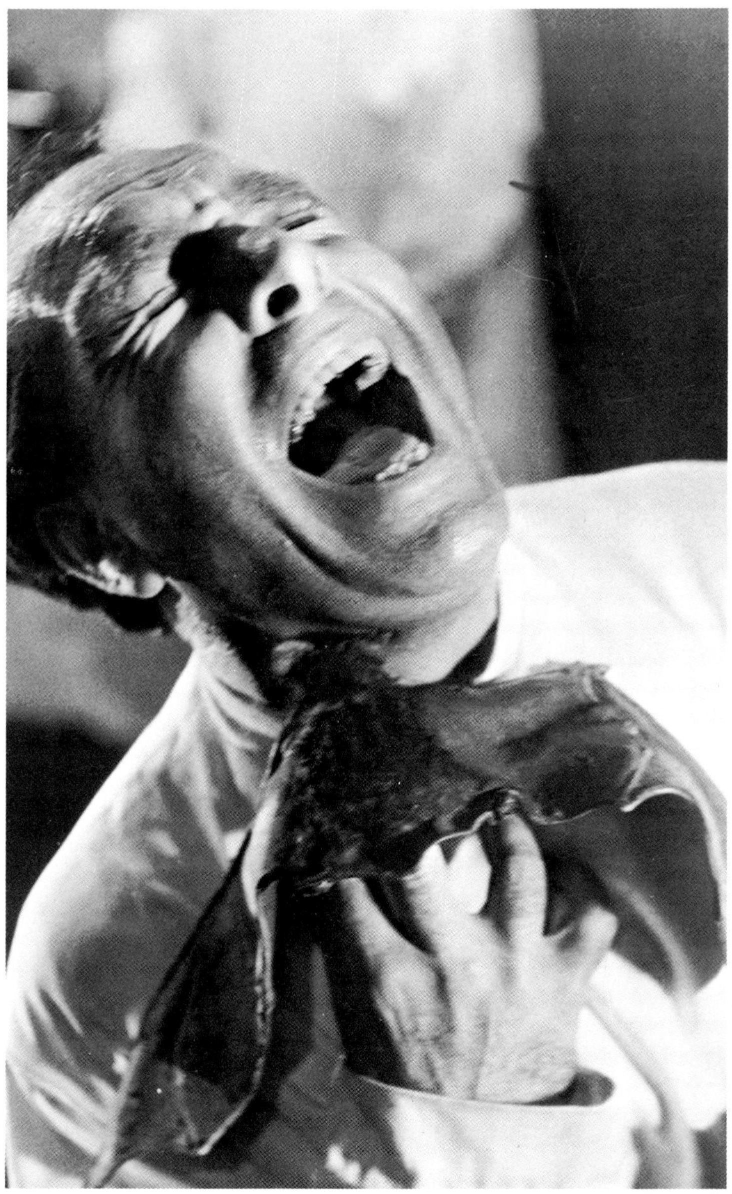

Peter Cushing was back as Van Helsing in *The Brides of Dracula* (1960). Baron Meinster (David Peel) has been victimized by Dracula and now needs the blood of young girls. Martita Hunt played his mother and procuress, the Baroness Meinster, but her son incestuously attacks her and she turns into a vampire too. Then it's Van Helsing to the rescue. He takes care of the vampires, but in the process is bitten by Meinster, whereupon he cauterizes the wound with a white-hot poker. The film showed carnality without frontal nudity, which was something to say for it.

Noel Willman was a vampire, Dr Ravna, in *Kiss of the Vampire*, a British film of 1962. It was an intelligent treatment of the theme, well done in color, with many chilling sequences. Unfortunately, it can usually be seen only on TV – retitled *Kiss of Evil* – and the editing takes away much of the film's punch.

John Carradine was Dracula in the Wild West in *Billy the Kid Versus Dracula* (1963). In the film he vampirizes an Indian woman, the Indians revolt, Dra-

cula flees to the Bar-B Ranch, where he attacks Melinda Plowman, and the retired Billy the Kid (Chuck Courtney) kills the monster in a silver mine.

You can't keep a good monster down, and Christopher Lee reappeared in *Dracula – Prince of Darkness* (1966). He was now an established horror-film star, and not just a bit player in movies where a tall person or an expert fencer was needed. He went on to play the Count many times, often wearing the Dracula ring that Bela Lugosi had given him, as well as his red or yellow contact lenses.

In this film, Lee was revived by having blood poured on his ashes in a particularly grisly way. Four travelers are in a coach going through the Carpathian Mountains – Francis Matthews, Susan Farmer, Barbara Shelley and Charles Tingwell. They have been warned not to go near Karlsbad, where Dracula had lived. The coach driver is frightened and kicks them out, so they walk to the castle. Dracula's servant, Klove, drags Tingwell to the coffin and slits him open. His blood falls on Dracula, who revives and vampirizes Shelley. The Count's newest victim goes to a monastery where Farmer is hiding and bites her. At the end, Dracula drowns trying to cross running water – a nice switch.

The Polish director Roman Polanski tried his hand at a vampire film – *The Fearless Vampire Killers* (1967), which was retitled *Dance of the Vampires.* Out of the Transylvanian snows come Professor Ambronsius (Jack McGowran) and his assistant Alfred (Polanski). Observing the pallid natives, they know that vampires are near, and after some hanky-panky with an innkeeper's daughter (Sharon Tate), they go to the castle, where they are trapped. The dead from the graveyards attend a ball that night. They also find Sarah, the innkeeper's daughter, there and try to escape with her, but find that they are spreading the curse of vampirism themselves.

Christopher Lee showed up in his contact lenses and fangs again in 1968. This time it was in *Dracula Has Risen from the Grave*. His first victim is found stuffed into a church bell, which enrages the discoverer, the local priest. Finally, Lee falls over a wall and impales himself on a crucifix.

Lee was back in *Count Dracula* (1970), playing opposite Herbert Lom (who would score as a star opposite Peter Sellers in the 'Pink Panther' films), but this was strictly a grade-Z production. That same year, Lee made *The Scars of Dracula*, which was another case of dribbling blood on the vampire's ashes. At the end, he is struck by lightning and falls over the ramparts of the castle in flames. A third 1970 appearance by Lee was in *Taste the Blood of Dracula*, and it seemed that every time he played the Count he was given less to do. This time the setting was transferred from Transylvania to Victorian England.

Then, also in 1970, came *The Vampire Lovers*, a film featuring frontal nudity for the first time in a vampire picture; it also featured explicit lesbianism. Ingrid Pitt went straight for her victims' breasts in a ruination of Sheridan Le Fanu's story 'Carmilla.' Peter Cushing, as usual, staked the vampire and then beheaded her.

A trio of rather fun vampire films came out in the early 1970s, all starring Robert Quarry and all set in Los Angeles's hippie community. The first was *Count Yorga, Vampire* (1970), in which the sophisticated and clever vampire establishes a coven in LA. George Macready was the vampire hunter, Professor Rightstat. In *The Return of Count Yorga* (1971), which also starred Mariette Hartley, the Count goes out for more blood, wreaking havoc on a local orphanage. Finally,

ABOVE: Mariette Hartley being kidnapped by the vampire coven in *The Return of Count Yorga* (1971). This was long before she appeared with James Garner in her camera television commercials.

LEFT: *Countess Dracula* (1971) begins to deteriorate, as Nigel Greene, saber in hand, watches tensely.

OPPOSITE: Dracula has brought consternation to this youth – and who could blame the boy? *Dracula A.D. 1972* (1972).

in *The Deathmaster* (1972), he leads a group of unsuspecting hippies who don't know that their guru is a vampire named Khorda.

In *Lust for a Vampire* (1971), Yutta Stensgaard played the part of Mircalla, a vampire who rises from the dead when the blood of a peasant girl drips into her coffin. She finishes off Ralph Bates when his crucifix doesn't work (one wonders why) and goes on to attack the breasts and occasionally the throat of Pippa Steele. There is a fire in the castle, but she survives until a blazing beam falls and stabs her to death.

Peter Cushing came back in *Twins of Evil* (1971), as the witch hunter Gustav Weil. Madelaine and Mary Collinson played the twins, one of whom had been turned into a vampire by Count Karnstein (Damien Thomas). All Cushing had to do was to cut off the head of the errant twin.

Countess Dracula (1971) was a retelling of the old legend of Countess Elisabeth Bathory of Transylvania, who delighted in the slow torture and murder of some 650 girls, sinking her teeth into their bodies and drinking their blood in a desperate effort to retain her youthful beauty. In the film, she was named Countess Nasady and bathed in the blood of virgins. But when she tried to marry her daughter's lover, her body disintegrated.

In *Grave of the Vampire* (1972) a vampire seduces a college coed, who bears him a child. The little monster suckles by drinking blood from her breast. The film ends with a confrontation of the now grown son with his father, who is teaching at a college and plotting to vampirize his students.

Lee was back as Dracula once more in *Dracula AD 1972* (1972). It begins in Chelsea, where Dracula is brought back to life by his disciple, Johnny Alucard, in the deconsecrated Church of St Botolph's. He is later defeated by a descendant of Van Helsing (Peter Cushing). The film was confusing, especially because it was unnerving to see good old Dracula in this 1970s youth setting.

RIGHT: Laurence Olivier, as Dr Van Helsing, is about to finish off Frank Langella, as Dracula, in *Dracula* (1979).

OPPOSITE: Frank Langella repeated his triumphal Broadway role as the Count in *Dracula* (1979).

BELOW RIGHT: William Marshall was at his best as the vampire in *Blacula* (1972).

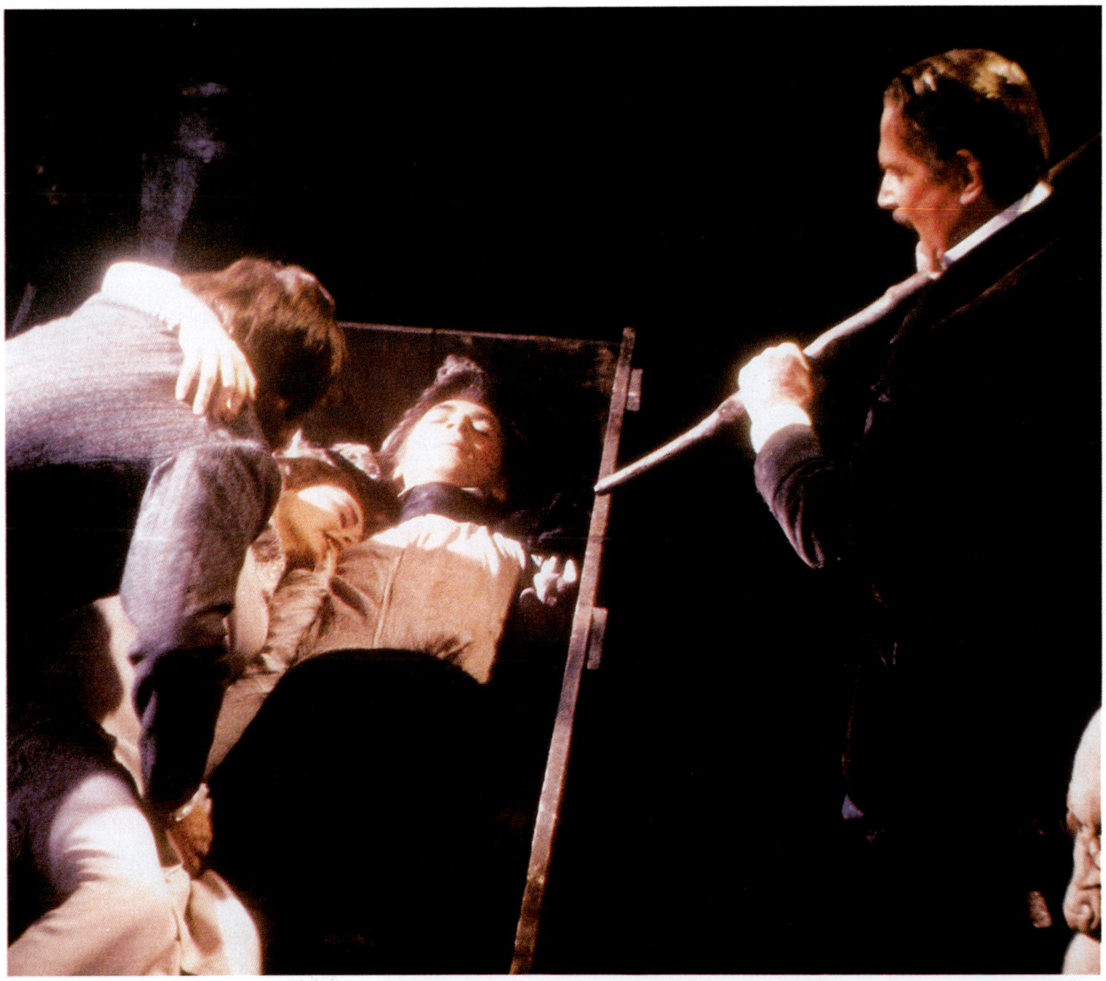

A most unusual vampire movie was *Blacula* (1972). Admittedly, it was a black exploitation film about an African prince who was bitten by Dracula and is now stalking the streets of Los Angeles. But it had some fine things going for it. There were shocks and wonderful dialogue and there was the acting of William Marshall, whose ringing Shakespearian delivery and innate dignity made the picture worth watching. Also, there was one of the best endings in any vampire film. Throughout the film, Marshall has resisted biting his true love, because he knows the hell of being a vampire. When he realizes that he will no longer be able to resist the temptation he commits suicide by walking into the sunlight. A much less successful sequel, *Scream, Blacula, Scream*, was released in 1973.

The Satanic Rites of Dracula (1973) was a mess. In an attempted modernization of the subject, Christopher Lee played a modern business magnate who turns into a vampire.

Frank Langella as Dracula and Laurence Olivier as Van Helsing appeared in *Dracula* (1979). This was an adaptation of the old play, in which Langella had been so successful in its Broadway revival of the 1970s.

Another remake of 1979 was *Nosferatu, the Vampyre*, in which Klaus Kinski played Count Orlock. Highly touted while it was in production, it just seemed to disappear shortly after it was released. Beautifully photographed in striking color, it was an homage to the earlier film. The problem was that it

ABOVE: Count Orlock's ghostly boat docks in Bremen and out come the hordes of plague-ridden rats in *Nosferatu, the Vampire* (1979).

LEFT: Dracula (John Carradine) asks Dr Edelmann (Onslow Stevens) for a cure for his disease of vampirism, which keeps him confined to his coffin in *House of Dracula* (1945).

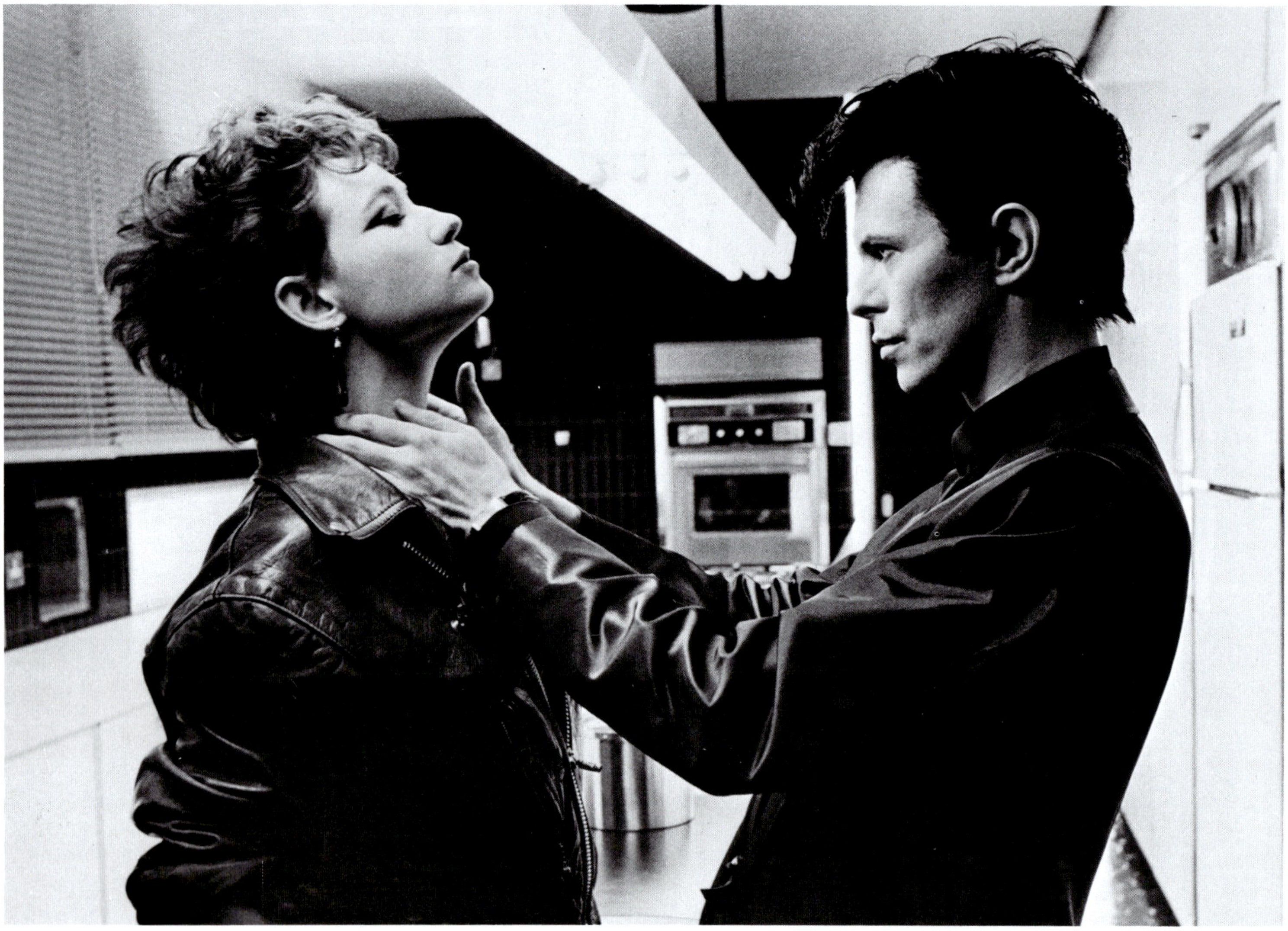

was too much like the earlier film – slow-paced and not too well acted.

Another beautifully photographed vampire film that seemed to get lost was *The Hunger* (1983). In this strange treatment of the theme, Catherine Deneuve, of all people, was a vampire (and the most beautiful one of all time). She causes her lover, David Bowie, to age right before our eyes until he dies of senility, and then practices her wiles in a lesbian relationship with Susan Sarandon. Deneuve comes out of all this unscathed, a nice touch.

If any vampire movie can be called fun to watch, it is *Fright Night* (1985). It is about a vampire (Chris Sarandon) who moves in next door to Charley Brewster (William Ragsdale). Brewster enlists the aid of an over-the-hill screen star, Peter Vincent (Roddy McDowall), who has been forced to work in television as the host of a horror-movie series, and even then has been fired because he shows the classics instead of the blood-and-gore thrillers. It has some fine touches, such as Sarandon whistling 'Strangers in the Night' when out on the prowl, and Ragsdale's apprehensively decorating his room with crucifixes and garlic. McDowall summarizes the feelings of an older generation when he says, 'All the people of your generation want to see is demented madmen running around in ski masks hacking up young virgins.'

ABOVE: Catherine Deneuve, as a vampire, works her wiles on her lover, David Bowie, in *The Hunger* (1983).

RIGHT: Deneuve and Bowie in happier days, before he turned old almost overnight in *The Hunger* (1983).

OPPOSITE TOP: As a young vampire, David Bowie mesmerizes a young woman (Ann Magnuson) in *The Hunger* (1983).

OPPOSITE BOTTOM: After the death of David Bowie, Catherine Deneuve begins a lesbian vampire affair with Susan Sarandon in *The Hunger* (1983).

Roddy McDowall, as the aging horror-television-show host, fights off a monster in the vampire comedy-horror picture *Fright Night* (1985).

Another kind of creature that comes back from the dead in horror movies is the mummy. The ancient Egyptians believed that the physical body was essential to the human personality, and a dead person could not go on to an afterlife without it. So they had to preserve the corpse as best they could.

In 1932 the cameraman Karl Freund turned his hand to directing movies, teaming with Boris Karloff to do *The Mummy*. This human form, though dead for 3700 years, made one of the most eerie of movie monsters when it rose from its sarcophagus. Freund had been the photographer of *Dracula*, and previously, in Germany, of *Der Golem*, and Karloff got another splendid makeup job from Jack Pierce in this production.

The basic story of *The Mummy* involves an ancient Egyptian of the lower class of priests, Im-Ho-Tep, who falls in love with the Princess Anck-Es-En-Amon. The princess dies, and Im-Ho-Tep tries to get the Scroll of Thoth from the temple in order to bring her back to life. But the priests and the pharaoh are put out by this and sentence the poor man to be buried alive – denying him his funeral service. So he spends the next few centuries guarding his long-dead sweetheart's mummy.

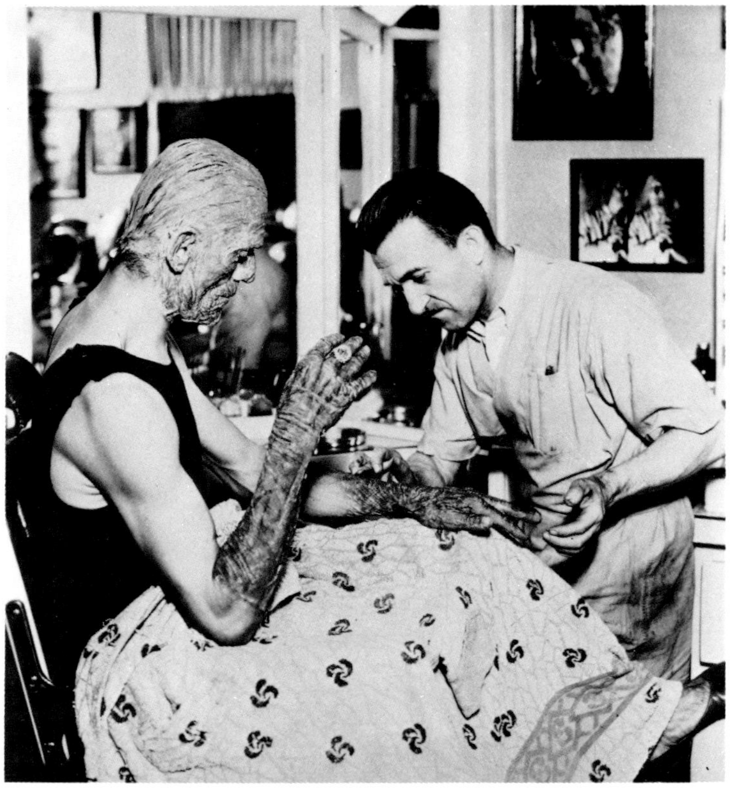

RIGHT: Boris Karloff as Im-Ho-Tep in *The Mummy* (1932), wearing his marvelous Jack Pierce makeup job. Little does Bramwell Fletcher (left) suspect that Karloff will soon come out of the coffin to pay him a visit.

OPPOSITE TOP: Jack Pierce at work on making up Karloff for *The Mummy* (1932).

OPPOSITE BOTTOM: Karloff as Im-Ho-Tep shows up to threaten young archaeologist Bramwell Fletcher.

BELOW: Karloff with his love, the Princess Anck-Es-En-Amon, in *The Mummy* (1932).

LEFT: Lon Chaney Jr got a chance to play the mummy in *The Mummy's Tomb* (1942). Here he is with Turhan Bey, the newly appointed High Priest – his master – contemplating the unconscious Elyse Knox.

BELOW: Elyse Knox and John Hubbard are apprehensive in *The Mummy's Tomb* (1942).

OPPOSITE: In *The Mummy's Hand* (1940), Tom Tyler played the mummy, whose name had been changed from Im-Ho-Tep to Prince Kharis.

The rest of the film takes place in modern times. We see the still-living Im-Ho-Tep in the disguise of a terribly wrinkled Egyptian scholar, Ardet Bey (Karloff played a dual role in the film). The body of the princess is taken to a museum in Cairo, and Ardet Bey tries to bring her back to life with the Scroll of Thoth, but is discovered before he can bring this off. Bey then finds a beautiful young girl named Helen, whom, for some reason, he believes to be the reincarnation of his lost love. When he approaches her to explain the idea, she calls on the goddess Isis for help. The goddess conveniently hears the prayer and turns the old man to dust.

Some interesting scenes from the film were cut – all of them flashback scenes of the reincarnation of the princess at various points in history, as viewed in reflections from a misty pool. She had lived with the Vikings, been a medieval princess and frolicked with the nobility of France.

The Los Angeles Times raved about *The Mummy*. '*The Mummy* beggars description. It is one of the most unusual talkies ever produced.' Karloff then went on to make a British film, *The Ghoul* (1933). In it he played a cataleptic Egyptologist who returns from the dead to reclaim a stolen ring.

In 1940 Universal Studios decided to bring the mummy back. Again, they selected a minor cowboy actor (remember Glenn Strange in the Frankenstein remakes?), Tom Tyler, to be the monster. The main reason he was chosen was that in all those wrappings he looked a lot like Karloff, and that meant that clips from the original film could be used to cut down on the budget. In *The Mummy's Hand* he played only the mummy, not the dual role.

A few other changes were made. Im-Ho-Tep has been promoted to a prince, and his name has been changed to Kharis. The princess is no longer called Anck-Es-En-Amon, but Ananka. Kharis had not stolen the Scroll of Thoth, but rather some precious tana leaves that would supposedly bring the dead back to life. Finally, he was not only buried alive, but also had his tongue cut out.

Two scientists arrive in Egypt and find the tomb of the princess and the mummy of Kharis. They decide to take Ananka back to America, but before they can get away, Kharis kills one of them. The other scientist succeeds in taking the princess to a museum in a small New England town.

Meanwhile, back in Egypt, the High Priest of the Temple of Amon-Ra (George Zucco) prepares to take Kharis to America so that the body of Ananka can be returned to her tomb. The High Priest is careful to take a supply of tana leaves with him to feed to the mummy. The fluid from three leaves will keep Kharis alive, while the fluid from nine will permit him to move and give him tremendous strength. The priest

LEFT: Finally, it was Christopher Lee's turn to be the mummy. Here he is as Kharis in his better days in *The Mummy* (1959).

OPPOSITE TOP: Peter Cushing, as a scientist, tries to do in Christopher Lee, as Kharis, in *The Mummy* (1959).

OPPOSITE BOTTOM: Kharis and the reincarnation of Princess Ananka (Yvonne Furneaux) enter the swamp in *The Mummy* (1959).

and the mummy arrive in New England and, although Kharis is able to kill a few people, he is eventually destroyed by fire.

As we might expect, Lon Chaney Jr got his chance to be the mummy too. In 1942 he appeared in *The Mummy's Tomb*. The High Priest (George Zucco again) is now an ancient man, so he must appoint a new leader, and Turhan Bey is the man. Kharis, of course, is badly maimed from the fire, but by the time Bey arrives in New England, the mummy is up to trying to get Ananka back to Egypt again.

In the meantime, the new High Priest has fallen in love with a local girl and sends Kharis, the mummy, after her. The usual thing happens – the villagers come after them with torches and the building goes up in flames, as does the mummy.

Zucco never gave up. In 1944, in *The Mummy's Ghost*, he made John Carradine the High Priest. Ananka's mummy is on display in the museum, and the High Priest takes Kharis (Lon Chaney Jr) there. Kharis touches Ananka, who crumbles to dust.

The High Priest and Kharis find a young college girl – an exchange student from Egypt – whom they think is the reincarnation of Ananka. Add to that the fact that the High Priest has fallen in love with her, and it is obviously the time to send Kharis after her. He plans to feed the girl (and himself) on tana leaves and make them both immortal. Kharis doesn't think much of the plan, but he does kidnap the girl. Then he turns on the priest, kills him, grabs the girl again and heads for the swamp. As he stumbles along, the girl in his arms changes into an ancient hag, and they both disappear in the quicksand.

Chaney also starred in *The Mummy's Curse* (1944). The scene is the same swamp, now drained, 25 years later. Peter Coe has been named the new High Priest and gives Kharis some tana leaves. Ananka returns from the swamp in the form of a young girl. Kharis carries her to an abandoned monastery, where the caretaker tries to make love to her. The mummy can't stand this and pulls the building down on them, as Ananka turns into a mummy again.

Then, true to form, Hammer came onto the scene with *The Mummy* (1959). Christopher Lee was Kharis, buried alive for defiling the memory of his beloved Princess Ananka (Yvonne Furneaux). He is revived in 1895 to protect the tomb of the princess, but a scientist (Peter Cushing) has shipped the mummy of Ananka to London. Kharis is strengthened by the Scroll of Thoth and goes after her. The scientist's wife turns out to be Ananka's reincarnation, so Kharis picks her up and carries her to a swamp, where he is shot dead and all is well.

In *Blood Feast* (1963), a madman tries to revive an Egyptian goddess, and blood, viscera and human body parts are all over the screen. In *The Curse of the Mummy's Tomb* (1965), Dickie Owen was the mummy.

The Mummy's Shroud (1967) featured Roger Delgado as Hasmid, who brings the mummy of Prem (Eddie Powell) back to life. The mummy catches the hero (David Buck) and the heroine (Maggie Kimberley) in a deserted museum (why are museums in movies always deserted?). After they try bullets and hatchets to no avail, the mummy crumbles to dust when Kimberley intones the words from the Sacred Scroll. The publicity department went wild: 'Beware the beat of the cloth-wrapped feet.'

Blood From the Mummy's Tomb (1972) was taken from Bram Stoker's story 'Jewel of the Seven Stars' and was a mishmash of Egyptiana: a probing severed hand even crawled about under the influence of a sacred jewel. Queen Tara's spirit enters Valerie Leon to avenge herself on the desecrators of her tomb.

The final 'back from the dead' monster is the zombie. According to the American writer W B Seabrook, a zombie is 'a soulless human corpse, still dead, but taken from the grave and endowed by sorcery with a mechanical semblance of life.' He claimed to have seen them working in the Haitian fields and described them as dull and plodding, 'with the eyes of a dead man, not blind, but staring, unfocused, unseeing.'

Probably the first film about these creatures was *White Zombie* (1932), in which Bela Lugosi played, not a zombie, but Legendre, the master of the living dead. He is introduced to the audience by a close-up of his eyes, superimposed over his figure, as he watches some unsuspecting visitors approach in a coach driven by one of his zombies. The role suited him, as he had little dialogue and was wholly evil.

In the picture, the heroine, Madge Bellamy, watches some Haitians bury a body at a crossroads so that it cannot be possessed by a sorcerer. Then a bunch of zombies appear, lurching down a hill on their way to work in the sugar cane fields. Bellamy gets married, but on her wedding night Lugosi drugs her so that even her husband thinks that she is dead. Lugosi revives her and takes her to his castle, telling his zombie bodyguard to kill her husband. The film has a great ending. The husband escapes and throws Lugosi over a cliff, and all of the faithful zombies jump over the cliff after him.

A stranger-than-average zombie film was released in 1936. Called *Revolt of the Zombies*, it featured zombies who were all Cambodians. A war-time zombie film

ABOVE: Madge Bellamy has a tender moment with her husband-to-be, John Harron, in *White Zombie* (1932).

LEFT: Dick Purcell waits for something to happen at a Voodoo ceremony as Joan Woodbury and Henry Victor look on in *King of the Zombies* (1941).

OPPOSITE: Bela Lugosi and John Carradine experimenting with some horrible rituals in *Voodoo Man* (1944).

was *King of the Zombies* (1941), in which Henry Victor produced troops of zombies to be used as spies by foreign agents. The latter plot was given a flipflop in *Revenge of the Zombies* (1943). In the swamplands of the Deep South, John Carradine is busy creating an army of invincible zombies for the Axis Powers. He turns his wife, Veda Ann Borg, into a zombie, but she takes command of the army of the living dead and has him killed.

I Walked with a Zombie (1943) had a plot that was a combination of Jane Eyre and a series of newspaper articles about voodoo on a Caribbean island. It took place in the Haitian cane fields, where Frances Dee is a young nurse hired to look after a planter's sick wife. The people on the island think the wife is a zombie, and she and the nurse seek the aid of the local voodoo priest. The pacing of the film is filled with exquisite terror, from the time that the nurse and her half-zombie patient see a gigantic silent black man to their view of a voodoo doll hanging from a tree.

Lugosi was back with the zombies in *Voodoo Man* (1944). He played the part of a man who had touching devotion to his zombie-wife and performed harrowing experiments with unsuspecting girls to try to cure her. Then he appeared in a real clinker – *Zombies on Broadway* (1945) – in which he was a doctor in the West Indies who produced zombies by injection, while Broadway public-relations men tried to palm him off as a genuine voodoo victim.

In *Valley of the Zombies* (1946), despite the title,

there was only one zombie. It told the story of a mad scientist, Ian Keith, who worked hard bringing a body back to life only to find out that it was already a zombie.

The Zombies of Mora-Tau (1957) were the guardians of an underwater treasure. But when it was destroyed, they vanished. This juvenile hodge-podge, also called *The Dead That Walk*, starred the never-to-be-forgotten Gregg Palmer, Allison Hayes and Autumn Russell. Allison Hayes returned the same year, 1957, in *The Disembodied*, in which she played Tonda, the Voodoo Queen. She tried to murder John E Wengraf and ended up falling in love with Paul Burke (better known as a lead in the television series 'Noah's Ark,' 'Naked City' and 'Twelve O'Clock High'). Eventually, she was killed in a voodoo ritual.

Voodoo Woman (1957) was a film about a deranged scientist trying to change a woman into a zombie. It starred Marla English and Tom Conway (better known as 'The Falcon' in the 1940s films and as the brother of George Sanders).

One of the most truly frightening of the zombie movies was *Carnival of Souls* (1960). This low-budget shocker, which starred Candace Hilligoss, opens with a car filled with young kids plunging off an amusement park pier into the water. Hilligoss gets out of the car and swims to the surface, only to be confronted by scores of undead people who are having a good time on the carnival rides at the park. They turn on her, and after what seems a lifetime of horror, the film ends with a scene in which the car is being pulled from the water. Inside are the dead bodies of the young people, including that of Hilligoss, who had not escaped at all.

A bunch of Roman zombies showed up in *War of the Zombies* (1963). This was an Italian production whose

BELOW: A group of the undead from *The Zombies of Mora-Tau* (1957) escorting their princess.

RIGHT: Another member of the undead comes out of his grave in *Plague of the Zombies*.

NORMAN WARD.
12TH FEB. 1860. · AGED 28 YEARS.

only redeeming feature was the appearance of John Drew Barrymore, the son of John Barrymore of Jekyll and Hyde fame. That same year appeared the picture with the worse title in zombie-film history – *The Incredibly Strange Creatures Who Stopped Living and Became Mixed-up Zombies*

Plague of the Zombies (1966) transplanted zombies from the West Indies to Cornwall, England, and had them working in a tin mine instead of the sugar cane fields. John Carson played Squire Hamilton, who raised his slaves from the dead. Unfortunately, the mine exploded and everyone got killed.

One of the sleaziest zombie films was Del Tenney's *I Eat Your Skin* (1970), which told of an adventurer battling a horde of laboratory-made zombies on a tropical island. It had been made to run on a double bill with *I Drink Your Blood* (1970).

But no discussion of zombie pictures would be complete without mentioning the master of them all – George Romero. This director started out making films in 1968. He had made most of his money up to that point by doing commercials for ketchup and pickle products. Then he decided to make the film *The Night of the Living Dead* (1968). The movie told the story of a space experiment that sets off high-level radiation, which activates recently buried bodies, turning them into man-eating monsters. Even shot in black and white, it was a gory picture. It starred such

ABOVE: The father and mother, holed up in the basement of a farmhouse, hiding from the undead creatures in *The Night of the Living Dead* (1968). They are worried about their sick daughter, not knowing that she will die and then come back as a zombie, only to kill and begin to eat her mother.

LEFT: Hordes of the living dead search hungrily for living human flesh in *Day of the Dead* (1985).

OPPOSITE: An undead meets his fate in *Dawn of the Dead*.

unknowns as Judith O'Dea and Duane Jones, plus a bunch of amateurs, some of whom were friends and relatives of Romero. It became a cult film, and although he made it on $114,000 ($60,000 plus $54,000 on credit), it earned more than $1 million in its first two years.

One of the strange things about *Night of the Living Dead* was that it was made in Pittsburgh. Indeed, a Pittsburgh butcher supplied most of the entrails eaten by the zombies. When he was asked, 'Why Pittsburgh?' Romero answered 'I like the beer.' Romero wrote, co-directed, photographed and edited the film, which was shot in 30 days, mostly on weekends.

The picture had murky photography, graphic violence and acting that was either amateurish or nonexistent. It outraged some people, especially *Variety*. The film 'casts serious aspersions on the integrity and social responsibility of its Pittsburgh-based maker . . . [It raises] doubts about the future of the regional cinema movement and about the moral health of filmgoers who cheerfully opt for this unrelieved orgy of sadism.' But the fact was, it was a real chiller.

Romero followed this with *Dawn of the Dead*, a horror film sardonic enough to let its zombies go shopping in the huge mall they have taken over. It was in that all-American mall, complete with fountains and Muzak, that the blue-faced dead and the living had it out.

Then came *Day of the Dead* (1985), with enough spilled guts and severed limbs to satisfy anyone. But most of the film took place underground, where the normals were hiding from the zombies, and a lot of the movie was devoted to windy argument about how they were going to get out alive.

The truth of the matter is, at least as far as back-from-the-dead creature films are concerned, that the shudders and screams have turned into smiles and titters.

SELF-MADE MONSTERS

Probably the most familiar self-made monster was the hellrake and murderer Edward Hyde, who, of course, was the alter ego of Dr Henry Jekyll. They first appeared in Robert Louis Stevenson's story 'The Strange Case of Dr Jekyll and Mr Hyde.' Stevenson let Jekyll speak for himself as he made the transition: 'Late one accursed night, I compounded the elements, watched them boil and smoke together in the glass, and when the ebullition had subsided, with a strong glow of courage, drank off the potion. The most racking pangs succeeded; a grinding in the bones, deadly nausea, and a horror of the spirit. Then these agonies began swiftly to subside, and I felt younger, lighter, happier in body . . . I knew myself to be wicked.'

Dr Jekyll then described his new body: 'Edward Hyde was so much smaller, slighter, and younger than Henry Jekyll. Evil was written broadly and plainly on the face. Evil had left on that body an imprint of deformity and decay . . . Edward Hyde, alone in the ranks of mankind, was pure evil.' Well, he brought it on himself.

The original story, of course, went like this. Dr Jekyll, a lovable character, represents the urge to do good that is present in most men. Mr Hyde, on the other hand, represents the evil that is also present in all of us. Jekyll has invented a potion that will turn him into Hyde, and he drinks the stuff. Fortunately, he also has discovered another concoction that will turn Hyde back into Jekyll. This goes on for a time, back and forth, until Jekyll finds out that, in the form of Hyde, he has committed a murder. At this point he decides to try to kick the habit.

The problem now is that he finds himself turning into Hyde without taking the potion, so he has to take double doses of the antidote in order to turn back into Dr Jekyll. The final blow comes when he runs out of one of the ingredients in the brew and finds himself unable to change back again into his former sweet self. So he commits suicide.

Probably the primary reason for the popularity of the Jekyll and Hyde films – and the story was filmed over and over – was that, in the early days of the movies, motion pictures were thought of as evil influences on the minds of people in the audience, and were often denounced from pulpits all over the land. So what could be more natural than to film a story in which there was such a clear separation between good and evil? Dr Jekyll is all good and Mr Hyde is all bad. Add to this the fact that, in the end, good was able to eliminate evil.

The 1908 production of *Dr Jekyll and Mr Hyde*, made by Selig Polyscope in the United States, was a pretty primitive film. The producers gathered a company of actors who were touring in a play based on the Stevenson novelette, let them act on a Chicago stage, and filmed their actions. Each scene in the movie even opened with a rising curtain. The dual lead role was played by Richard Mansfield.

The next version of the tale was *Den Skaebnesvangre Opfindelse*, released in the United States as, of course, *Dr Jekyll and Mr Hyde* (1910). This was made by a Danish film company named Nordisk (The Great Northern Company), and, unfortunately, ended with the old cop-out – it was all a dream.

In 1912 Thanhauser Studios came out with another American version, *Dr Jekyll and Mr Hyde*, starring James Cruze, who later went on to become a fine director after he broke his leg and found that it inhibited his acting. Also in the production were Henry Benham and Marguerite Snow, Cruze's wife. The unusual thing about this version is that, for the only time in history, two actors were used for the two title roles. The director of the film was Lucius Henderson, who decided to shoot the whole film from a fixed camera position, with no changes of lighting. Mercifully, his picture was a one-reeler and so was over before the audience could get up the courage to demand its money back.

The year 1913 gave us a bumper crop of films about the strange duo. There was the German picture called *Der Anderer* and a British movie, *Dr Jekyll and Mr Hyde*, shot in a primitive color process called Kineto-Kinemacolor. Another American version was made by Universal Studio's Carl Laemmle Sr, starring King Baggott and Jane Gail. One reason that this one was not much of a success was that the dual roles of Jekyll and Hyde require a master actor: Baggott was not in the same league with some later Jekyll-Hydes – John Barrymore, Fredric March, Spencer Tracy.

There are those who argue that the first important horror film to be made after World War I was *Dr Jekyll and Mr Hyde* (1920), produced by Famous Players.

ABOVE: John Barrymore, as the young Dr Jekyll, ponders his problem as Brandon Hurst looks on in *Dr Jekyll and Mr Hyde* (1920).

RIGHT: John Barrymore, as the evil Mr Hyde, hangs out in a bar with his crony, Louis Wolheim, in *Dr Jekyll and Mr Hyde* (1920).

OPPOSITE: Barrymore, as Mr Hyde, woos Martha Mansfield, his innocent friend, in *Dr Jekyll and Mr Hyde* (1920).

PREVIOUS SPREAD: Oliver Reed gave a touching performance as the wolf man in *The Curse of the Werewolf* (1961).

The title roles were played by the gifted Shakespearian actor John Barrymore. The director, John Stuart Robinson, adapted the Stevenson story for the screen and introduced an element of sex to the screenplay. Indeed, there were touches of Oscar Wilde's decadent character Dorian Gray, as well as exotic dancing by Nita Naldi, who had been a Ziegfeld Girl, in the film. And where the original Hyde of the novelette was a mere animalistic killer, in this picture he became a sadistic sex murderer.

In the film, Dr Jekyll is a virginal young gentleman in Victorian England who is coaxed by his friends into going to a stag party. Here, his sexual interest is aroused and, naturally, so is the same instinct in Mr Hyde.

Barrymore, at the time, was one of the top actors in the film world, and he milked the transformation scene for all that he could get out of it. The camera focuses on Dr Jekyll, full face. Slowly he raises the evil brew to his lips and drinks. His body stiffens, his face assumes a look of pain. Then he falls from his chair to the floor (out of range of the camera). At this point the camera was stopped while the actor donned his ugly makeup; then shooting started again. When the actor gets up – behold! – he is Mr Hyde. Barrymore added to the effect of the makeup by distorting his features – so much so that once he dislocated his jaw.

Barrymore was great. In the film, made on Long Island in the Paramount Studios, he became handsome, dashing Jekyll and a horrifying, fanged, taloned Mr Hyde. He was able to appeal to his feminine admirers – and there were millions of them – as Jekyll and to perform some fantastic emoting and scenery-chewing as Hyde. Altogether, this was an ideal setup for him.

This picture was so successful that a rival producer, Louis B Mayer, made a quickie version that same year. It starred Sheldon Lewis, and was a cheap imitation – so cheap that it was updated and shot on New York streets, rather than in a studio, thus eliminating the expense of scenery and nineteenth-century costumes – and had the additional drawback of including the old cop-out again. Jekyll awakes and finds that the whole thing was a dream.

Almost lost in the 1920 Jekyll-and-Hyde shuffle was a German picture, *Der Januskopf*. This starred the great actor Conrad Veidt, and Bela Lugosi played a bit part as a butler. The director, F W Murnau, realized that the original story was still in copyright, so he altered details and called the characters Dr Warren and Mr O'Connor: the film was the last of the silent movies on the subject.

Fredric March was the next Jekyll and Hyde, in the 1932 version directed by Rouben Mamoulian. He was the first actor (and the only one to date) to win an Academy Award for appearing in a monster film: he and Wallace Beery (in *The Champ*) shared the Oscar for best actor. This *Dr Jekyll and Mr Hyde* was the

ABOVE: In another version of *Dr Jekyll and Mr Hyde* (1932), Fredric March won an Academy Award for his performance. Here he is as Mr Hyde, strangling Miriam Hopkins.

LEFT: Fredric March, as Dr Jekyll, calls on the cheap floozie he is enamored of, Miriam Hopkins, in *Dr Jekyll and Mr Hyde* (1932).

OPPOSITE: Miriam Hopkins can't adjust to the fact that Fredric March has changed into Mr Hyde in *Dr Jekyll and Mr Hyde* (1932).

first sound movie based on the Stevenson story and, aside from the top-notch performance by March, the most outstanding thing about the movie was that the camera looked Jekyll right in the face all during his transformation into Hyde. And without the help of a photographic laboratory.

Mamoulian would never disclose how the change was effected, but it was done with no cuts or dissolves, probably with the lighting. Perhaps the lines and shadows were put on March's face in red, then shot with red filters, killing the shadows. Then the filters were removed, and the camera whirls, blurring our vision. We see the final result when March looks into the mirror.

There was a similarity between March's performance and the interpretation of the monster role that Karloff had given us in *Frankenstein*. Both Hyde and the monster were primitive men looking for pagan fulfillment. March's Hyde drinks the pouring rain gleefully in the same way that Karloff's monster

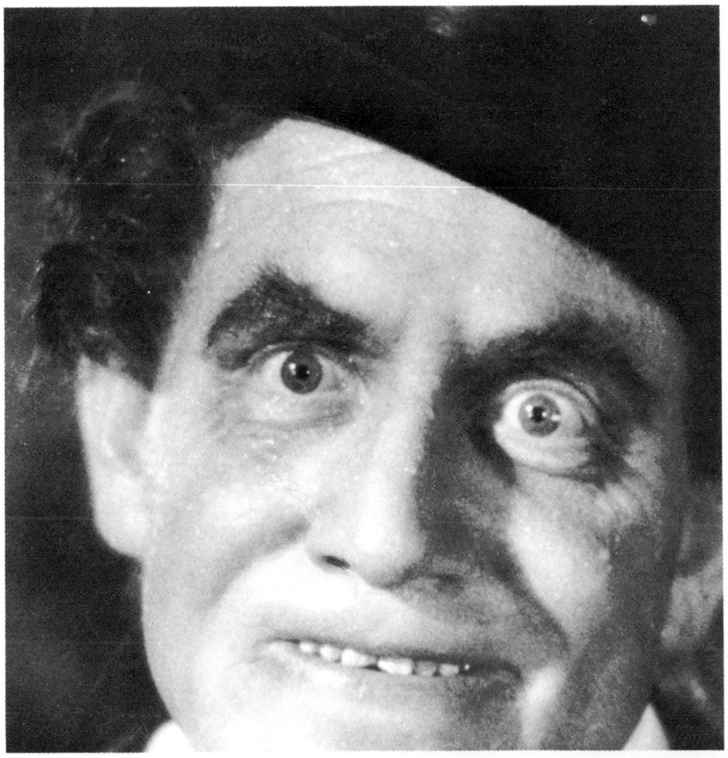

stood in awe of the first sunbeam that he saw. Add to this an assortment of weird sound effects, including a beating heart, and the film came out as a landmark version of the old story. Indeed, in spite of the fact that the 1941 edition starred Spencer Tracy, Ingrid Bergman and Lana Turner, March's film was the better of the two.

This is not to say that Tracy was bad as the heroes of *Dr Jekyll and Mr Hyde* (1941). Even those critics – and there are a few – who claim that this was the worst job of acting he ever turned in (his Jekyll was not interesting and his Hyde was not frightening, they say) admit that Tracy was never terrible. Tracy used a minimum of makeup – mostly fake eyebrows and eye shadow – and let his own talent supply the rest of the personality of Hyde.

But the script was dreary, and the director (Victor Fleming, fresh from his triumphant direction of *Gone With The Wind*) went in for a lot of dream sequences that tended to slow down the action.

Hollywood, used to bringing monsters back to life and drumming up offspring of horror characters, decided to do the same thing with Jekyll and Hyde. Even though Jekyll lived and died a bachelor in the

ABOVE: From opposite left: Three views of the transformation of Spencer Tracy from Dr Jekyll to Mr Hyde in the 1941 version of *Dr Jekyll and Mr Hyde*. Tracy used a minimum of makeup – mostly fake eyebrows and eye shadow.

RIGHT: Ingrid Bergman was Tracy's love in *Dr Jekyll and Mr Hyde* (1941), and here she is getting worried – small wonder.

OPPOSITE BELOW: Spencer Tracy in his laboratory in *Dr Jekyll and Mr Hyde*.

LEFT: There were creepy moments in *Daughter of Dr Jekyll* (1957).

OPPOSITE: Ralph Bates and Martine Betwick were *Dr Jekyll and Sister Hyde* (1971). The picture was better than the idea sounds.

BELOW LEFT AND RIGHT: The transformation in *The Two Faces of Dr Jekyll* (1960), sometimes known as *House of Fright*.

Stevenson tale and all the film versions, the producers gave him an heir. Louis Hayward played the title role in *The Son of Dr Jekyll* (1951). In this film he was not a mad scientist, but rather a young man merely trying to prove that his father was innocent of his crimes. The only horror in the film was when Hayward dreamed he was turning into Mr Hyde.

Then came *Daughter of Dr Jekyll* (1957), starring Gloria Talbott, who thinks she is cursed with the inheritance of being half-human, half-monster. She was not the monster, however. It was her guardian, an old friend of Dr Jekyll, who turned into a fiend from time to time.

Then, again, Hammer Studios could not resist. Their film, called *House of Fright* in the United States and *The Two Faces of Dr Jekyll* in England, came out in 1960. Loaded with sex, the film told the story of a certain Dr Jekyll (Christopher Lee) who is cheating on his wife. In the form of Hyde, he tries to make love to her. From that point on, the story gets further and further away from Stevenson, and the result was a box-office bomb.

The movie did have one interesting thing going for it, however. The personalities and appearances of the two characters were reversed. Dr Jekyll was a sinister, gruff, unapproachable bearded man. Mr Hyde was a smooth, charming and clean-shaven man. One critic said, 'If a classic is to be tampered with, it should at least be done with wit and competence.'

A French version, *The Testament of Dr Cordelier*, was released in the United States as *Experiment in Evil* (1961). It was directed by the great Jean Renoir and starred the fine actor Jean-Louis Barrault. In this film, based on the Stevenson tale, Opale (Hyde) is part killer, part clown character and more of an anarchist than a beast.

Christopher Lee was back as Jekyll and Hyde in *I, Monster* (1970). This time they were called Dr Charles Marlowe and Edward Blake. Despite the performances of Lee and Peter Cushing, this was another bomb.

Dr Jekyll and Sister Hyde (1971) starred Ralph Bates as Jekyll, who turns into Sister Hyde, played by Martine Betwick, which saved on makeup and special-effects costs. It had no thrills, but it was fun.

There was even an exploitation version in 1976 – *Dr Black and Mr Hyde*, starring Bernie Casey. Consider the publicity release: 'A Monster he can't control . . . has taken over his very soul,' 'The fear of the year is here' and 'See what ain't. See a HAINT.'

It shouldn't come as any surprise to learn that man, since the dawn of time, has been nervous around wolves. Probably our ancestors used to huddle in their caves, listening to the far-off cries of these beasts. What could be more natural than to dream up stories in which men turned themselves into wolves and wandered around the countryside looking for fresh meat? And with a few exceptions, the legends of werewolves indicate that the creature brings his strange state upon himself with various ointments and incantations. Most wolf-man films credit the hero's change into a beast to the bite of another werewolf – probably a case of confusing werewolves with vampires.

The first werewolf picture, called, naturally enough, *The Werewolf*, was made in the United States in 1913. But actually it was a wolf *girl* film and was based on an old Navajo legend. Watuma, an Indian girl, comes back to life 100 years after her death to look for the ghost of the evil man who had killed her lover. To accomplish this, she decides, for some reason or other, to turn herself into a wolf.

The wolf *man* did not arrive on the scene until 1935. One of the reasons for this long delay was probably that there was no piece of fiction to tie the script to, as was the case with Frankenstein, Dracula, and Dr Jekyll and Mr Hyde. At any rate, in that year *The Werewolf of London* made his appearance.

The werewolf of London is really an eccentric botanist who is attacked by a real werewolf while on an expedition. The purpose of this trip is to discover a rare plant called the *Marifasa lupina*, which blooms only in the moonlight. The botanist brings the plant back to London and proceeds to wait for it to bloom. Then a Japanese scientist appears, asking for the plant (Warner Oland, who, although of Swedish descent, became rich playing Orientals – Charlie Chan 16 times). It turns out that this Japanese is really the werewolf who attacked the botanist; he wants the plant because it cures the dreaded disease of lycanthropy. But the botanist is now a werewolf, too, and is killed by a silver bullet as the Japanese gets away with the plant.

BELOW: Henry Hull in *The Werewolf of London* (1935).

RIGHT: Hull (right) fights Warner Oland.

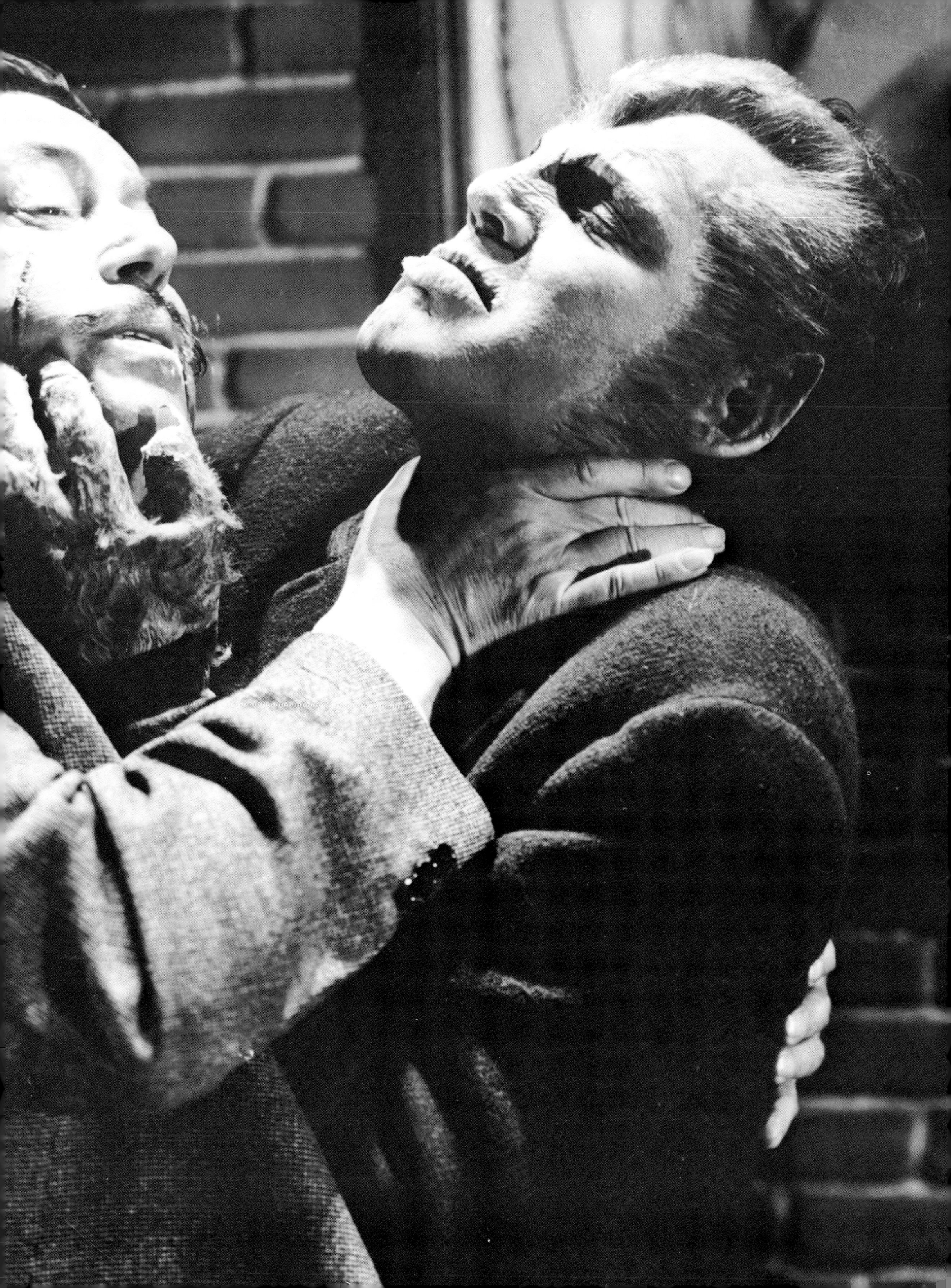

The film, from Universal Studios, starred Henry Hull as the botanist. But it was not the best of all werewolf pictures, since it was really a takeoff from the Jekyll-and-Hyde films. Here we have a kindly scientist who is bitten by a werewolf and keeps being transformed into a savage beast. Then, too, Hull refused to wear effective makeup or undergo the long process of transformation, which limited the horror of the film. The change was done with a tracking shot, not stop-motion. Hull's transformation was shown as he passed from room to room.

When they counted their money, the studio owners found out that this picture was not a financial success. But in 1941 the studio decided to try again, and hired writer Curt Siodmak to create another lycanthrope for them. The result was *The Wolf Man*.

Jack Pierce, of *Frankenstein* fame, was the makeup man responsible for the horrible appearance of the wolf man, who was played by Lon Chaney Jr. It is said that it took five hours per day to apply the makeup, and when the changes took place on camera, it really became complicated. As the hero changes into the

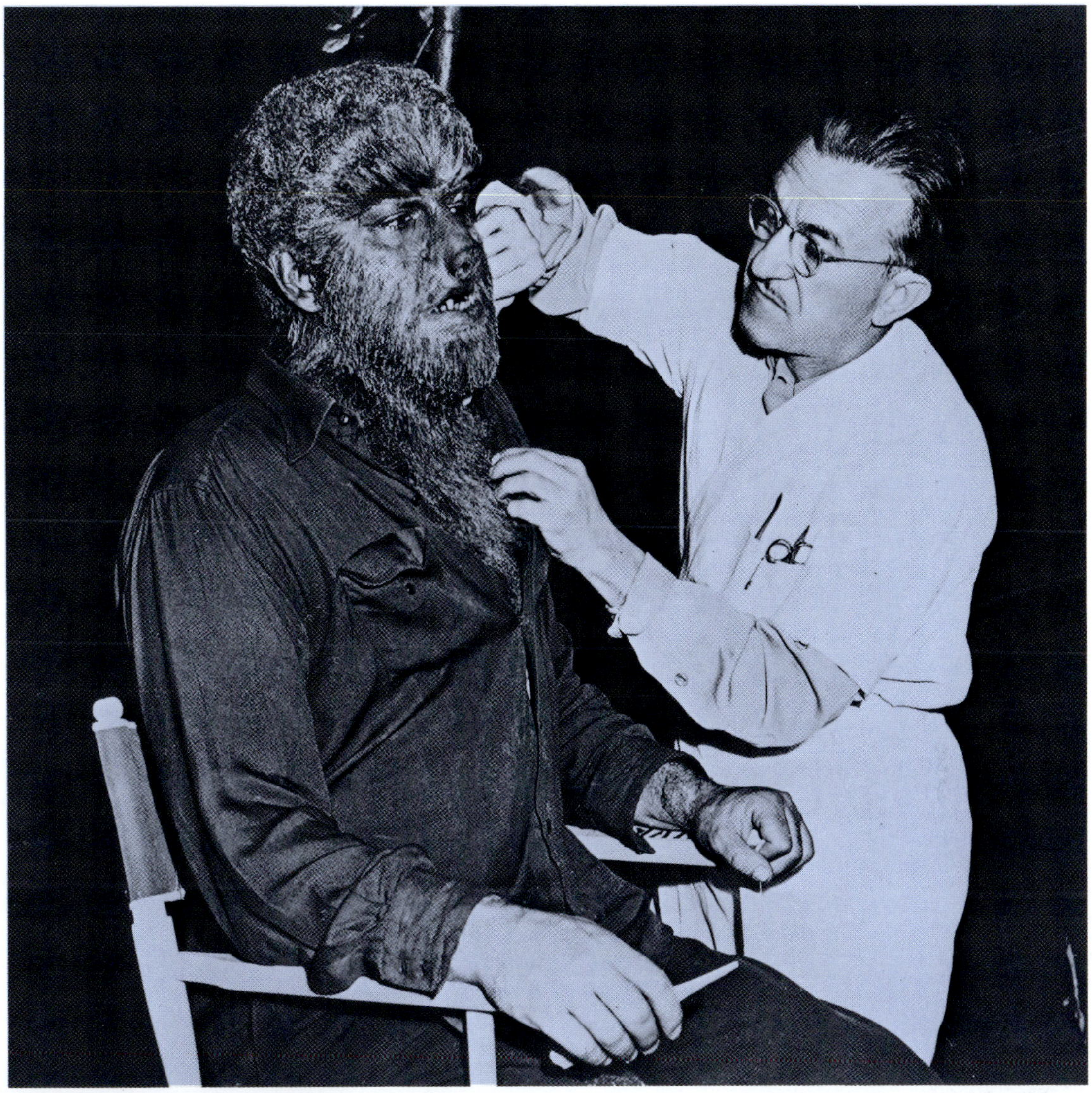

OPPOSITE AND LEFT: Maria Ouspenskaya and Lon Chaney Jr in *The Wolf Man* (1941).

ABOVE: Jack Pierce makes Chaney up for *The Wolf Man* (1941).

wolf man, yak hairs (that's right, yak hairs) were glued to his face in little clumps. Then the film was exposed a few frames, then more hairs were added, more film exposed, until the whole hairy face and the furry hands were visible.

The Wolf Man is the story of Lawrence Talbot, a happy college student who goes back to the home of his ancestors somewhere in Transylvania – the ancient home of horror. Bram Stoker may have started this mysterious reputation when he put Castle Dracula there. Perhaps it was due to the superstitious people who lived there, who were influenced by the large Gypsy population with their tales of werewolves and vampires. At any rate, Transylvania is the logical home of the mad scientist and the monster. It is an area with dark mountains, swamps, gloomy forests and lots of fog – just the place for a story of horror.

Here, in approximately the same region made famous in the Frankenstein films, Talbot goes out for a moonlight stroll. He breaks up a fight between a werewolf and a beautiful young girl, only to be bitten in the process. He then becomes a werewolf himself.

Talbot starts having what he thinks are dreams about killing people. Worried, he consults an old Gypsy woman (Maria Ouspenskaya), who recites the now-classic bit of doggerel:

Even a man who is pure in heart
And says his prayers by night
May become a wolf when the wolfbane blooms
And the autumn moon is bright.

Maleva, the Gypsy, now tells Talbot that her own son, who is a werewolf, was the one who had turned Talbot into a wolf man. The proof is a pentagram that appears in the palm of his hand. Her other wonderful news is that he can return to normal only by being killed with a silver bullet, or some other silver object. But, of course, that means that he will be normal but dead.

Talbot picks his victims when he sees the mysterious pentagram in the palms of their hands. The pentagrams that Talbot sees are illusions, of course, and are merely indications of who the next victim will be. Naturally, he begins to dread the coming of the full moon, during which time he will become a wolf. Finally, he is killed by his own father, who clubs him to death with his silver-headed cane.

This picture about the college boy (college boy? Chaney was 35 years old at the time) from Llanelly, Wales (Chaney certainly had the wrong accent for that), was an instant success when it was released. And part of the credit for the success goes to two other masters of horror – Bela Lugosi, as the son of the Gypsy, and Claude Rains as the senior Talbot.

John Howard inherited lycanthropism in *The Undying Monster* (1942). London was the setting for this story of a werewolf on the prowl in which the wolf man was not seen until the closing minutes.

Lawrence Talbot (Lon Chaney) was brought back again in the previously mentioned *Frankenstein Meets the Wolf Man* (1943). He fought with the monster (played not too well by Bela Lugosi). Actually, Chaney did not fare very well in these pictures, either. With all that makeup on, about the only acting he could do was to stare agonizingly at the full moon – waiting for nature to take its course. In this film, Talbot brings the Frankenstein monster back to life, only to have (in his wolf suit) a fight with him in the final reel. At the end of the fight, both monsters supposedly drown – but they are not dead, of course.

We had a female lycanthrope in *Cry of the Werewolf* (1944). It was Nina Foch, and when she turned into a wolf it was off-screen; her stand-in was what seemed to be a real wolf.

ABOVE RIGHT: Stephen Crane and Osa Masson in a scene from *Cry of the Werewolf*– Nina Foch is on the prowl again.

RIGHT: John Howard as the werewolf in *The Undying Monster* (1942).

OPPOSITE: Lon Chaney Jr is after Evelyn Ankers in *The Wolf Man* (1941).

After *Frankenstein Meets the Wolf Man*, Universal came out with *The House of Frankenstein* (1944), also previously mentioned. In this one, the monster returns the favor and brings the wolf man back to life. This time our furry friend is killed by a silver bullet, but he returned again in 1945 in *The House of Dracula*, in which he is alleged to have been cured of lycanthrophy.

The Werewolf (1956) starred Steven Ritch in a juvenile treatment of the theme. He was a victim of radiation, turned into a wolf man, who was given time to say good-bye to his family before being shot by Don Megowan.

Maybe the bottom of the barrel was reached with *I Was a Teen-age Werewolf* (1957). Herman Cohen, 29-year-old producer, had studied the results of a poll that said that 70 percent of the movie-going public was within the 12- to 25-year age range. So he decided to appeal to the young, and invested $150,000 in the picture, which grossed $300,000 in a short time. The star was Michael Landon, long before he went on to 'Bonanza' and 'Little House on the Prairie' on television, and the doctor who turned him into a werewolf while looking for a shield against radiation was Whit Bissell, who had caused so much trouble in *I Was a Teen-Age Frankenstein*.

Lycanthropus (1961) was also known as *I Married a Werewolf* and *Werewolf in a Girls' Dormitory*. It was an Austrian/Italian film featuring Curt Lowens in the dual role of werewolf and school superintendent. The only redeeming factor was the hit song 'The Ghoul in School.'

The Curse of the Werewolf (1961), made by Hammer, is probably the most intelligent of the wolf-man films, in spite of the fact that the fiend is perhaps too wavy-haired. It combines the horror of the werewolf story with an almost anthropological approach to the legends of lycanthropy. Add to that a magnificent performance by Oliver Reed as the werewolf. The film was set in eighteenth-century Spain, where a beggar rapes a mute servant girl who gives birth to a werewolf. The baby is adopted by a nobleman, who later has to kill him with a silver bullet made from a melted-down crucifix. Reed was wonderful in conveying the agony of a man who tries to avoid his fate.

Paul Naschy starred in three wolf-man films made in Mexico in the early 1970s. The first was *The Fury of the Wolf Man*, or *La Furia del Hombre Lobo* (1970). He played Waldemar the Wolf Man and was killed by a silver bullet. In *La Noche de Walpurgis* (1970) Walde-

Curt Lowens played a school superintendent who turns into a wolf man in *Werewolf in a Girl's Dormitory* (1961).

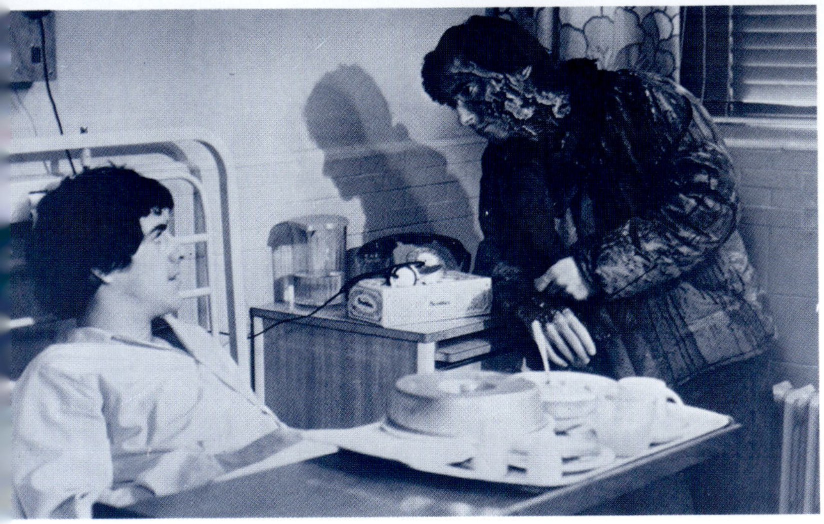

LEFT: David Naughton's dead friend visits him: *An American Werewolf in London*.

ABOVE: Naughton turns into a werewolf in *An American Werewolf in London* (1981).

mar was back. In this one, he kills a witch who acts like a vampire before getting another silver bullet himself. In the United States this film was known as *Werewolf Versus the Vampire Woman*, and in Britain as *Shadow of the Werewolf*. The third Waldemar film was *Dr Jekyll and the Werewolf* (1971). This time Hyde shared the werewolf's body, but got his silver bullet for the third time.

Peter Cushing played the part of a police pathologist in *Legend of the Werewolf* (1974), and David Rintoul was the werewolf. It had good makeup and transformation scenes, but otherwise was done on the cheap.

In *An American Werewolf in London* (1981), theater patrons were treated to the best transformation from man to werewolf ever put on screen. Though it was standard werewolf fare, the film contained one unusual element – humor. The title was a tipoff, and so was the name of the director – John Landis – whose first big film was the wild comedy *Animal House*. There have been plenty of horror films so inept that they have been very funny indeed. There have been many others that have been parodies or satires of traditional horror films. But films that combine real horror and real humor are rare, and it is rarer still that the combination works as well as it does in *American Werewolf*. Having the lead character, David Naughton, carry on a series of conversations with his dead and rapidly rotting friend is a bold, and often hilarious stroke. Even the choice of background music, 'Blue Moon,' is funny. Yet the terror is there, and the ending, when the werewolf is killed, brought a tear to many eyes.

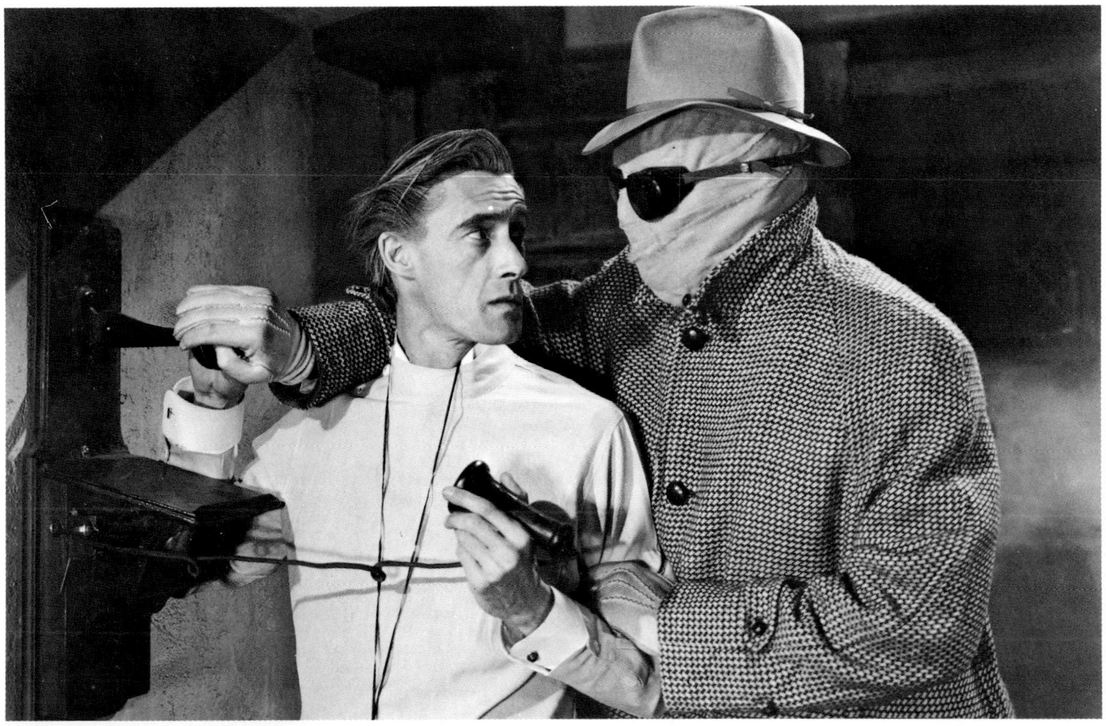

RIGHT: Jon Hall (right) comes to wreak vengeance on John Carradine in *The Invisible Man's Revenge* (1944).

OPPOSITE: Claude Rains ponders his fate in *The Invisible Man* (1933).

BELOW: Claude Rains and Gloria Stuart starred in *The Invisible Man* (1933).

Michael J Fox brought his considerable natural charm to another telling of the werewolf story in *Teen Wolf* (1985). This was no *I Was A Teen-Age Werewolf*; indeed, it had warmth and humor. It was the story of a high-school kid who periodically changes into a gentle wolf, and was probably the only time audiences will be treated to the spectacle of a wolf break-dancing.

One of the few psychotics who actually turned himself into a monster was found in H G Wells's ghoulish novelette *The Invisible Man*. Boris Karloff pulled essentially the same kind of stunt that Bela Lugosi had done before when the time came for James Whale to film the story. Karloff didn't want to be invisible until the end of the picture, so the part was given to Claude Rains. This launched Rains's movie career, much as Lugosi's turning down the Frankenstein monster role had been so helpful to Karloff.

The Invisible Man (1933) is the story of a mysterious stranger who turns up in a small English village. His hands are encased in gloves, and his head is completely covered with bandages. He wears a pair of dark glasses, and seems to be a chemist who is diligently looking for an unknown formula. It turns out that the man is a Dr Griffin, who has discovered a batch of chemicals that will turn flesh and bone and blood into a state of invisibility. Unfortunately, it also makes the subject insane. Griffin is full of plans to dominate the world, and he derails trains, robs banks and murders people – all in his invisible state. When he is finally caught and shot, he returns to visibility.

The trick photography in the film was fantastic. Imagine watching a man unwind the bandages around his head and finding that there is nothing underneath. The transformation in *The Invisible Man* was probably done with a combination of double exposure (exposing the film twice) and masked negative (blotting out the exposure of the man's head on the film and letting the second half of the double exposure shine through).

This trick was picked up again in *The Invisible Man Returns* (1940). In this film, Vincent Price is not psychotic, but rather makes himself invisible in order to track down a murderer. And in *The Invisible Man's Revenge* (1944), Jon Hall was made invisible by a doctor who wanted his estate. He then kills the doctor after being refused visibility.

But enough of these people who brought it on themselves. There are plenty of other people who brought it on the innocent.

THE HUMAN FIEND

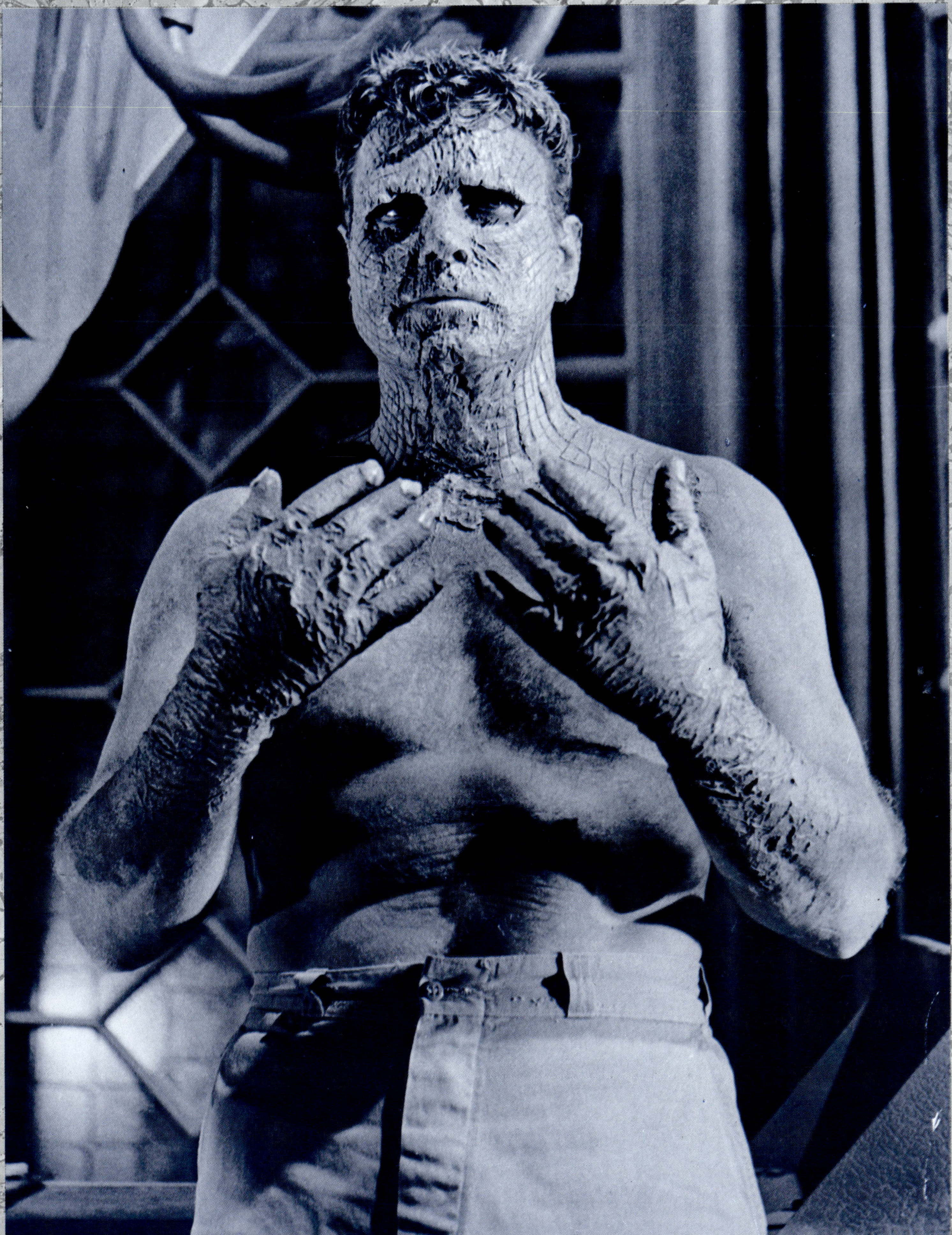

The basic reason for the popularity of the movies starring crazed doctors who run around doing atrocious things to animals, plants and even human beings, is apparently the ingrained suspicion that most people have toward science itself. And they come by this suspicion honestly: it's been around for a long time. The early scientists were content to sit around and discuss their subject matter with each other, and so were no threat to the established beliefs of the day. But suspicion began to rear its ugly head when these learned men began to hang out in their laboratories, performing experiments that, while they were not blasphemous, at least produced results that might cause their fellow men to question long-established ideas. The scientists were almost forced to go underground, writing up their experiments so that laymen could not understand them.

Even today, deep down, the common man retains his suspicions of the man in the white laboratory jacket. Although we applaud the results of modern science – the polio vaccine, transplant surgery, the landing on the moon – we are secretly not surprised at the failures of science: excessive chemical insecticides, radioactive pollution, the side effects of modern drugs. The scientist is still a man apart.

One of the most fearsome of these mad doctors was Dr Moreau, in the chilling novelette *The Island of Dr Moreau*, by H G Wells. His research involved painful surgery on animals in the hope of turning them into humans. In the book, the hero looks on these creatures of Dr Moreau for the first time and observes:

> One was evidently a female. The other two were men. Their skins were of a dull pinkish drab color, such as I had seen in no savages before. They had fat, heavy, chinless faces, retreating foreheads, and a scant bristly hair upon their faces. Never before had I seen such bestial looking creatures. . . . Each of these creatures, despite its human form, its rag of clothing, and the rough humanity of its bodily form, had woven into it, into its movements, into its whole presence, some now irresistible suggestion of a hog, a swinish taint, the unmistakable mark of the beast.

Oh, those mad scientists. Where would horror films be without them?

Possibly the first mad-scientist film told of the creation of ape monsters. It was *The Doctor's Experiment, or Reversing Darwin's Theory* (1908). This was followed in 1915 by *Heba the Snake Woman* (turning a

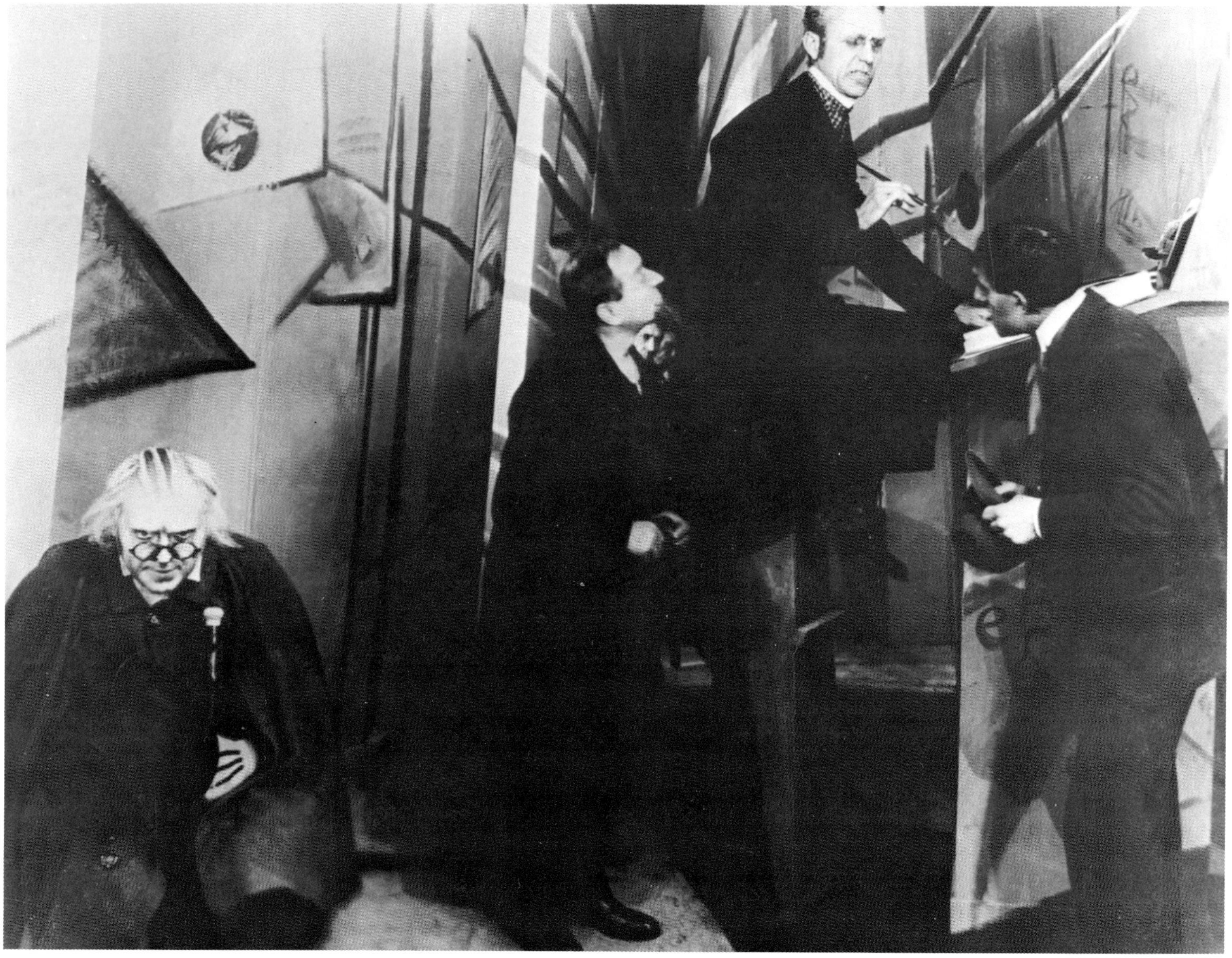

OPPOSITE AND ABOVE: Two scenes from *The Cabinet of Dr Caligari* (1919).

PREVIOUS SPREAD: One of the creatures from *The Alligator People* (1959).

woman into a snake) and in 1919 by *The Beetle*, in which a man becomes an insect.

From the popularity of mesmerism and hypnotism came stories of the sleepwalker, or somnambulist. Here we have a monster who has been put into a deep sleep by a mad doctor and forced to do the bidding of his master. An added part of the story is that the sleepwalker has enormous strength and can feel no pain. The greatest of films about a somnambulist was the first one ever made – *The Cabinet of Dr Caligari* (1920).

In 1913 Hans Janowitz, a young Czech writer, experienced something that was eventually to have a profound effect on the world of horror films. He was attending a fair in Hamburg, Germany, and noticed a strange man lurking about some bushes in a park. When he read the papers the next day, he learned that a young girl had been brutally murdered at the spot where he had seen the prowler. Janowitz attended the funeral of the murdered girl and saw the mysterious man again. He had no proof that the man had been the murderer, and, as far as the police were concerned, the case was never solved.

A few years later, Janowitz met a young poet, a former Austrian infantry officer named Carl Mayer. He told his story to the poet, who, in turn, told Janowitz of his experiences with an army psychiatrist who had made fun of Mayer's philosophical ideas because he felt that the young officer was mentally ill. The two writers decided to collaborate on a story. They called it *The Cabinet of Dr Caligari*, and took it to a German film company, Decla, to show to the producer Erich Pommer. He immediately bought the script for something in the neighborhood of $200. Before we can assume that Janowitz and Mayer were robbed, we must remember that the story may not have been completely original. There is an old German folk tale, dating from the eleventh century, of a dishonest

LEFT: The somnambulist, Cesare, played by Conrad Veidt, comes to kidnap the heroine, Jane, played by Lil Dagover, in *The Cabinet of Dr Caligari* (1919).

BELOW: Cesare can't bring himself to kill Jane, so he carries her off, eventually becoming so exhausted by the pursuing townsfolk that he dies.

monk who had a sleepwalking slave committed to do his evil bidding.

Fritz Lang was offered the directorship of the movie, but turned it down, and it was taken over by Robert Wiene. The result was one of the first full-length pictures involving a mad scientist – Dr Caligari. He controlled the mind of a sleepwalker, Cesare, and often forced him to do a bit of business that later became almost a requirement in monster movies: the somnambulist would sneak into the heroine's bedroom and carry her off. Of course, she was usually dressed in a long white robe.

The story of *The Cabinet of Dr Caligari* starts with a traveling fair that is set up in the village of Holstenwall. Caligari, with his hypnotized somnambulist, wants to open a fortune-telling booth. The town clerk is cruel and insulting to Caligari, and the next day the poor official is found murdered. Guess who did it. At any rate, Caligari opens his booth, exhibiting Cesare, who lives in a coffin-like cabinet. Alan and Francis, two students, attend the show in Caligari's booth, and Cesare predicts that Alan will die before morning. When Alan is killed, Francis tries to convince the police that Caligari and Cesare are to blame, but they will not pay any attention to him. If they had, the story would have been over before it had really begun.

Next, for some reason, Cesare is sent out to murder Francis's girlfriend, Jane. But, as we might guess, she is too beautiful to be murdered, so Cesare merely kidnaps her. Jane's vocal chords are her salvation. Attracted by her screams, a crowd starts chasing the somnambulist. He drops Jane, runs away, and dies of exhaustion and exposure in a nearby wood. Caligari then escapes, and Francis follows him. The last part of the story reveals that Caligari is really the director of an insane asylum and is nuttier than his patients. Francis exposes him, and Caligari is put into a strait jacket.

That's the way the story went, but by the time Wiene got through with it, some changes had been made. The film opens with a scene in which Francis is sitting on a park bench, talking to an old man. Jane walks by, looking as if she, too, were a somnambulist. Francis explains that they have had quite an experience, and begins to tell the original story. At the end of the film, Caligari is revealed as the director of the insane asylum, all right. But Francis, Jane and the somnambulist are patients there, and the events of the picture were merely the products of Francis's demented mind.

The film was a sensation. The eerie expressionist

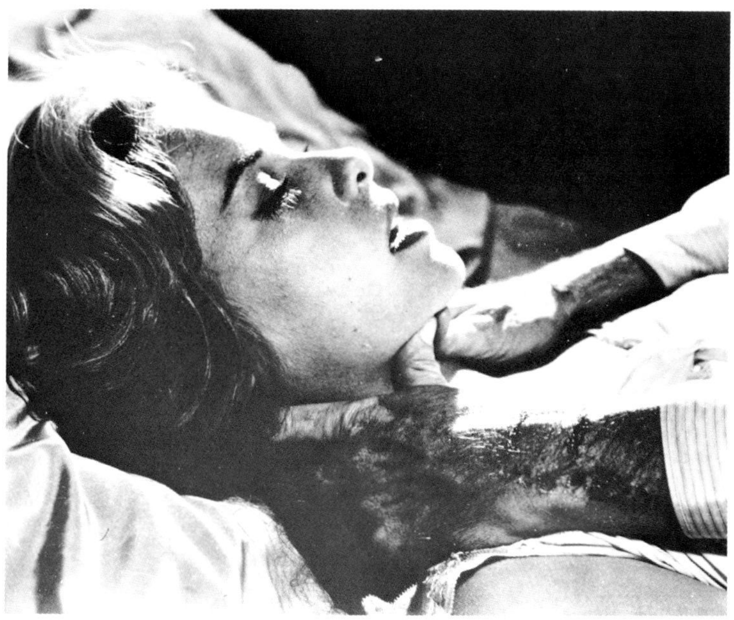

sets – except for the prologue and epilogue scenes – looked like black-and-white cubist paintings and were extremely effective in giving a dreamlike quality to the action. This may have been a fortunate accident, however. The movie-makers were forced, because of poverty, to use any cheap material they could lay their hands on.

The actors were also made up with the stark white and deep black of the sets, and the interpretations of Werner Krauss as Caligari and Conrad Veidt as Cesare (both of them appearing in their first picture),

RIGHT: Charles Laughton (right), Arthur Hohl, Richard Arlen and Leila Hyams in *Island of Lost Souls*.

OPPOSITE LEFT: Burt Lancaster played Dr Moreau in the remake of *The Island of Lost Souls*, which was retitled *The Island of Dr Moreau* (1977).

OPPOSITE RIGHT: Strangulation by the hands of the murderer grafted onto the pianist's arms is imminent in *The Hands of Orlac* (1960), also known as *Hands of the Strangler*, a remake of the 1925 classic.

BELOW: Charles Laughton, as the evil Dr Moreau (right), repels the insurrectionists in *The Island of Lost Souls* (1933). Bela Lugosi is the man-beast in the center.

were terrifying. The film gives to the audience the feeling of observing a terrible nightmare.

Lon Chaney Sr played a mad doctor in a tongue-in-cheek spoof called *The Monster* (1925). The odd thing about the film was that it satirized a type of movie that had not been invented yet. Chaney was a semicomic scientist who arranged that automobile accidents would happen near his laboratory so that he would have dead bodies to work on.

Robert Wiene and Conrad Veidt worked together again in an Austrian film, *Orlacs Hande* (1925), also called *The Hands of Orlac*. In this goody, a concert pianist loses his hands and a strange scientist gives him a new pair. Anyone can guess the rest – the new hands are those of a murderer and take over the pianist's brain, turning him into a murderer, too.

The theme in *The Cabinet of Dr Caligari* has been copied over and over again since the film was first seen. In *The Bells* (1926), Boris Karloff played a hypnotist with a slave – the first of many Caligari-type movies. In *The Magician* (1926), Paul Wegener played a character based on Aleister Crowley, the famous occultist. In this picture he hypnotized Ruth Terry and carried her off to his castle to extract her blood for his experiments in the creation of life.

H G Wells's great story *The Island of Dr Moreau* was made into a movie and released as *The Island of Lost Souls* (1933). Dr Moreau was played by Charles Laughton, a talented English actor who had yet to make his big splash as Captain Bligh in *Mutiny on the Bounty* (1936).

As in the original story, Moreau felt called upon to change animals of all types into men and women, or reasonable facsimiles of them. This was done by performing horrible vivisections. The most successful of his experiments is a girl named Lola, a fine panther woman. She and the doctor, however, have disagreements because, among other things, he forgets that she has a naturally feline nature. In the interests of self-preservation and science, Moreau has patiently taught his animal men and women to be unaggressive. Then he makes the mistake of ordering an ape

LEFT: Vincent Price, as the mad disfigured artist, watches his wax museum go up in flames in *House of Wax* (1953), a Technicolor remake of *The Mystery of the Wax Museum* (1933).

OPPOSITE TOP: Bela Lugosi is properly frightened in *The Black Cat* (1934), but he will get his revenge.

OPPOSITE BOTTOM: A theater poster for *The Black Cat* (1934).

BELOW: Lionel Atwill was the mad artist in *The Mystery of the Wax Museum* (1933).

man to commit murder, and the monsters discover that they are able to revolt. And revolt they do.

Under the leadership of Bela Lugosi (wearing hairy makeup that makes him look like a magnet dipped in iron filings), they take Moreau prisoner and haul him off to the torture chamber of a laboratory, where they begin to operate on him. Turn about is fair play. But the whole island catches fire and destroys every living thing except the hero and heroine who, of course, are able to escape. For some reason or other, this film was banned by the censor in Great Britain. It might have been because of pressure by the Royal Society for the Prevention of Cruelty to Animals.

It is possible that a popular phrase first saw the light of day in *The Island of Lost Souls*. Laughton and his human captives are having dinner inside his fortress, as the human animals are having a meeting outside. Drums are beating and low murmers can be heard from the beasts. Laughton looks at his guests and utters the deathless line: 'The natives are restless tonight.'

The Mystery of the Wax Museum was perhaps the only important horror film ever made by Warner Brothers. It was released in 1933, directed by Michael Curtiz, and starred another British actor, Lionel Atwill, as well as Fay Wray, who had another of her patented screaming roles. The film tells the story of a

mad artist who kills people, dips them in wax, and behold – another work of art. One of the important features of the movie was that it was shot in the two-color Technicolor process.

Bela Lugosi and Boris Karloff teamed up again in *The Black Cat* (1934), which had nothing at all to do with the Edgar Allan Poe story. It concerned a vengeful doctor (Lugosi) who seeks out the Austrian architect and devil-worshipper (Karloff) who had betrayed his country in World War I. It was set in a modernistic but crumbling castle that is blown up just as Lugosi is skinning Karloff alive.

The Hands of Orlac was remade and released as *Mad Love* (1935). In this version, Hungarian-born Peter Lorre made an impressive American screen debut as Dr Gogol, who grafted the hands of a murderer onto the pianist, Colin Clive.

The Raven (1935) was reminiscent of Chaney's film *The Monster*. Bela Lugosi runs a quiet little country clinic complete with an Edgar Allan Poe torture chamber in the basement. Boris Karloff, an escaped murderer, hopes that Lugosi will use his skill as a plastic surgeon to change his face. But after the operation, his face is a mess: one side is horribly scarred, the lips are twisted and one eye is lower than the other. The film had stunning sets and full-blooded dialogue. For example, when Lugosi taunts Karloff about the murder that Karloff has committed, the criminal seems almost like an embarrassed schoolboy who has been caught by the truant officer. 'Well, after all, he was in my way, and there was the acetylene torch in my hand.' Lugosi reminds him that he had thrust the flames into the man's eyes. 'Well, there are some things you can't 'elp doing.'

Karloff was framed and executed in *The Walking*

Dead (1936). He is brought back to life, however, by a professor (Edmund Gwenn, long before he became so lovable as Kris Kringle in *The Miracle on 34th Street* in 1947). Karloff swears vengeance on those who sent him to his death. Then in *The Man Who Lived Again* (1936), retitled *The Man Who Changed His Mind*, he became the scientist who learns how to transplant brains from one human being to another.

Karloff's third 1936 film involving mad scientists was *The Invisible Ray*, in which he played the part of Dr Janos Rukh, who had been contaminated by 'radium X' from a meteorite while on an expedition to the Mountains of the Moon in Africa. His brain disintegrates slowly, and he dies as a glowing monster – falling from a window and exploding on impact.

Karloff's last mad-scientist film of the 1930s was *The Man They Could Not Hang* (1939). In this one, he was again the executed man brought back to life who resolves to get revenge on those who had him hanged.

Humphrey Bogart had his turn at being a mad scientist in *The Return of Dr X* (1939), another resuscitation film. Bogart was an executed child murderer, Dr Maurice Xavier, who has been brought back to life, but needs frequent transfusions of human blood to stay that way. The only decent thing about the movie was Bogart's makeup with its waxy features and white-streaked hair.

Karloff was a mad scientist who had a date with a noose in *Before I Hang* (1940). This time he trans-

ABOVE: Bela Lugosi played a mad doctor in *The Raven* (1935). Here he contemplates the stuffed bird who played the title role.

RIGHT: Mad doctor Boris Karloff examines a possible brain donor in *The Man Who Lived Again* (1936).

OPPOSITE: Peter Lorre made his American film debut in *Mad Love* (1935), a remake of *The Hands of Orlac*. He played Dr Gogol, who performs the hand transplants. It also starred Frances Drake.

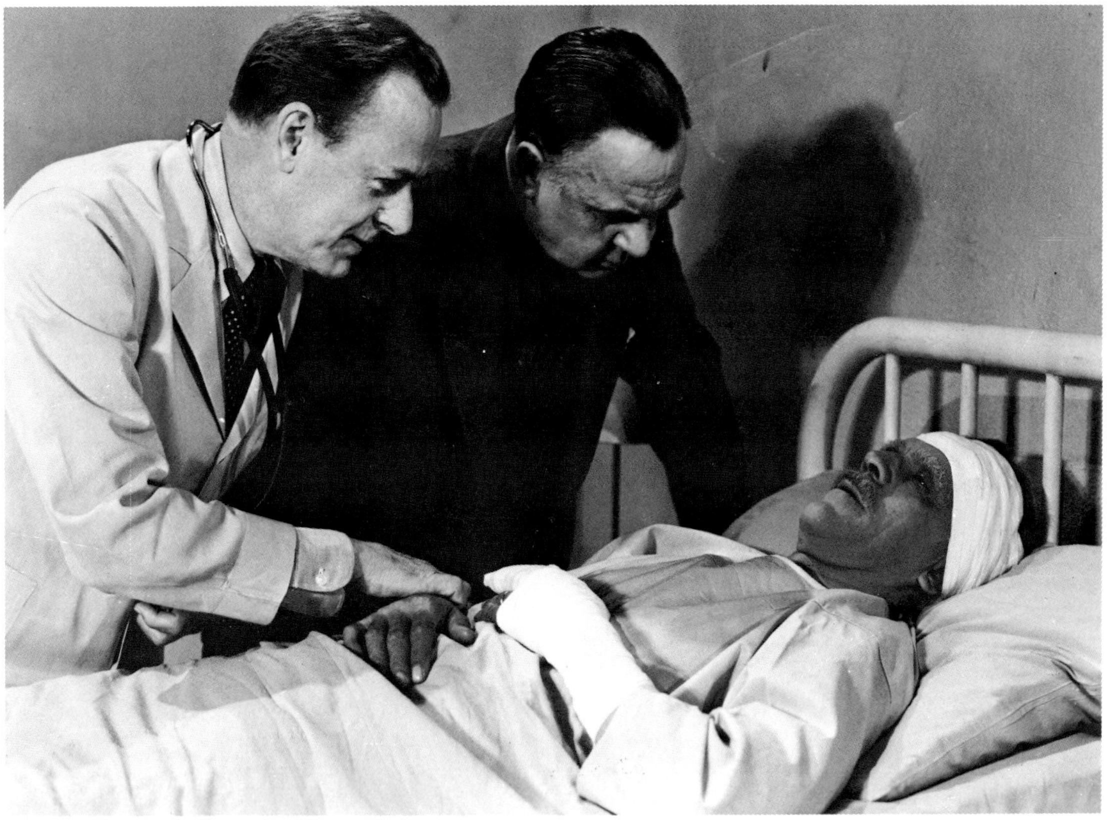

LEFT: Boris Karloff was frozen in *The Man with Nine Lives* (1940). He gets out of the hospital, but his brain is completely altered.

OPPOSITE TOP: Bela Lugosi on the prowl in his ape suit in *The Ape Man* (1943).

OPPOSITE BOTTOM: A theater poster for *Dr Cyclops*.

BELOW: Lionel Atwill was a mad scientist again in *Man Made Monster* (1941). Here he is about to give Lon Chaney Jr his electrical treatment.

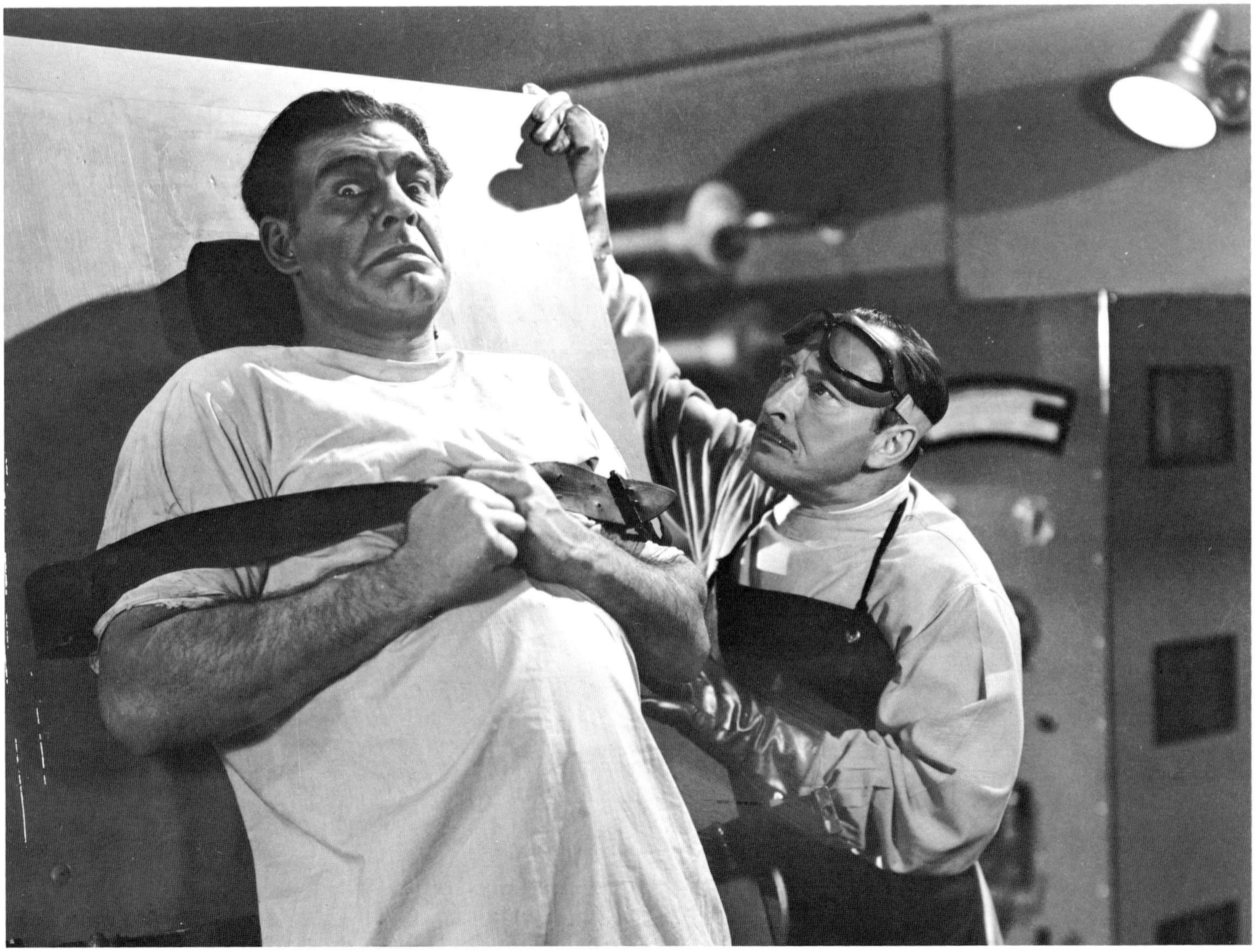

forms himself into a young man to escape being hanged by injecting himself with the blood of a condemned murderer. Unfortunately, this makes him go on a killing rampage, and he finally returns to prison of his own volition.

Karloff played a mad doctor twice more in 1940. In *The Ape* he is looking for a cure for polio and finds that he needs human spinal fluids for his experimentation, so he kills an ape and dresses in its skin to go looking for victims. In *The Man With Nine Lives*, he thinks he has found a cure for cancer by freezing his patients, but he accidentally locks both himself and his patients in the freezer. When he is thawed out seven years later, he goes berserk. Both of these films were hokey, but fun.

Lugosi's mad-doctor turn came again with *The Devil Bat* (1940). In this one, he trains bats to kill his victims for him. And he uses the smell of a special shaving lotion so the bats can find the person to kill. Naturally, he gives the shaving lotion to his enemies as a gift.

Dr Cyclops (1940) was one of the better crazy-scientist movies. In it, Albert Dekker played the part of Dr Thorkel, who used a uranium isotope to shrink animals and natives in the South American jungle. A group of explorers happens along and he shrinks them, too. But once they break his glasses (recalling the Cyclops legend), he is helpless, and they resume their normal size. The film was in Technicolor, and the special effects make it a classic of its kind.

The Invisible Woman (1941) starred the former Jekyll and Hyde, John Barrymore, as the mad doctor and Virginia Bruce, the former Busby Berkeley showgirl, as the woman he makes invisible. Oddly enough, this was really a screwball comedy. An example of

RIGHT: Aquanetta, the *Jungle Woman* (1944), being rescued, but not from a fate worse than death.

OPPOSITE: Bela Lugosi needed the vital fluids from young girls in *The Corpse Vanishes* (1942), and sometimes he had to take matters into his own hands.

BELOW: Mad scientist George Zucco giving orders to the zombie he has created – David Bruce, in *The Mad Ghoul* (1943).

Lionel Atwill's several roles as the mad scientist was the film *Man Made Monster*, also made in 1941. In this picture he doses Lon Chaney Jr with so much electricity that he walks around in a perpetual glow and has to wear a rubber suit. The monster eventually kills the scientist, carries off the girl, and dies when his suit snags on a barbed-wire fence, which drains him of all his electrical energy.

Lugosi was back in *The Corpse Vanishes* (1942). This time around he has to kill girls for their vital fluids, which he injects into his aged wife in order to keep her young and beautiful. Also in 1942, in *Dr Renault's Secret* (which had nothing to do with an automobile), J Carroll Naish was turned into an ape with a human face.

Universal Studios tried to start another horror series about an ape woman named Paula Dupree (played by Aquanetta, who was born Burnu Davenport). It started with *Captive Wild Woman* (1943). Dr Sigmund Walters (John Carradine) injects some hormones into a circus orangutan and then puts his lady assistant's brain into the head of the beast. The result is a beautiful woman who turns into an ape when she gets excited. She kills Walters and eventually is shot to death herself. But was she really dead? The next time around, in *Jungle Woman* (1944), Dr Fletcher (J Carroll Naish) brings her back to life and beauty. And the silly girl turns back into an ape again and dies. Next, Dr Stendhal (Otto Kruger) gives her corpse another transfusion in *Jungle Captive* (1945), but she gets shot again. This time she – and the series – remained dead.

For some reason or other, Bela Lugosi tried to turn himself into a monkey in *The Ape Man* (1943). To do this, he had to go on a killing spree to get the necessary spinal fluid to turn himself back into a human. In this film, he wore almost the same makeup as he had in *The Island of Lost Souls*.

George Zucco invented a special gas to turn David Bruce into a member of the living dead in *The Mad Ghoul* (1943). But he had to give him a heart transplant every so often and was forced to become a grave robber.

Another seeker of perpetual youth was Nils Aster in *The Man in Half Moon Street* (1944). He wanted to remain a perpetual 35-year-old and replaced his glands with new ones every so often. Naturally, he had to commit murder to get the glands, but he missed a fix and aged 50 years in a matter of minutes. He died, of course.

Gale Sondergaard was angry in *The Spider Woman Strikes Back* (1946). She worked out a complicated scheme of revenge on local ranchers whom she felt were occupying land that was rightfully hers. She advertised for companions, then drugged them, siphoned off their blood and fed it to giant carnivorous plants. From the plants, she brewed a poison that killed off the other ranchers' cattle, and all of them had to file for bankruptcy.

The Mystery of the Wax Museum (1933) was remade in 1953 and called *House of Wax*. It starred Vincent Price as the insane proprietor of the waxworks and was shot in 3-D. Charles Bronson had a minor role under his real name, Charles Buschinski. Phyllis Kirk and Fay Wray supported.

The mad scientist Dr Boronski filled children with radiation that turned them into either geniuses or zombies in the British film *The Gamma People* (1955). Walter Riller was the scientist and Paul Douglas (again, the obligatory American actor) played the part of the journalist who defeated him.

Bela Lugosi's last film was *Bride of the Monster* (1955). He played the part of Dr Eric Vornoff, who

BELOW: Gale Sondergaard (left) starred in *The Spider Woman Strikes Back* (1946).

RIGHT: Paul Douglas played the part of an investigative reporter in *The Gamma People* (1955).

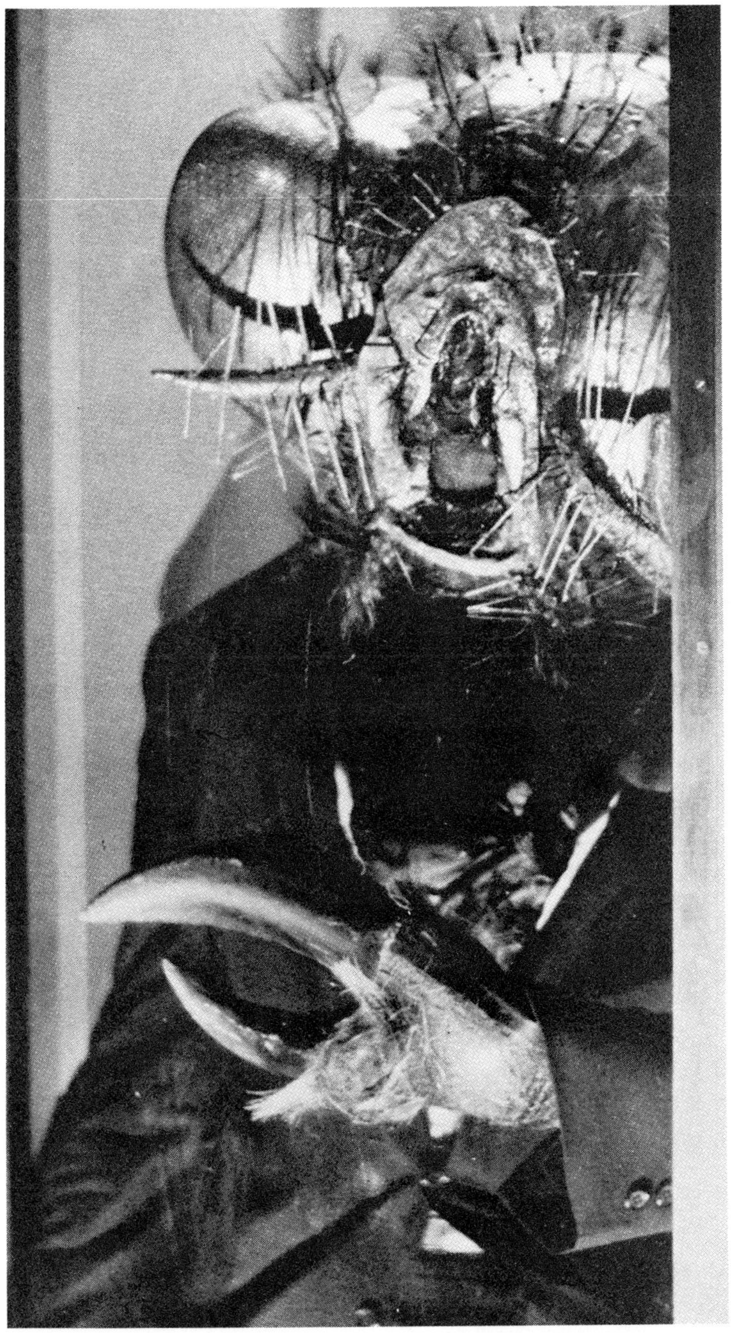

the film, the scientist does away with himself, with his wife's help, by squashing his ghastly head in a hydraulic press, so that no one will ever know the nature of his experimental failure. The fly with a human head ends up being trapped in a spider's web, hit with a rock and squashed, too. Nobody bothered to explain how the scientist with the fly's head retained his own human brain, especially since the man's head on the fly's body was able to speak.

Then came *The Return of the Fly* (1959), in which Vincent Price (who had been a family friend in the previous film) played the part of the scientist's son. He tried the same experiment and became a monster himself. As we have seen in the Frankenstein family, some people never learn. Then there was an English movie, *The Curse of the Fly* (1965), in which Carole Gray screamed like a latter-day Fay Wray, but the less said about that the better.

In *The Alligator People* (1959), George Macready tried to regrow limbs on an amputee by injecting him with a serum made from alligators. Naturally, he turns into a reptile-man. It was an above-par chiller, but the real star was the makeup man.

LEFT: David Hedison was the scientist who accidentally turned himself into an insect in *The Fly* (1958).

BELOW: One of the victims of *The Fiend Without a Face* (1958), being attacked by monsters.

tries to create superstrong and supersized monsters by radiation, only to be eaten by his own giant octopus. The film was done so much on the cheap that a photographic enlarger was used in the role of the radiation machine.

In *The Fiend Without a Face* (1958), a scientist works on materialized thought and produces monsters from his own subconcious. The result was crawling brains and spinal cords that jumped on their victims to suck their brains out.

The Fly (1958) was the first horror film in CinamaScope. It was the story of a scientist who develops a machine that will transport matter instantaneously from place to place. The big problem arises when he tries to transmit his own body across the width of the laboratory. There is a fly in the ointment – a real fly in the machine, that is. At the end of the experiment, he is intact, but with the fly's head and foreleg on his body, while the fly has his head and arm. At the end of

Michael Gough starred as the scientist in *Konga* (1960). He was the one who creates a giant ape by injecting a monkey with a secret serum. As might be expected, the ape almost destroys London. Along the way, the scientist also created a giant plant. It's hard to believe, but the name of the picture was later changed to *I Was a Teen-age Gorilla*.

Michael Caine had a supporting role in *Dr Blood's Coffin* (1960), in which Kieron Moore played Blood. He keeps transplanting hearts into his patient until the poor man ends up as a rotting living corpse (played by Paul Stockman).

In *The Snake Woman* (1960), Susan Travers turns herself into a cobra and kills off her enemies – who had caused the death of her father, the mad scientist. He had tried to cure his pregnant wife of insanity by using snake venom, which accounts for his daughter's affliction.

The Hands of Orlac was filmed yet again in 1961. It was an English picture directed by Edmond T Greville, with Mel Ferrer as the pianist and Donald Wolfit as Dr Gogol, the sadistic surgeon.

The British movie *The Damned* (1962) was retitled *These Are the Damned*. In the film Alexander Knox is trying to breed a race of cold-blooded radioactive children; he keeps them in a cave waiting to inherit the world after World War III. There was also a secondary plot about motorcycling thugs, with Oliver Reed as

ABOVE: A couple of the cave-dwelling radioactive children in *These Are the Damned* (1962).

LEFT: A severed head (belonging to Kathleen Breck), being kept alive electronically, talks to Philip Gilbert and Anna Palk in *The Frozen Dead* (1966).

OPPOSITE BELOW: The kindly protective monster from *The Swamp Thing* (1982).

OPPOSITE TOP: The unlikely duo from *The Incredible Two-Headed Transplant* (1971).

the leader of the gang.

The mad scientist in *The Frozen Dead* (1966) was Dana Andrews. He finds a king-size freezer full of frozen Nazis and revives them in hopes of setting up a Fourth Reich. Then Cameron Mitchell played Baron von Weser in *The Bloodsuckers* (1966). He was a mad scientist who creates plants that eat meat. Finally, he ends up being chopped down along with his carnivorous trees. Frank Finlay, in *The Deadly Bees* (1966), trained his little insect pets to sting people to death, but they turned on him.

In a Mexican film, *La Horripilante Bestia Humana* (1970), or *Night of the Bloody Apes*, the mad Dr José Elias Moreno gives his dying son a gorilla's heart. The boy turns into an ape. That obviously was a mistake, so the doctor gives his son another transplant – this time from a lady wrestler.

The head of an insane murderer is attached to the head of a mental retardate in *The Incredible Two-Headed Transplant* (1971). Bruce Dern starred, and one critic commented, 'Which head made this film?'

Louis Jourdan played the madman in *The Swamp Thing* (1982). He transforms one of his scientist assistants into a green slimy monster that roams the swamps, looking for his former girlfriend, Adrienne Barbeau. He is a gentle monster, however, in this film that asks the question, 'Can a busty young woman who hates bugs and reptiles find true happiness in the arms of a gruesome monster?'

That about wraps up the highlights in the long parade of human fiends. But there must be many more waiting in the wings for their chance to touch our hearts.

SERVANTS OF THE DEVIL

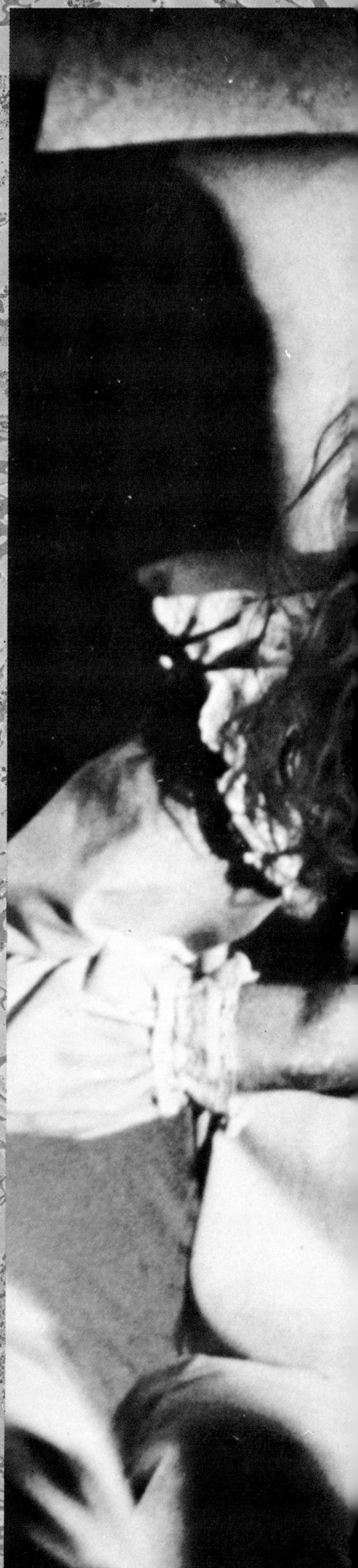

The legend about a human being selling his soul to the devil for some special favors is an extremely old one. It is based on the ancient belief that the Prince of Darkness is greedy for human souls, and anyone is fair game. One of the oldest stories is that of young Proterius, who was supposed to have lived in the fourth century. He signed a pact with the devil to win the hand of his master's daughter, and was saved when St Basil forced the devil to give back the paper.

The most famous pact-signer was Johann Faust, the half-mythical philosopher who died in 1541. His story has been told many times in plays (Johann Wolfgang von Goethe's *Faust* and Christopher Marlowe's *Dr Faustus*) and operas (Charles Gounod's *Faust* and Arrigo Boïto's *Mephistofele*). Depending on whose version of the story we read, Faust either beat the devil or he didn't. One group of writers gets him off the hook, after a life of youth and love, while another group has a more startling story to tell. They say that Faust was urged to break his promise, but he replied: 'The devil has honestly kept the promise that he made to me, therefore I will honestly keep the pledge that I made and contracted with him.' About midnight on Faust's last day on earth, it is said, there came a storm, accompanied by sounds of hissing and whistling as though from thousands of snakes. When the neighbors came out of their houses the next morning, all that remained of Faust was a pitiful pile of flesh in the yard. In his study, however, they found blood all over the place, brains and teeth on the floor, and his eyeballs pinned to the wall.

The first film about a pact with the devil was *Faust* (1900). This was followed by other versions of the tale in 1903 and 1904, but no prints of these pictures remain. The French did it in 1905, and it was redone in 1907, 1909, 1911 and 1921. The only version that has survived, and it was probably the best of all, was the *Faust* of 1926, a superbly styled version of the legend. It was a German film, directed by F W Murnau, that starred Emil Jannings, the great actor who would become the first star to win an Academy Award – for *The Way of All Flesh* (1927).

Another pact movie was *The Student of Prague* (1913), starring our old golem friend, Paul Wegener. Here we have a poor student named Baldwin who signs up with a representative of the devil, the wizard Scapinelli. He is rewarded with the girl of his dreams in exchange for all rights to his image in the mirror.

ABOVE: Emil Jannings, as Mephistopheles, fondles a servant girl (Yvette Guibert) in *Faust* (1926).

LEFT: Gosta Ekman, as the aged Faust, yearns to become young again in *Faust* (1926).

OPPOSITE TOP: Mephistopheles transforms the old man into a youth in *Faust* (1926).

OPPOSITE BOTTOM: *The Student of Prague* (1913) was based on an old German legend about a man who sold his reflection to the devil and bought it back only at the expense of his life.

PAGE 143: Max von Sydow, as *The Exorcist* (1973), contemplates the possessed Regan (Linda Blair).

In this German film, Baldwin beats the girl's boyfriend in a duel by the use of magic. But this angers the girl's family and Baldwin loses out to the devil. The film was so successful that it was remade in Germany in 1926 starring Conrad Veidt.

Adolphe Menjou made a bargain with the devil in *The Sorrows of Satan* (1927), but the next great pact-with-the-devil film was *All That Money Can Buy* (1941). It was based on the short story by Stephen Vincent Benét, 'The Devil and Daniel Webster,' about a poor New England farmer, Jabez Stone (James Craig), who gives in to the devil's promises of wealth. Walter Huston played Mr Scratch, the devil, in a great performance). Anne Shirley played Mrs Stone, who is saddened by the advances made toward her husband by a seductive devil's assistant (Simone Simon) – sent by Scratch to keep Stone on the crooked and wide path to damnation. Stone becomes the richest man in the state of New Hampshire, but when it is almost time for him to give up his soul, he sends for the legendary orator Daniel Webster (Edward Arnold) to help him out of the jam. Webster convinces Scratch that Stone deserves a jury trial. Just for fun, Scratch agrees, but with two provisos – *he* gets to select the judge and jury, and if Webster loses, he has to accompany Stone to hell.

Scratch summons his judge and jury from hell – the judge is the same who sentenced American witches to be hanged, and the jury consists of twelve of the worst cutthroats, brigands and criminals in American history – Benedict Arnold, Simon Girty, pirates and murderers. The trial lasts all night, ending with Webster's impassioned speech about patriotism and how the jury cannot let Stone be abducted by an alien power. Stone is acquitted, but Scratch grins and tells Webster that his punishment is fitting: he will never be elected president.

The film was a visual delight, with Huston's sparkling performance almost matched by Arnold's Daniel Webster. It was a magic act in more ways than one, and used Hollywood's whole bag of cinematic tricks.

Some would argue that the greatest satanic-pact movie of all time was *The Picture of Dorian Gray* (1945), taken from the short novel of the same name written by Oscar Wilde in 1891. Young handsome Dorian (played by Hurd Hatfield) is having his portrait painted. He admires his youth and beauty in the painting and wishes that he might stay forever as he is in the picture. Now the plot thickens. The years go on and Gray remains unchanged. He leads a depraved life, but not a wrinkle appears upon his face. Yet after each crime, each vicious act that he commits, the portrait changes, becoming over the years a thing of horror. Dorian can no longer stand to look at the painting and hacks away at it with a knife. But in so doing, he destroys his own soul, and falls dead before the portait. When his friends find his body there, the painting appears as it was in the beginning. But his remains on the floor are 'withered, wrinkled and loathsome of visage. It was not until they had examined the rings that they recognized who it was.'

George Sanders was elegant as Gray's sardonic friend Lord Henry, and a young Angela Lansbury (aged 20) made her debut as one of his innocent female victims. Her rendition of 'Little Yellow Bird' was extremely moving. But much of the critical acclaim was due to the magnificent paintings by the Albright Brothers of poor Dorian withering away.

Dame Edith Evans sells her soul to the devil to find the secret of winning at cards in *The Queen of Spades* (1948). Anton Walbrook is a poor Russian officer who wants her secret, but she dies of fright. At the end, Walbrook turns over the final card to win himself a fortune – it is the Queen of Spades, and Evans's face is on the card – she is determined to haunt him. The style of the film was impressionistic and the acting was suitably extravagant.

René Clair directed his own version of the Faust legend in France in *La Beauté du Diable* (1949), starring Gérard Philippe. In this film, the two main characters agree to change places.

LEFT: The magnificently disgusting painting of Dorian Gray as an old man was created by two Chicago artists – the Albright Brothers – for *The Picture of Dorian Gray* (1945). Only the statue of the cat remained constant as the painting became more depraved and ugly.

OPPOSITE TOP: The trial of Jabez Stone, from *All That Money Can Buy* (1941). Jabez Stone (James Craig), Daniel Webster (Edward Arnold) and Mr Scratch (Walter Huston) face the judge (H B Warner). The film was also called *The Devil and Daniel Webster*, as was the original story by Stephen Vincent Benét.

OPPOSITE BOTTOM: Mr Scratch (Walter Huston, left), tempts Jabez Stone (James Craig) by making vast sums of money appear out of thin air and offering him a contract for his soul in *All That Money Can Buy* (1941).

LEFT: Thomas Mitchell (left) as the politician, Audrey Totter as a prostitute and Ray Milland as the devil in *Alias Nick Beal* (1949).

OPPOSITE TOP: Richard Burton makes his pact with the devil as *Dr Faustus* (1967).

OPPOSITE BOTTOM LEFT: Elliott Gould (right) played Devlin in *The Devil and Max Devlin* (1981). Here he tries to recruit a young boy (Adam Rich) for the devil.

OPPOSITE BOTTOM RIGHT: Bill Cosby was assistant devil Barney Satin in *The Devil and Max Devlin* (1981).

BELOW: Peter Cook and Raquel Welch starred in *Bedazzled* (1967) with Dudley Moore.

In a gangster version of the Faust legend, *Alias Nick Beal* (1949), Ray Milland played the devil. He corrupted an honest politician (Thomas Mitchell) with the help of a whore (Audry Totter).

There was a Spanish Faust film in 1957, *Faustina*. But in this version, the hero becomes the heroine through a pact with the devil.

Peter Cook starred in a camped-up version of the Faust story in *Bedazzled* (1967), a picture that critics either loved or hated. Starring with him in this film about a short-order cook who is saved from suicide by a Mr Spiggott, who offers him seven wishes in exchange for his soul, were Dudley Moore and Raquel Welch. Some critics said that it resolved itself into a series of threadbare sketches for the stars. But then there was the other point of view, as exemplified by the comment: A 'cult film updating the Faust legend [that] is as sacrilegious as *The Singing Nun* and usually funnier.'

Richard Burton directed himself in *Dr Faustus* (1967). Based on the Marlowe play, this version was flat, dingy and uninspired. Critic John Simon said, 'It is of an awfulness that bends the mind.' Judith Crist reported that 'It turns out to be the story of a man who sold his soul for Elizabeth Taylor.'

Of all people, Bill Cosby was in a pact-with-the-devil film, *The Devil and Max Devlin* (1981). Devlin was played by Elliott Gould, and Cosby was the devil's left-hand man who offers to invalidate Devlin's contract if

LEFT: A woman who wants to become a witch confronts the devil in *Witchcraft Through the Ages* (1922).

OPPOSITE: The devil's messengers arrive on earth in *Les Visiteurs du Soir* (1942).

BELOW: The devil looks on as a nun says her prayers in *Witchcraft Through the Ages* (1922), a Swedish film about Satanism.

he will bring him three innocents willing to sign their souls away.

Satanism, devil worship and witchcraft were not often tackled in the early days of the movies, usually for censorship reasons. One of the first attempts was *Leaves from Satan's Book* (1920). This Danish film was directed by Carl Dreyer, with Helge Nissen, and told, in episodic form, some of the devil's activities throughout history: tempting Christ, at the Spanish Inquisition, during the French and Russian Revolutions. Although some of it was propagandistic, much of it was quite effective.

In another Scandinavian film, *Witchcraft Through the Ages* (1922), the Swedish director Benjamin Christensen gave audiences a unique and still horrifying film that reconstructed pagan ritual with such care that it was almost a handbook of diabolism. It was a fascinating 'documentary' investigation of the history of witchcraft.

Les Visiteurs du Soir (1942), made during the German occupation of France, had Jules Berry, as the devil, send messengers to earth to corrupt two lovers, but the mission fails. Even when they are turned into stone, their hearts continue to beat. Of course, it was propaganda – the devil was Hitler, and the heartbeat was the spirit of France – but it was still moving and well made.

Carl Dreyer made another Danish devil-worship film in 1943, *Day of Wrath*. An old woman is burned as a witch in a seventeenth-century village. As she is being executed, she curses the clergyman who judged her. He dies, and his mother accuses his widow, who is in love with another man, of using witchcraft to kill him. It was a depressing, harrowing – and spellbinding – melodrama.

In *The Seventh Victim* (1943), Kim Hunter goes to New York in search of her sister, who is under the influence of Satanists who practice devil worship and black magic. The problem was that the censorship of the time made the plot so obscure that it was difficult to follow. Still, it was an off-beat Val Lewton chiller that was genuinely eerie.

A French film, *The Witches of Salem* (1957), originally titled *Les Sorciers de Salem*, told of the 1692 witch trials in Salem, Massachusetts. It starred Simone Signoret and Yves Montand, but tried so hard to make a statement about the parallel Senator Joseph McCarthy witch hunts of the 1950s that it fell on its face.

The Curse of the Demon (1957), made in England as *The Night of the Demon*, was based on M R James's story 'Casting the Runes.' Dana Andrews, as an occultist, unleashes unspeakable horror when he discovers an ancient magic stone that releases a giant medieval devil.

Devil worship, reincarnation and possession were all the thing in *Back From the Dead* (1957). In this picture, Peggy Castle played a wife possessed by the spirit of her husband's dead first spouse, but the cliché-ridden production made everything seem ridiculous.

The British movie *City of the Dead* (1960), retitled *Horror Hotel* in the United States, told the story of a Massachusetts woman burned as a witch in old Salem who was still 'alive,' running a local hotel and luring unwary strangers into becoming sacrificial victims. Christopher Lee played Professor Driscoll, who is a member of the group at a Witches' Sabbat on Christmas Eve. He helps to make a human sacrifice of the heroine, Venetia Stevenson, while her lover, Dennis Lotus, is quite put out.

Ingmar Bergman both wrote and directed *The Devil's Eye* (1960). In this film, an old proverb is quoted: 'A woman's chastity is a stye in the eye of the devil.' So when the devil (Stig Järrel) has a sore eye, he sends Don Juan (Jarl Kulle) up to earth from hell to seduce the virgin Bibi Andersson. It was a shoddy movie, but once in a while the genius that is Bergman's showed through.

Black Sunday (1961), made in Italy as *La Maschera del Demonio*, was retitled in Great Britain as both *The Mask of the Demon* and *Revenge of the Vampire*. It was the story of the one day in each century that Satan

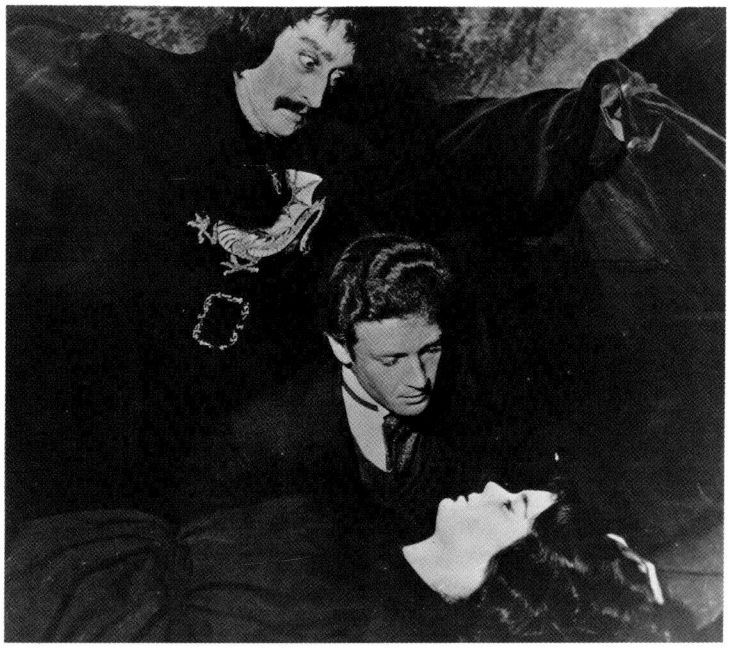

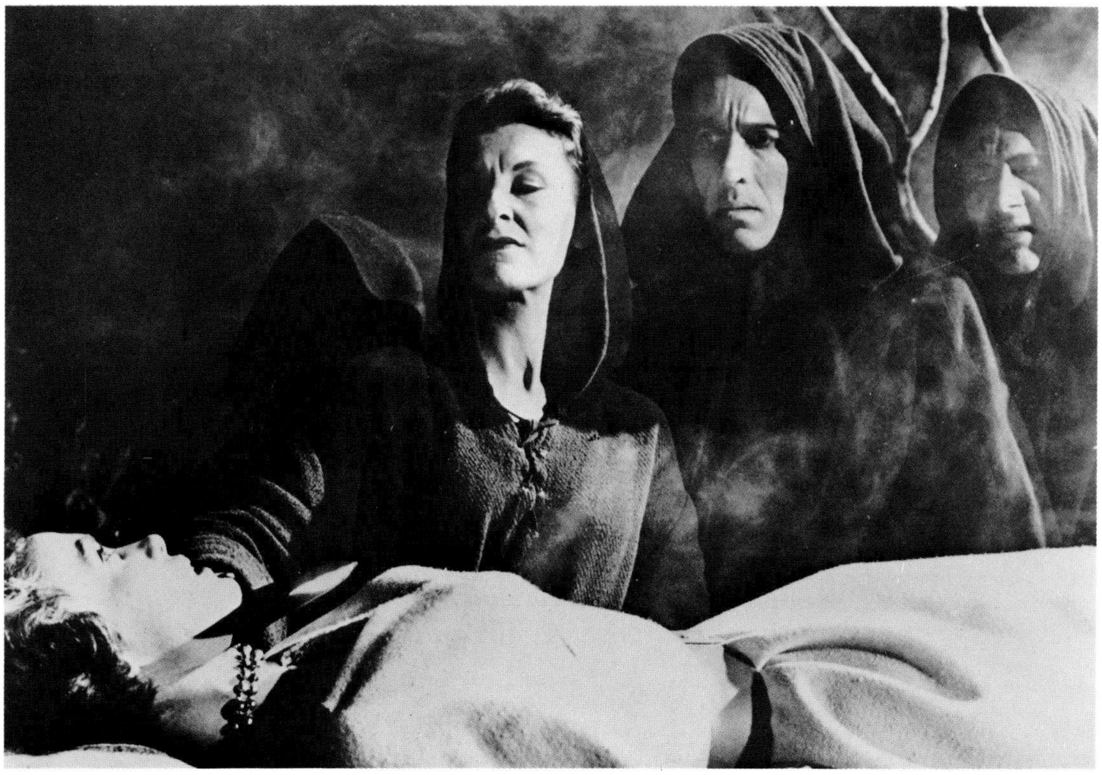

ABOVE: A Satanist and a love-smitten young man contemplate the catatonic Princess Asa (Barbara Steele) in *Black Sunday* (1961).

LEFT: Christopher Lee (center) assists in the intended sacrifice of Venetia Stevenson by the witches' coven in *Horror Hotel/City of the Dead* (1960).

OPPOSITE: The devil in *Curse of the Demon* (1957).

ABOVE: Jack Nicholson and Sandra Knight in *The Terror*.

LEFT: Sandra Knight and Boris Karloff in *The Terror*.

OPPOSITE: A deranged Lon Chaney Jr confronts Jill Dixon in *Witchcraft* (1964), a film about Satanism in England.

roams the earth. Barbara Steele played the part of Princess Asa, a suspected witch. As the townspeople applaud, the executioner nails a metal devil mask, which has spikes protruding on the inside, to her face. The shock of this scene was so powerful that the picture was not released in most countries until many years after the film's production. Asa is then placed in a coffin with a cross cut into the lid in such a way that the sun will form the sign of the cross on her face. Strangers disrupt this arrangement, and the trouble begins. Asa escapes in the form of the modern-day Princess Katia, and starts vampirizing the neighborhood.

It was a beautifully atmospheric production, based on Nikolai Gogol's book *The Vij*. Mario Brava, the director of the picture, when asked why he specialized in horror, replied, 'I am a frightened man. If I am alone at home, I turn on all the lights. *La Maschera* had all the things in it that frighten me.'

A British movie, *Night of the Eagle* (1962), was released in the United States as *Burn, Witch, Burn*. It told of witchcraft entering the lives of a teacher in a medical school and his wife, caused by a jealous witch, and starred Janet Blair and Peter Wyngarde in a genuinely chilling and frightening production.

The Terror (1963) was one of Roger Corman's superquickies. Boris Karloff played the part of Baron von Leppe – a crazy recluse living in his castle and mourning his dead wife. A woman resembling his wife (Sandra Knight) wanders in. André Duvalier (Jack Nicholson, of all people) also fancies her, and in the end Karloff drowns in the cellar of the castle and Duvalier saves the girl, only to have her turn into a decaying corpse in his arms as he tries to kiss her. Corman had hired Karloff for only two days, and shot all the scenes in which he appeared in that time. Several other directors were used to finish the movie, which took another 90 days. They were Francis Ford Coppola (everyone has to start somewhere), Monte Hellman, Dennis Jakob and Jack Hill. The publicity department went wild: 'Dracula . . . Frankenstein . . . House of Wax . . . Pit and the Pendulum. Now a new classic of horror comes to the screen.' A classic it wasn't.

Witchcraft (1964) was a standard plot of witch-cult happenings in an English village, and starred Don Sharp and Lon Chaney Jr. It told the tale of the accidental unearthing of a 300-year-old witch by bulldozers, and the family of witches who start to take revenge on their long-time enemies. The witch and her coven were eventually destroyed by boiling oil.

There had been many attempts to film Poe stories, but, as with the Karloff-Lugosi *The Black Cat*, the films usually had Poe's title and that was about all.

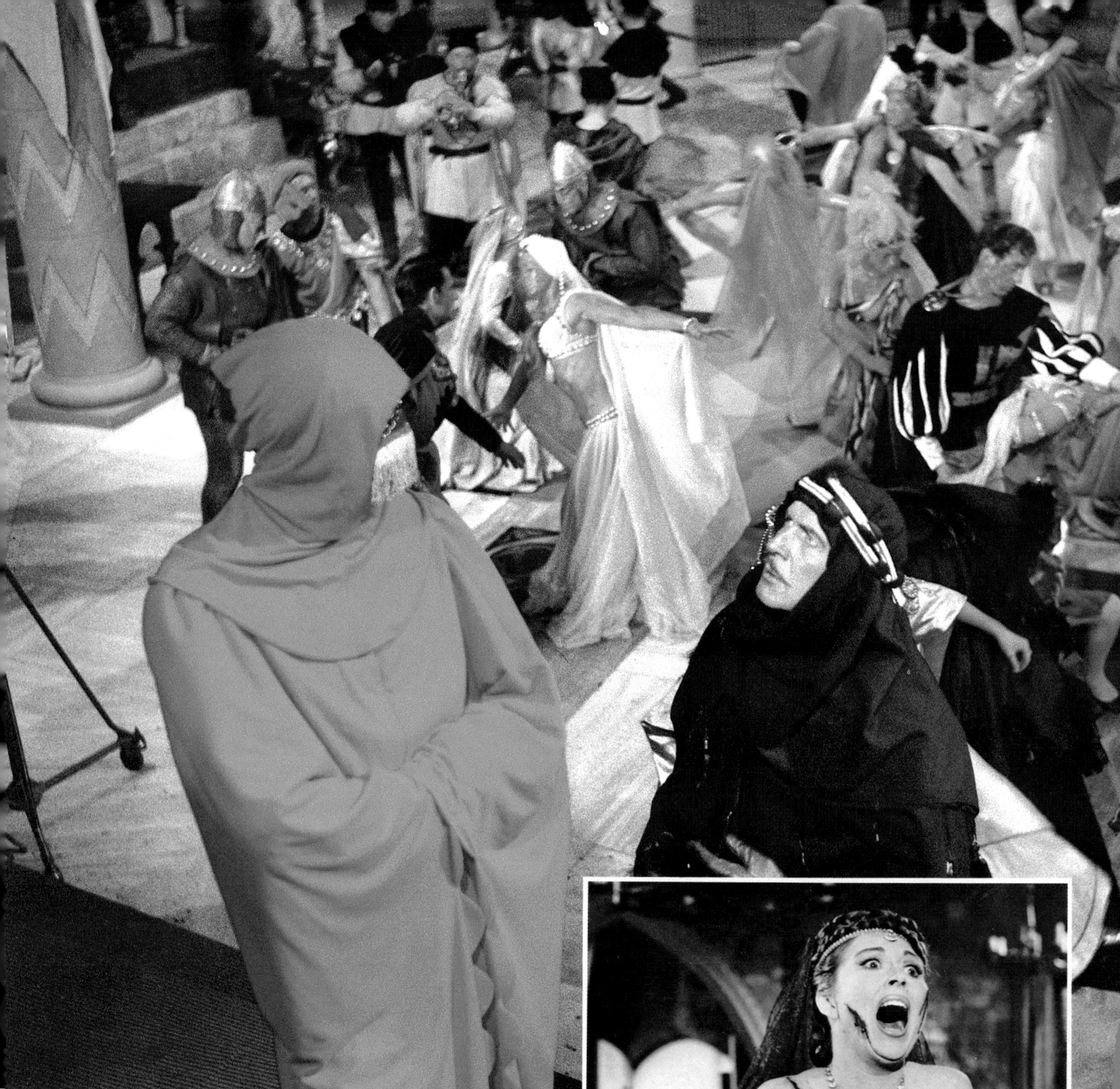

Then Roger Corman decided to do Poe's *The Masque of the Red Death* (1964), and this one was different. It was a stylish distillation of two Poe stories set in an eerie, timeless castle. For Corman, this was an extravaganza. Not only did he have a slightly bigger than usual budget to work with, but he set the film in England, where he could use magnificent settings on the cheap. Vincent Price played Prince Prospero, a devil worshipper who is stalked around the castle by hooded death figures, and Hazel Court was the heroine. The plague is raging outside, and when the prince holds a ball, death is the uninvited guest. Everybody dies. It was often a visually striking movie, and some of the scenes of devil worship were so effective that they were cut by the British censor.

Four scenes from *The Masque of the Red Death* (1964):
ABOVE: The Red Death (the plague) comes to the ball and confronts Vincent Price.

OPPOSITE BOTTOM: Hazel Court meets her fate.

ABOVE RIGHT: Vincent Price as Prince Prospero.

RIGHT: Hazel Court, as Juliana, calls on the evil spirits in her black-magic rites.

The Devil's Own, taken from Peter Curtis's novel *The Witches* (1966), starred Joan Fontaine and Kay Walsh. Fontaine lives in West Africa, where she is driven to a nervous breakdown by voodoo (West Africa is a strange place for that). She returns to England, where she discovers that Walsh is the head of a witches' coven, worshipping the devil in a country village. Of course, Walsh is thwarted by Fontaine. It combined chintzy horror with predictability.

Another pair of fine talents wasted in a sub-par thriller was Deborah Kerr and David Niven in *Eye of the Devil* (1967). The Marquis de Bellac (Niven) is obsessed by a family tradition of pagan self-sacrifice and abruptly leaves his wife in Paris to 'do what he

LEFT: Torin Thatcher, as a priest, protects Deborah Kerr from a Satanist in *Eye of the Devil* (1967).

OPPOSITE: A pregnant Mia Farrow and her husband, John Cassavetes, contemplate baby furniture for the upcoming event in *Rosemary's Baby* (1968).

BELOW: Kay Walsh leads her group in a rite of witchcraft in *The Devil's Own* (1966).

must' at his ancestral estate near Bordeaux, where devil worship and human sacrifice are taking place to ensure an abundant grape harvest. Niven volunteers himself for the sacrifice and is shot by the arrow of David Hemmings. In addition to Niven, Kerr and Hemmings, the cast included Emlyn Williams, Flora Robson, Donald Pleasance and Edward Mulhare, but not even this all-star assemblage could rescue the movie.

Then came *Rosemary's Baby* (1968), based on the Ira Levin novel of the same name. John Cassavetes and Mia Farrow are a young couple, very much in love, but little does Rosemary (Farrow) know that her husband is involved in witchcraft with Sidney Blackmer, as the head of a coven, and Ruth Gordon, as a witch. Farrow, unconscious, is impregnated by the devil, and much of the picture concerns her debilitating pregnancy and her growing fear of what she may be carrying. She delivers the little demon, but is told that the baby died at birth. The movie ends when Rosemary finds the baby in the apartment of witches Maurice Evans and Gordon, and after a horrifying glimpse of it, begins crooning to the creature with motherly love.

It was an unusual horror film in almost all respects. While it had its moments of humor, its greatest merit is director Roman Polanski's ability to give ordinary activities a sinister twist and to entrap the audience in a growing feeling of paranoia. The story is not played out in a ruined castle in Transylvania or at some time in the distant past. It is happening here and now, in an apartment in Manhattan, and the audience gets the feeling that it really could have happened, that it really did happen. There is a strong performance by Mia Farrow as the unfortunate Rosemary and wonderful characterizations by Ruth Gordon (who won the best supporting actress Academy Award) and Maurice Evans. While the tension in *Rosemary's Baby* is almost overwhelming, nothing gruesome happens on the screen, nothing to cause anyone in the audience to hide his or her eyes or to run from the theater.

The Devil Rides Out (1968) was a taut filming of Dennis Wheatley's novel of the same name. The Duc de Richleau (Christopher Lee) comes to the assistance of a young friend who has fallen under the spell of Mocate (Charles Gray), an ultra-evil Satanist. The film was also titled *The Devil's Bride.*

A virtually unknown cast appeared in *The Brotherhood of Satan* (1970), unless you count L Q Jones and Strother Martin. The movie took place in a small town in the United States where Charles Bateman and Anna Capri were trapped by the forces of evil. The sheriff was Jones, who also co-produced, and Martin was the leader of a witches' coven. The coven's job was to capture children so that the more elderly witches could be reborn in them. It was quite a claustrophobic movie – fresh and intriguing – with imaginative touches, as when a possessed doll kills a couple while they are reading the Bible together.

A British picture, *Satan's Skin* (1970), was released in the United States as *The Blood on Satan's Claw* and told the story of the devil in a seventeenth-century English village. In 1670 a farmer unearths a skull with one eye intact, and a demon is the result. It possesses the children of the village, and these cherubs offer it human sacrifices. They are overcome by religion, but not before several grisly scenes are presented, such as the surgical removal of a patch of devil's skin from the leg of a young girl – without an anaesthetic, needless to say. Altogether, it was implausible and unpleasant, but not without style. It starred Patrick Wymark, Linda Hayden and Barry Andrews.

Vincent Price starred with Elisabeth Bergner and Hugh Griffith in another British film, *The Cry of the Banshee* (1970), in which Price played the part of a sixteenth-century English magistrate, a witchfinder. He burns a lot of young women for witchcraft, but Bergner (who for some reason chose this role to make her screen comeback), a witch, curses him and sends a devil in the form of a wolf to destroy him.

Curt Jurgens and Barbara Parkins were the evil ones in *The Mephisto Waltz* (1971). Based on the novel of the same name by Fred Mustard Stewart, it told the story of two fiends who make a pact with the devil. Jurgens is a concert pianist, dying of leukemia, and he needs a new body to carry on his art. Now enters an aspiring pianist (Alan Alda), living happily with his wife (Jacqueline Bisset). Naturally, Alda is the victim, and Bisset can't understand why he spends so much time at the piano. It was complex mumbo-jumbo with plenty of style.

RIGHT: Mia Farrow wonders where the scratches came from after being raped by the devil while under a spell in *Rosemary's Baby* (1968).

OPPOSITE LEFT: The devil in the form of a wolf arrives to destroy Vincent Price in *The Cry of the Banshee* (1970).

OPPOSITE RIGHT: Curt Jurgens played dying pianist Duncan Ely in *The Mephisto Waltz* (1971). Here he is with his Labrador dog, Robin, who is the incarnation of the devil.

BELOW: Pregnant Mia Farrow worries while husband John Cassavetes calmly reads the paper in *Rosemary's Baby* (1968).

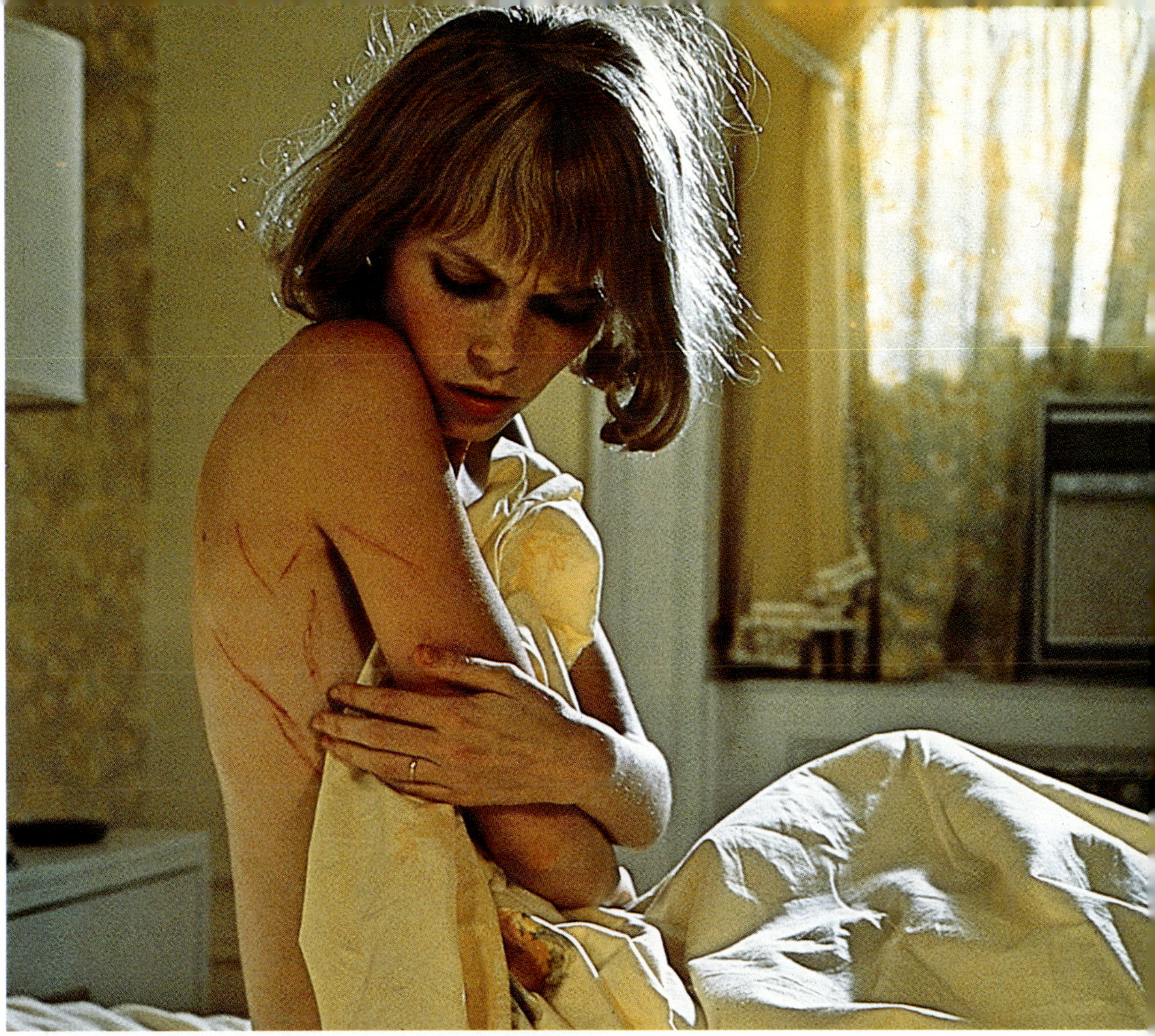

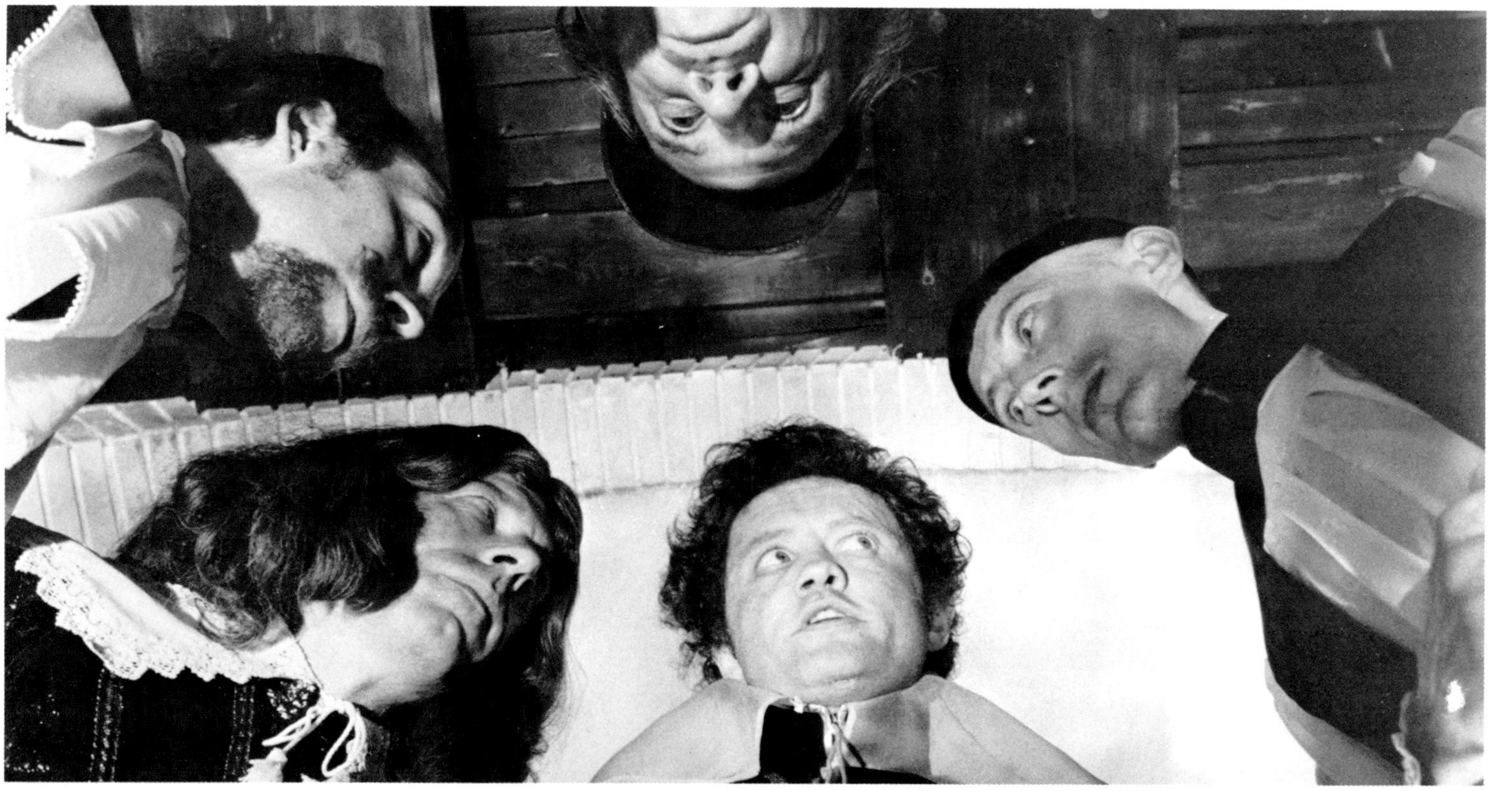

One of the wildest devil movies of all time was *The Devils* (1971), based on a stage play of the same name by John Whiting and on Aldous Huxley's novel *The Devils of Loudon*, which, in turn, was based on an actual occurrence in France in 1633. Father Urbain Grandier, the handsome and worldly priest of the small town of Loudon in central France, was accused by the prioress of the local Ursaline convent of bewitching her and several nuns. In the presence of their confessors, and later before huge crowds, the nuns threw themselves into convulsions, cursed God, lifted up their petticoats and coarsely invited sexual overtures from the shocked but fascinated onlookers.

ABOVE AND TOP: Oliver Reed and his enemies, plotting against him, in two scenes from *The Devils* (1971).

OPPOSITE: Grandier (Oliver Reed), although a priest, marries himself to a local beauty in *The Devils* (1971).

At Grandier's trial, the prosecution produced a pact allegedly made between him and the devil. Grandier was convicted as a witch and burned to death. Later it was discovered that Grandier had offended the all-powerful Cardinal Richelieu, and the nuns' spiritual advisors had coached them in the proper 'possessed behavior' at the beginning, although they must have believed that they were possessed at the end.

Oliver Reed played the part of Grandier, and Vanessa Redgrave was Sister Jeanne, the nun who led the other sisters in unspeakable perversions, tortures, humiliations, degradations and sadism. It was a technically proficient mess – sacrilegious and in terrible taste. The critic Stanley Kauffmann spoke for his colleagues: '[Ken] Russell's swirling multi-colored puddle . . . made me glad that both Huxley and Whiting are dead, so that they are spared this farrago of witless exhibitionism.'

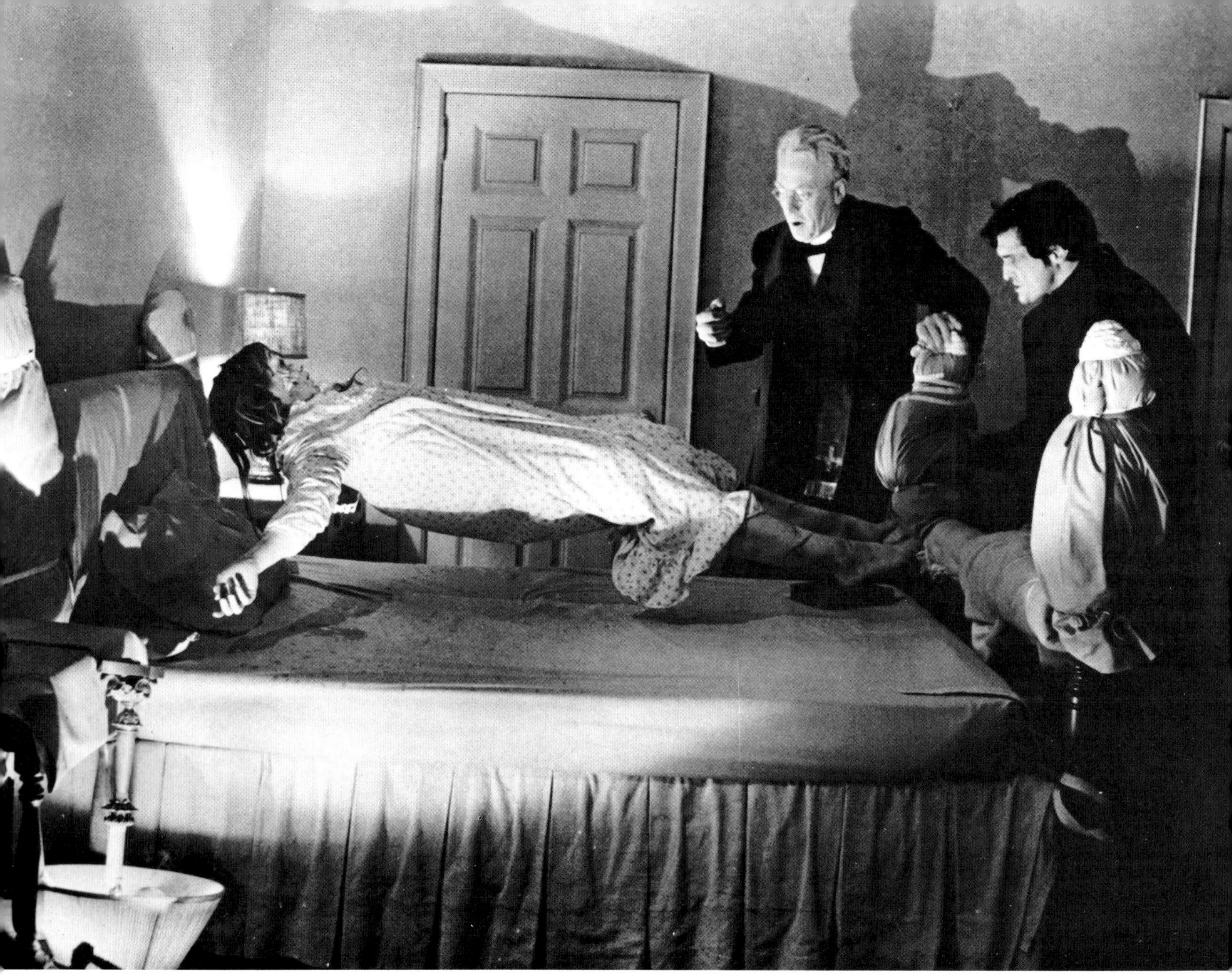

Then came the picture everyone was looking forward to – *The Exorcist* (1973). This shocker was based on the novel by William Peter Blatty. Like *Rosemary's Baby*, William Friedkins' *Exorcist* was also based on a best-selling book, and the book itself was allegedly based on a true story. It is doubtful that either the book or the movie bore any significant relationship to anything that actually happened, but the fact that it was supposed to be somehow true did give the film an extra advantage in the area of publicity.

The film tells the story of a young girl, Regan, played by Linda Blair, whose body becomes possessed by a demon – the demon's voice is that of veteran actress Mercedes McCambridge and is the most consistently creepy element of the film. The demon causes the girl to do many strange things. She can turn her head completely around, she levitates, she causes the bed to rock back and forth, she curses, she vomits (although it looks like pea soup), she develops self-inflicted wounds. Regan's mother (Ellen Burstyn) finally gains the help of an exorcist – a priest played by Max Von Sydow, who struggles to free the girl from the devil.

The film's release was preceded by an extraordinary amount of publicity, and it quickly became the biggest box-office grosser of any horror film in history. People lined up around the block in all sorts of weather to buy tickets. *The Exorcist* was the most talked-about film of its day, a movie that people just *had* to see, if they could stand it. For years, studio publicists had issued claims that this or that horror film was so terrifying that members of the audience fainted or fled the theater screaming. The same sort of claims were made about *The Exorcist*, and at least some of them appeared to be true. The difference was that instead of being frightened out of the theater, people had to leave because they were feeling disgusted or sick.

The criticism that the film had 'gone too far' did not keep people away from the theater one bit. If the public wanted horrific shock, the movie makers were ever ready to give it to them. Actually, *The Exorcist* has a lot more going for it than a couple of shocking scenes. It is a well-acted, tightly directed film that holds up, and can now be considered a genuine horror classic.

Following close on the heels of *The Exorcist* was the Italian film *The Anti-Christ* (1974). In this rip-off, Ippolita (Carla Gravina) terrifies her father (Mel Ferrer) by becoming possessed. She becomes hideous and develops sores all over her body. Her eyeballs vanish,

she levitates, she vomits what looks like a mixture of spinach and vegetable soup. George Coulouros was the priest who couldn't exorcise her, and Arthur Kennedy was her bishop. At the end, Ferrer forces her to embrace a cross and all is over.

Another rip-off was a second Italian picture of 1974, *Beyond the Door*, made as *Chi Sei?* (British title, *The Devil Within Her*). Juliet Mills was possessed this time, and even made pregnant by the devil (shades of *Rosemary's Baby*). Here it came again – vomiting, head rotating, levitation, foul language.

In *It's Alive* (1974), a film that almost everyone hated, a newborn baby turns out to be a vicious demon sent by the devil: it kills all the hospital staff members in the delivery room and disappears from sight. At the end, it is found by its father in the sewers of Los Angeles. The picture, starring John Ryan, Sharon Farrell, Andrew Duggan and Guy Stockwell, does seem to be egregiously gory, but the relationships between the father, mother and first-born son, and the father's realization that he could not kill the monster because it was his son, were moving in the highest degree.

Many good horror films have had their imitators, but the not-so-good *It's Alive* had one too. It was the British film *I Don't Want to Be Born* (1975), released in the United States as *The Devil Within Her*. In this

ABOVE: Christina Raines tries to protect herself when she is haunted by walking corpses in *The Sentinel* (1976).

RIGHT: Special-effects man Rick Baker and his creation, the 'baby', from *It's Alive* (1974).

OPPOSITE: The possessed Regan (Linda Blair) levitates as Father Merrin (Max von Sydow, center) and Father Karras (Jason Miller) attempt the exorcism in *The Exorcist* (1973).

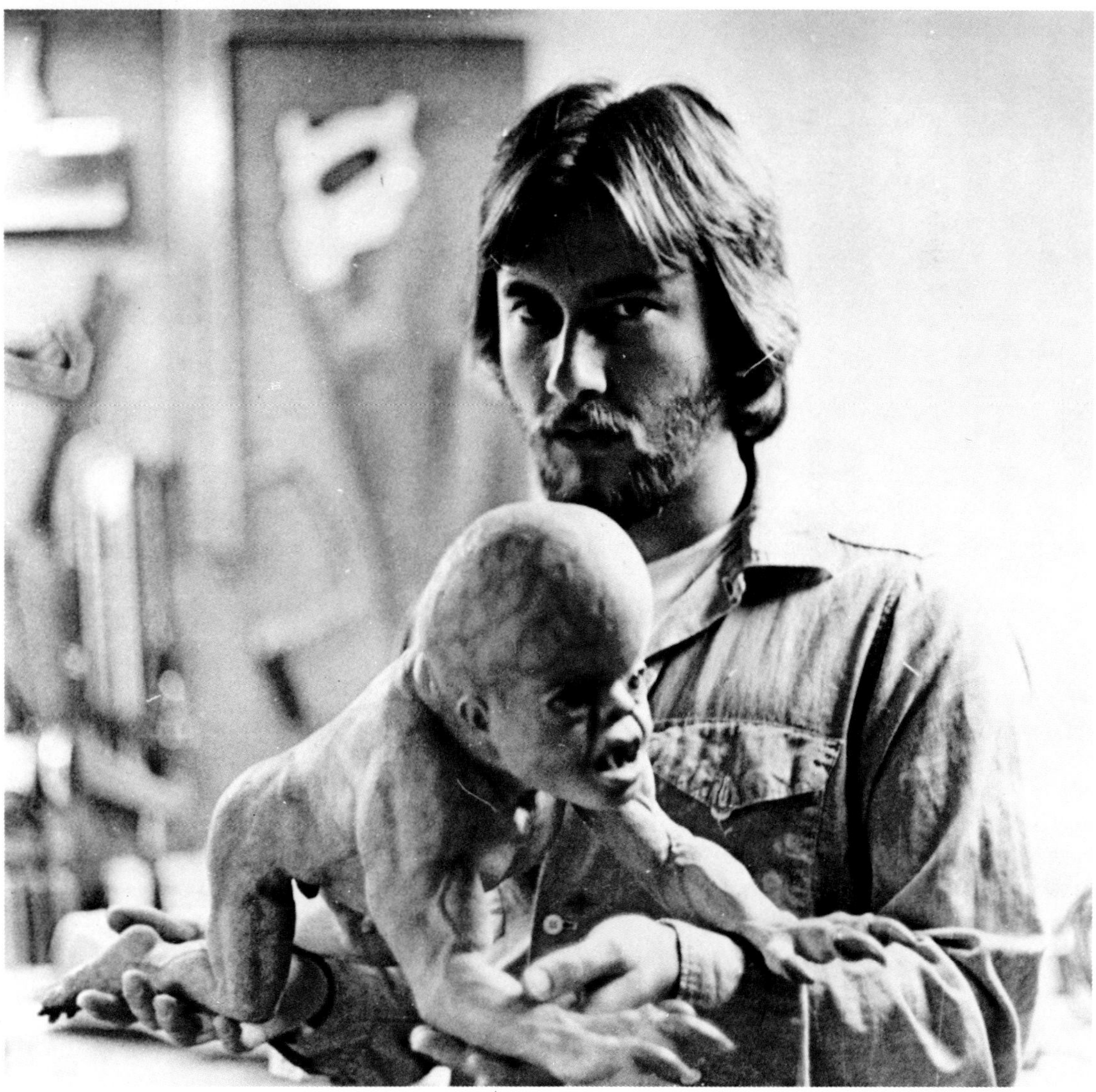

movie, which starred Joan Collins, Ralph Bates and Donald Pleasance, it was an ex-stripper who gave birth to the devil-baby that goes on a murderous rampage. It was without any sign of redeeming social importance.

The Devil's Rain (1975) featured Ernest Borgnine as the leader of a group of Satanists in a deserted town in the American West. He is looking for a sacred book listing people who had been promised to the devil; if he can't find it, their souls will not be delivered as promised. At the end, the rain dissolves the devil worshippers. With Borgnine in the film were Ida Lupino, Eddie Albert, William Shatner and Keenan Wynn, which only proves that even the best actors can figure in the cast of an exploitation movie that had more nastiness than logic.

The Sentinel (1976), although some critics thought that it was a direct steal from *The Exorcist* and *Rosemary's Baby*, was at least a modish theft. Starring Chris Sarandon, Christina Raines, Martin Balsam, John Carradine, José Ferrer, Ava Gardner, Arthur Kennedy, Burgess Meredith, Eli Wallach and Jerry Orbach, how could it be completely bad? In the film, a disturbed girl has something to be disturbed about. She lives in an old apartment house that is haunted by walking corpses. The house turns out to be the gateway to hell, and her boy friend is the sentinel at the gate.

Peter Cushing was Baron Corofax, who led a coven of devil worshippers in *The Devil's Men* (1976). The setting was a small Greek island, so what could be more natural than that the devil appeared to them as a fire-breathing minotaur – half man, half bull. Donald Pleasance was an Irish priest who faces the worshippers with a cross, whereupon they explode.

In a German film, *To the Devil a Daughter* (1976), Christopher Lee, who appeared in so many foreign films because he is an expert linguist, played Father Michael Rayner – a Satanist. In the movie, an occult novelist is asked to take care of a girl who has been promised to Lee and his henchmen. It also starred Richard Widmark, Denholm Elliott and Honor Blackman and was a rather camp, but diabolical, thriller.

LEFT: The ferocious newborn baby monster in *It's Alive* (1974).

BELOW: Donald Pleasance was an Irish priest in *The Devil's Men* (1976).

The blockbuster devil film of 1976, however, was *The Omen*. It was another of the 'devil-child' movies, but this time the child really was the devil. In the picture, the anti-Christ was Damien (Harvey Stephens), whom Robert Thorn (Gregory Peck) had agreed to have substituted for his own stillborn child in Rome, at the prompting of the sinister Father Spiletto (Martin Benson). Thorn then becomes the American Ambassador to the Court of St James in England, where, five years later, Damien begins the reign of supernatural horror that was to take him to the White House. Director Robert Donner staged his first major shock effect impressively, with the child's nanny hanging herself in the middle of a birthday party for the boy; the scene gained much of its power from the contrast between the woman's fatal drop from an upper-story window right over the innocent children's party going on below the house on the sunlit lawn.

The nanny was replaced by the mysterious and unannounced Mrs Blaylock, chillingly played on a single note of evil by Billie Whitelaw. She arrives at the Thorn mansion and installs herself with the

LEFT: Lee Remick clutches her son after the governess has committed suicide in *The Omen* (1976).

ABOVE: Gregory Peck consults photographer David Warner about his mysterious photographs.

words, 'Fear not, little one, I'm here to protect thee.'

Importuned by a strange priest, Father Brennan (Patrick Troughton), who warns Thorn of impending evil as foretold in the Biblical Book of Revelations, the ambassador is plunged into a web of terror with young Damien as its calm and inscrutable center. Soon Father Brennan is dead, killed in the middle of a freak storm conjured up by the devil and transfixed by a falling lightning rod, which skewers him to the ground. In a carefully built-up scene, Thorn's wife Katherine, well played by Lee Remick, falls from a balcony in their home after Damien collides with her on his tricycle – an 'accident' planned by the child and Mrs Blaylock. Even before this the Thorns had sensed that there was something seriously wrong with the child – his refusal to enter a church and the effect he had on animals at a game reserve, where baboons had suddenly become hostile and attacked their car. But John Stride, playing an unctuous and useless psychiatrist, dismisses their concern for the child's behavior. Unwillingly enlisting the aid of a photographer, Jennings (David Warner), whose photographs appear to show forewarnings of his own death and those of the nanny and the priest, Thorn goes to Italy to find a badly scarred Father Spiletto, burned in the fire that had destroyed the Roman hospital in which Damien had been born, and learns from him his part in the Satanic plot to foist Damien on the Thorns.

After being set upon by vicious hounds from hell in a churchyard (a well-staged and frightening scene),

The first was *Damien: Omen II* (1978), in which Damien (Jonathan Scott-Taylor) is a teen-ager in a military school that his new parents, William Holden and Lee Grant, had sent him to. The second was *The Final Conflict: Damien III* (1981), where Damien tries to take over the world and is defeated.

At least *Omens II and III* had the excuse of being low-budget spinoffs, but *Exorcist II: The Heretic* (1977) was a major production, and has been called 'Perhaps the worst sequel of all time.' Linda Blair was back as the possessed girl, and Richard Burton was brought in as the exorcist. It seems that the girl has been repossessed (you can't keep a good monster down), and Father Burton must throw the rascal out again. The film was a disaster in every way. Preview audiences laughed and hooted. The film was taken back and completely re-edited. And still it provoked laughter. The fans of bad movies (yes, there are such people) voted it the second-worst movie of all time. (The worst movie on the list was a science-fiction film, *Plan Nine from Outer Space* – a real low-budget stinker of 1959.

LEFT: Sam Neill starred as Damien, the son of the devil, in *The Final Conflict: Damien III* (1981).

BELOW: Rossano Brazzi played a monk who was determined to destroy Damien in *The Final Conflict: Damien III* (1981).

Thorn and Jennings seek advice from the strange exorcist Bugenhagen (Leo McKern), to learn that Damien must be ritually slain in a church. Jennings, whose photograph had been marked with a strange line across the throat, dies, decapitated very convincingly by a sheet of plate glass, and Thorn returns to England to kill Damien. But the police follow him as he snatches the child from Mrs Baylock, kills her, and takes Damien to a church to murder him. Thorn is killed by the police before he can do the job, and the film ends with Damien attending his father's funeral with his new 'parents' – the President and First Lady of the United States.

In its way, *The Omen* was a powerful and intelligent piece of film-making. Gregory Peck gave one of his more-than-reliable performances, judging well the character's shading form total disbelief in the supernatural happenings around him to total commitment to the killing of his own son. But there were holes in the premise – for example, Thorn, although Ambassador to England, has to find his own place to live. And what happened to the other servants?

The film also inspired two sequels, each smaller and less frightening then the one that had gone before.

Hollywood redeemed itself with *Something Wicked This Way Comes* (1983), a Disney film, beautifully staged, atmospheric, an old-time horror movie based on Ray Bradbury's best-selling novel. Jason Robards Jr played the part of Mr Halloway, the librarian in a small Illinois town. One night in October, a mysterious carnival arrives, and Halloway's son and his friend, Jim Nightshade (Vidal Peterson and Shawn Carson), watch it unload. In reality, the carnival is the soul-buying establishment of Mr Dark (Jonathan Pryce), a servant of the devil who promises to make dreams come true in return for eternal torment.

Dark comes to town looking for the boys and asks Halloway if he knows them. Halloway pretends ignorance, even when he sees drawings of the boys' faces in the palms of Dark's hands. The boys hide and later meet Halloway in the library. In the meantime,

LEFT: Jonathan Pryce in *Something Wicked . . .*

ABOVE: Max von Sydow in *Exorcist II: The Heretic.*

several people in the community have sold their souls to Mr Dark. A one-legged former football star has been given a new leg; an old school teacher has been made young; a lonely barber has been given female companionship. Halloway reads in a back issue of the newspaper in the library of the carnival's previous visit to the town, and of a crippled girl who was suddenly able to run but later went mad.

Dark enters the library and the boys hide from him. He offers Halloway youth if he will give up the boys, but the old man refuses, so Dark finds the boys himself and takes them back to the carnival. Halloway follows and rescues his son in the house of mirrors. At the same time, Dark takes Jim to the carousel, which magically speeds into years past and future in its revolutions. As they are riding, lightning strikes Dark, who turns into an old man and dies looking like a skeleton. All the victims are released from their bondage and the carnival flies away in a tornado. It was an unusually effective contemporary treatment of an age-old theme.

HAUNTINGS

REDRUM

By and large, movies about ghosts have not fared too well. Although belief in ghosts is one of the oldest items in our folklore heritage, on the screen they just don't seem to work. Perhaps this is because film-makers have historically shied away from real ghost stories and have given us the rational explanation at the end of the films that these weren't really ghosts after all.

One of the earliest attempts to portray ghosts in motion pictures was *The Necklace of the Dead* (1910). The film was made in Denmark and, playing on old fears and tales of premature burial, it centered on an apparently dead girl who is buried with a valuable necklace around her throat. A thief opens the tomb in order to steal the necklace and is greeted with the spectacle of the girl stirring and very much alive.

The Ghost Breaker was an American stage thriller by Paul Dickey and Charles W Goddard about a girl who inherits a West Indian castle and finds herself up to her neck in ghosts, zombies and buried treasure. It was first made into a film in 1915 with H B Warner, and then in 1922 with Wallace Reid. In 1940, with the name slightly changed to *The Ghost Breakers*, George Wallace directed a talkie version for Bob Hope, and the result was an oddly successful combination of laughs with horror, with contributions by Paulette Goddard, Paul Lucas and Willie Best. The undead were described in the film as moving 'with staring eyes and no will of their own, performing what another tells them.' Hope, naturally, thinks they are Democrats. Marshall remade the movie under the title

ABOVE: Bob Hope spars with an apparition in rehearsal for his role in *The Ghost Breakers* (1940).

LEFT: Forrest Stanley is captured by Creighton Hale while Laura La Plante looks on in horror in *The Cat and the Canary* (1927).

OPPOSITE TOP: Left to right: Ruth Hussey, Alan Napier, Ray Milland and Cornelia Otis Skinner in *The Uninvited* (1944).

OPPOSITE BOTTOM Jerry Lewis in *Scared Stiff* (1953) – a remake of *The Ghost Breakers*.

PREVIOUS SPREAD: The young psychic in *The Shining* (1980), while in a trance, reads the word 'REDRUM' written in blood on the door – MURDER spelled backward.

of *Scared Stiff* (1953). This time it was a vehicle for Dean Martin and Jerry Lewis, and the results were hardly stimulating.

John Willard's stage thriller *The Cat and the Canary* opened on Broadway in 1922. It was a tale about an eccentric will read at midnight in a haunted house with secret panels, behind which a maniac lurks. It was first made into a film in 1927. Directed by Paul Leni, who had just arrived from Germany, it featured Laura La Plante, Creighton Hale and Forrest Stanley, who played the maniac. This version was a semi-surrealistic send-up, but it was an immensely stylish one. Rupert Julian directed the first sound version under the title of *The Cat Creeps* (1930), starring Helen Twelvetrees, Raymond Hackett and Gene Hersholt. Elliott Nugent wrote the script for *The Cat and the Canary* (1939), which gave Bob Hope his first starring role. This superbly staged, briskly paced remake also starred Paulette Goddard and Gale Sondergaard, as the sinister housekeeper.

The Uninvited (1944) starred Ray Milland and dealt with a young girl (Gail Russell) being possessed by the ghost inhabiting the English house that Milland and his sister (Ruth Hussey) have rented in Cornwall. Cornelia Otis Skinner stole the picture as the head of a lunatic asylum. Based on the Dorothy Macardle novel *Uneasy Freehold*, the film was probably Hollywood's first attempt at a serious ghost story. The movie refrained from showing the spirits – the evil spirit who sends out icy breezes and the good spirit who smells

RIGHT: Anthony Hopkins with the ventriloquist dummy that takes over his very soul in *Magic* (1978).

OPPOSITE: The young Dirk Bogarde played a series of menacing roles under his long-running contract with Rank before his dramatic mid-life career change in *Victim* (1961).

BELOW: Michael Redgrave caught in his dressing room by Allan Jeayes as his supposed dummy (John Maguire) is spouting off in *Dead of Night* (1945).

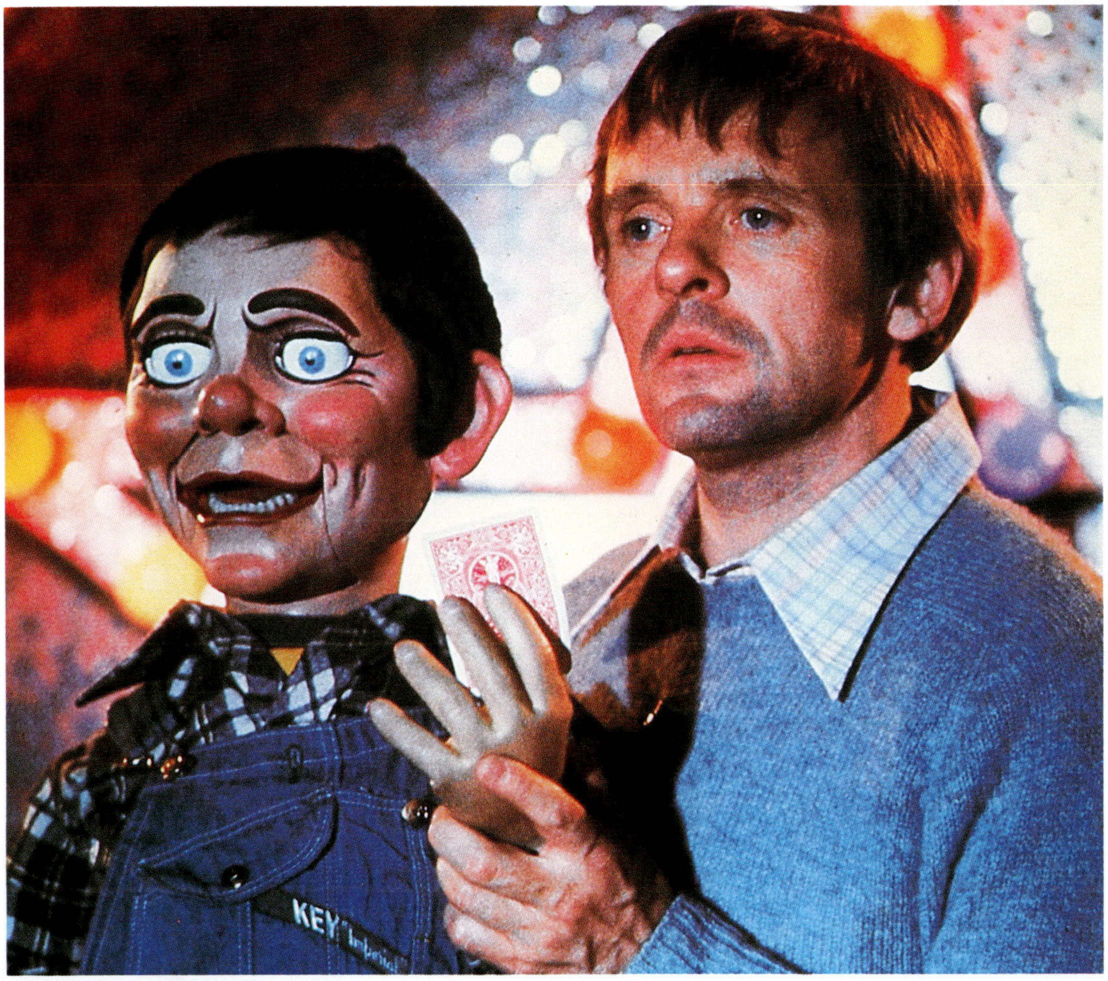

like mimosa. But the touches – the French doors swinging open for no obvious reason, the window suddenly shattering and the wine glass moving across the table during a séance – were spine-tingling.

In all, *The Uninvited* is an effective piece of subdued horror, though Milland – who was a year away from making his excellent *The Lost Weekend* (1945), for which he won the Academy Award for best actor – was still in the minds of audiences so much the strong and capable romantic leading man that his very presence tended to reduce the terror. A greater fear might have been communicated to and instilled in the viewer had someone not so rock-steady been faced with the ghosts.

Equally effective – even more so in the minds of many critics – was *Dead of Night* (1945). The film concerns a group of people who, spending an evening together in an old country house, pass the hours by telling each other macabre stories. Five yarns in all are spun, with three concerning ghosts, and a fourth, death. The fifth – and perhaps the one that has proven the most memorable of all – is an exercise in fright about a ventriloquist (Michael Redgrave) who comes to think of his dummy as alive and then is driven mad by the figure. Much the same theme was explored by Anthony Hopkins in *Magic* (1978), but, with some unnecessary gore thrown in for good measure, far less effectively.

Other fine pieces in the film include the story of a

young girl (Sally Anne Howes) who, while attending a party, hears a child crying in a room. She enters, sees a little boy, and comforts him with stories, only to learn later that he is the ghost of a youngster killed there years earlier. Then there is the tale of the young husband (Ralph Michael) driven to the brink of suicide by the odd reflections that he sees in a mirror before which its previous owner had killed himself. And, of course, there is the highly comic vignette about the two golfing friends (Naunton Wayne and Basil Radford). One is tricked by the other into suicide, but evens the score by coming back to haunt his chum's wedding night. The other story concerned a race driver who, recovering in the hospital after the crash, imagines a hearse whose driver tells him that there is always room for one more inside. When he is released from the hospital, he tries to board a bus whose conductor is the same man as the hearse driver, and who says the same thing. He reels back, and the bus drives on and plunges off a bridge into the river.

Equally frightening was the linking plot about an architect (Mervyn Johns) caught up in the recurring 'dreams' that are the tales told by the storytellers. It was neatly underplayed until its phantasmagoric ending, in which the architect, now wide awake, is summoned to the house, finds that it is real and is assailed by all the terrible creatures from his 'dreams.'

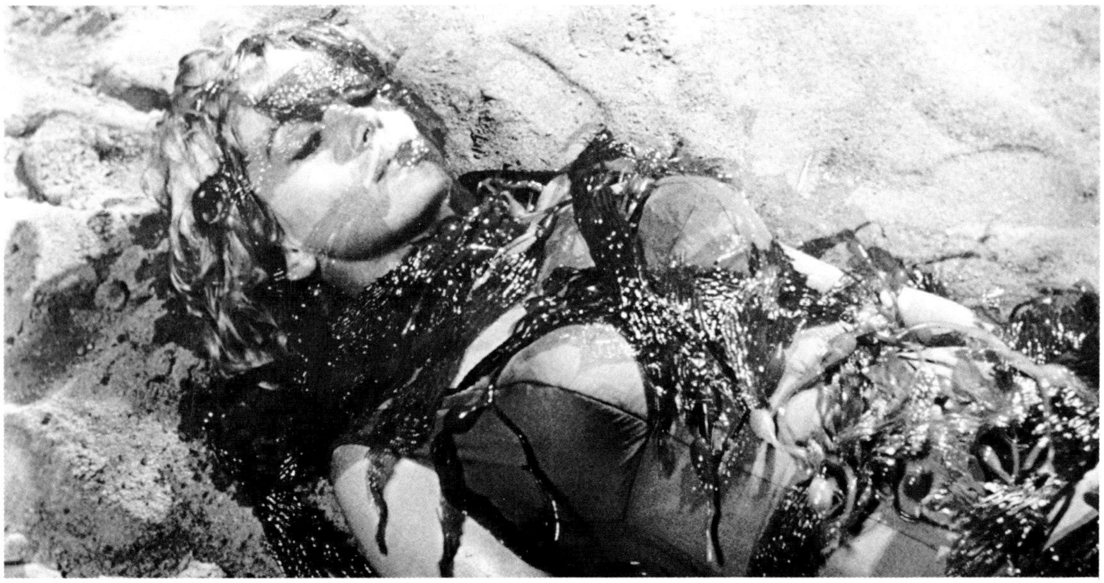

ABOVE: Gene Tierney and George Sanders in one of the early scenes in *The Ghost and Mrs Muir* (1947).

LEFT: The long-dead mistress who haunts the hero in *Tormented* (1960).

OPPOSITE TOP: Deborah Kerr, as the governess, and Pamela Franklin and Martin Stephens, as her haunted young charges, in *The Innocents* (1961).

OPPOSITE BOTTOM: Deborah Kerr, as the apprehensive governess, in *The Innocents* (1961).

For audiences who saw the film in its American release, the Sally Anne Howes and Wayne-Radford stories will be unfamiliar. (The golf story has been reinstated for television viewing.) Both were cut in the interests of saving time when the picture was sent to the United States. The American filmgoer was the loser.

In Nöel Coward's comedy *Blithe Spirit* (1945), a cynical novelist's second marriage is disturbed when the playful ghost of his first wife materializes during a séance. Of course, he is the only one who can see and talk to her. This most polished job of film-making starred Rex Harrison and Constance Cummings, but Margaret Rutherford, as the dotty medium, Madam Arcati, stole every scene she appeared in.

Gene Tierney and Rex Harrison appeared in another pleasant ghost movie, *The Ghost and Mrs Muir* (1947). Mrs Muir (Tierney) moves into a cozy house on the English coast and meets the shade of its former owner – a salty, bearded sea captain (Harrison). Over the years they fall in love, but obviously nothing can come of it until the three-handkerchief ending. Mrs Muir, now an old lady, dies, and the captain returns for her. She rises from her chair, looking young again, and they depart through the front door.

Richard Carlson suffered as the husband bedevilled by the seaweed-dragging spirit of a former mistress in *Tormented* (1960). This was a low-budget piece of hogwash about a guilt-ridden pianist dubious over his forthcoming marriage to a society girl.

One of the landmark films about ghosts was *The Innocents* (1961), adapted from the Henry James novel *The Turn of the Screw*. The subject of the original book was the idea that children, however pictur-

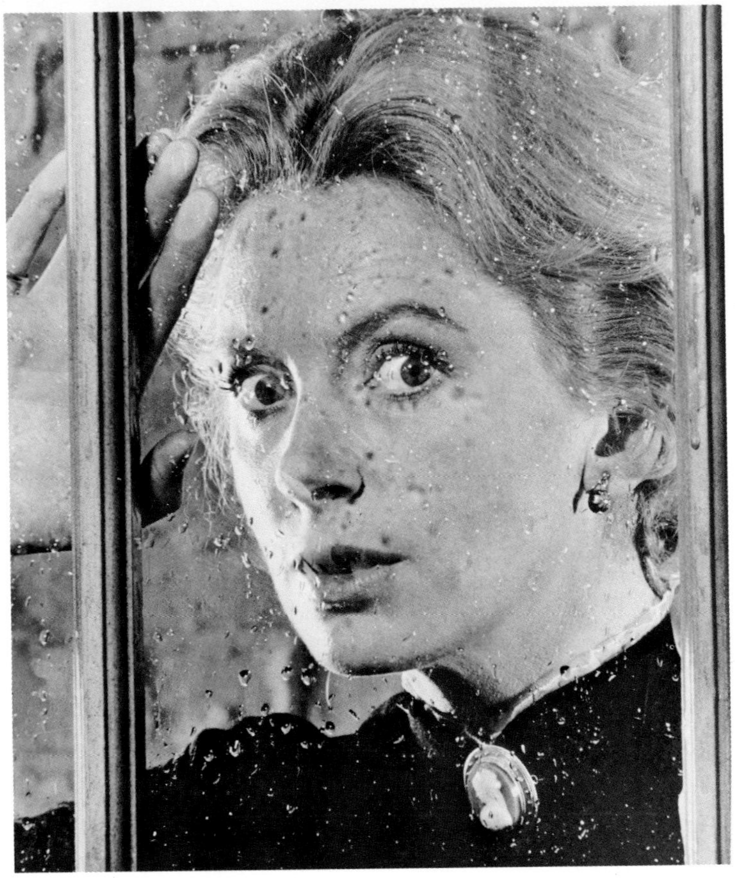

esque some precocious romance between boy and girl may be, are possibly incapable of handling 'adult' carnal knowledge without falling prey to evil.

The film told the tale of a spinster in Victorian times (Deborah Kerr) who becomes the governess of two children (Martin Stephens and Pamela Franklin). The boy and girl, brother and sister, attracted the atmosphere of an incestuous relationship. As the film continues, an indefinable sense of evil permeates the lovely setting. There appear to be people around the place about whom the neurotic young governess knows nothing. The children behave oddly. From the housekeeper, the Governess hears about two former servants – a man called Quint and Miss Jessel, the former housekeeper – who were vile people and are now dead. She is convinced that they are haunting the place and are using the two children for their own evil purposes. The governess vows to save the children, but the girl collapses in hysterics and the boy dies in her arms when she tries to exorcise him. In the book, the reader is left with the notion that the ghosts might have been the figments of the governess's imagination, but in the film the audience is led to believe that they are actually sharing the woman's real experiences.

Roger Corman made another Edgar Allan Poe story into a film in 1961. It was *The Premature Burial*, and starred Ray Milland, Heather Angel and Hazel Court.

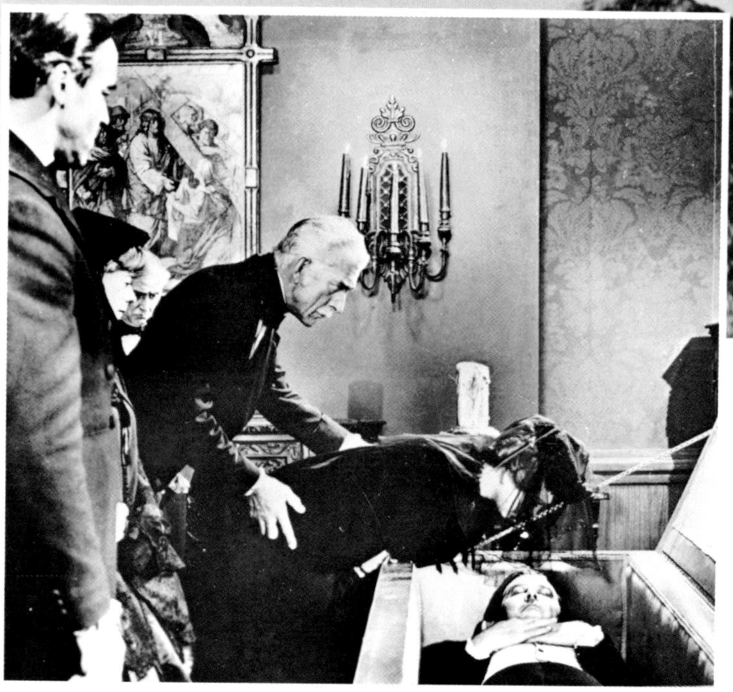

In it, Milland is terrified of being buried alive, but suffers just that fate. Later he reappears to wreak vengeance on his tormentors. Corman packed the film with contrivances, clinchés and gloomy decors and turned it into the ultimate in graveyard ghoulishness.

Claire Bloom and Julie Harris starred in *The Haunting* (1963), which had hints of lesbianism. Taken from Shirley Jackson's novel *The Haunting of Hill House*, the film told of an anthropologist, a sceptic and two mediums who spend the weekend in a haunted Boston mansion. It was a quite frightening but exhausting and humorless melodrama with a lot of suspense.

Another Roger Corman film of 1963 was *The Haunted Palace*, in which a nineteenth-century New Englander claims an old mansion as his inheritance and then is haunted by one of his evil ancestors. It starred Vincent Price and Lon Chaney Jr, but it was a slow, plodding horror comic. As Judith Crist said, it was 'for those of ghoulish bent, or lovers of the perfectly awful.'

Corman was back delving into Poe in *The Tomb of Ligeia* (1964), and this was probably his best foray into the works of that writer. Starring Vincent Price, Elizabeth Shepherd and John Westbrook, it told of a brooding Victorian widower (Price) who changes his dead wife first into a cat, then into the beautiful Lady Rowena. It was complex and fascinating, and a bit horrifying.

Joan Collins and Robert Hardy starred in *Dark Places* (1973). In it, a former mental patient inherits a mansion that was once owned by a man who murdered his wife and children. Naturally, the spirit of the murderer possesses the mental patient.

The Legend of Hell House (1973), in a way, was a takeoff on *The Haunting*, but was much more harrowing and frightening. Starring Roddy McDowall and Pamela Franklin, it was a story of occult phenomena,

LEFT: Lon Chaney Jr (left) and Vincent Price discover an unexpected treasure in *The Haunted Palace* (1963).

BELOW: A ghastly scene from *The Tomb of Ligeia* (1964).

BOTTOM: Julie Harris was the star of *The Haunting* (1963).

OPPOSITE TOP: The ghostly funeral procession in *The Premature Burial* (1961).

OPPOSITE BOTTOM: Alan Napier tries to comfort the distraught Hazel Court as she gazes at the supposedly dead Ray Milland in *The Premature Burial* (1961).

as four researchers agree to spend a week in a house known to be inhabited by spirits who have killed previous psychic investigators. It was one of the most absorbing ghost-breaker yarns on film. Pamela Franklin had so grown up from her child's role in *The Innocents* by now that she could be seduced by a lecherous spirit.

The Amityville Horror (1979) was advertised as based on a true story – but that is doubtful. It told of a haunted house in a Long Island community that was taken over by ghosts. Complete with blood running down the wall and many other special effects, the film starred James Brolin and Margot Kidder as the parents of the Lutz family, who were eventually forced to leave the evil place.

The Amityville Horror was so successful that along came *Amityville II: The Possession* (1982). This was not a sequel, but rather a prequel, explaining how the house got its reputation. It involved Burt Young as the father of a highly unfamily-like family who were the original residents. He beats his wife and children and his psychotic son (Jack Magner) retaliates.

Then came *Amityville II: The Demon*. Tony Roberts is a reporter who buys the house to expose it as a fake. But the devil in the basement doesn't like the idea, so

LEFT: Margot Kidder and her daughter beat a hasty retreat from their haunted house in *The Amityville Horror* (1979).

OPPOSITE: Shelley Duvall waits in the bathroom for her homicidal maniac husband in *The Shining* (1980).

BELOW: Shelley Duvall tries to comfort her novelist husband, Jack Nicholson, who is about to go off the deep end in *The Shining* (1980).

he starts playing deadly tricks on the inhabitants.

In *The Shining* (1980), based on the Stephen King novel, Jack Nicholson played the part of an alcoholic writer struggling for sobriety. He and his wife (Shelley Duvall) and their young son are the winter caretakers in an isolated Colorado mountain hotel, where the ghosts of former evil guests begin appearing to him. His child has the power of telepathy and sends thought messages for help. Finally, Nicholson becomes completely crazed and chops down a door, behind which his wife is hiding.

The Shining was supposed to be a major film event. Stephen King movies are always popular, and it was directed by Stanley Kubrick, acknowledged as one of the world's great directors, who had been working on the film for three years. Jack Nicholson was a fine actor as well as a hot film property. When *The Shining* was released, it turned out not to be quite the bone-chilling triumph that horror-movie buffs had been hoping for. No question that it contained many impressive moments and a couple of scenes that will linger in nightmares for years to come. Yet in the end there was a confusion about the film; too many promising beginnings became dead ends. Supernatural horror does not have to be entirely logical, but a script should have a certain internal consistency and coherence. To a degree, *The Shining* lacked this. Nicholson gives a bravura performance as the writer rapidly being transformed into an ax-wielding madman. But perhaps Nicholson's performance was a bit too bravura. Shelley Duvall, his pathetic and irritating wife, is really better. Whatever one thinks of *The Shining*, it is no formula horror film, turned out to make the quick dollar. It will be closely studied by those interested in films, horror and otherwise, for many years to come.

Ghost Story (1981) was based on Peter Straub's best-selling novel of the same name. The novel is a highly complex supernatural tale, with all sorts of literary allusions to other supernatural fiction. The film greatly simplifies Straub's plot, and turns it into a more traditional type of ghost story, though the female ghost is still a supernatural force rather than an old-fashioned 'haunt.'

Played against a New England setting, it is tautly told from beginning to end, with a climax (that could have reduced the whole film to silliness had it not been handled correctly) as close to shattering as you can get. The story centers on four elderly men who are hunted down by the ghost of a young woman whom they had injured as college students. Thinking her dead at the time, they had placed her in a car and then had rolled it into a pond, only to see her rise and stare at them, terrified, as the car sank to the depths, not to be retrieved for decades. The girl haunts their memories for the rest of their lives, and returns in their late years to take her revenge on them and theirs.

The film is shot in color – a dangerous undertaking, because the brightness can detract from the somber mood of a horror story. But such is not the case in *Ghost Story*. The color not once gets in the way and, at times, even contributes to the chilling mood. As can be expected when the names of the players are mentioned – Fred Astaire, Melvyn Douglas, John Houseman and Douglas Fairbanks Jr – the acting is flawless.

RIGHT: The father and mother begin to become frightened as their daughter communicates with ghosts through the television set in *Poltergeist* (1982).

OPPOSITE TOP: An eerie moment in *Ghost Story* (1981).

OPPOSITE BOTTOM: Fred Astaire contemplates the sins of the past in *Ghost Story* (1981).

BELOW: The mother saves her child from being kidnapped to the underworld by the dead creatures in *Poltergeist* (1982).

Poltergeist (1982) managed to be chilling and good-humored all at the same time. Craig T Nelson, Jobeth Williams, Oliver Robbins and Heather O'Rourke were the stars of this film about a family moving into a new subdivision that has been erected over a graveyard. The spirits get annoyed and start communicating through the television set to a little girl. Pandemonium then takes place, and we have ghastly scenes of people and things flying through the air, a séance performed by a very short medium and a horrible scene in which the mother tries to keep her child from being sucked into the mouth of hell – and fails. Everything turns out all right. The child is rescued when the mother goes to hell for her, and the family checks into a motel room – with the father carefully unplugging the television set and putting it outside the room.

Steven Spielberg, possibly the most successful director/producer of the 1980s, produced and wrote the book and screenplay for *Poltergeist*. The direction was by Tobe Hooper, who had gained some notoriety for *The Texas Chainsaw Massacre* – a gore rather than a horror film. *Poltergeist* is no *Chainsaw*, but eyebrows were raised when the movie was given a PG (Parental Guidance) rating instead of the expected R (Restricted). The picture, for example, contains one scene in which a man rakes back the flesh on his face to reveal the skull beneath, and there are several scenes of corpses in various states of decomposition. Indeed, partly decomposed corpses seem to be as much a feature of the horror films of the 1980s as the mad scientist and his hunchback were of the 1930s.

Will the blood ever cease flowing and the sadism finally go out of style? Motion-picture entertainment has always run in cycles and, unless tradition here is defied, things must one day change, with horror being played again, not for its shock value, but for the eeriness and the genuine, tingling fright that it once sought to achieve. But from the look of present-day box-office receipts, no one should hope for an alteration of course in the very near future.

A LOOK TO THE FUTURE

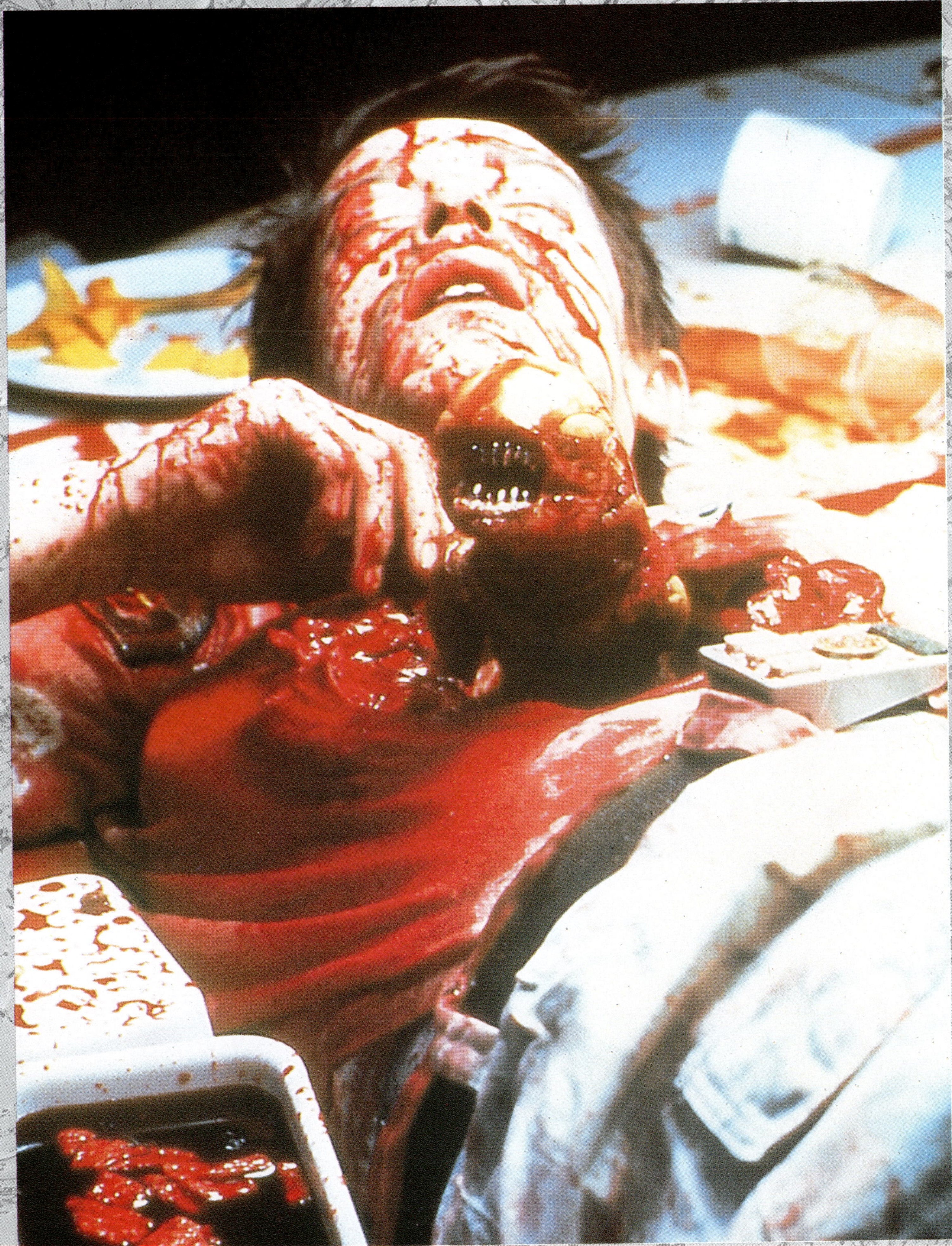

Horror movies have never been more than the unwanted stepchildren of the film industry. There have been a lot of good and a lot of bad supernatural movies. Some of them have been critically praised and others critically damned. But how have they fared in the reception of awards and recognitions for works that are especially meritorious, or that have marked a contribution to the motion-picture as an art form? The answer is – badly.

There have been a few awards for special effects, and we can't forget Fredric March and Ruth Gordon for their Oscars, but the horror film as such has been ignored. Completely overlooked by all the awards groups were such landmark productions as *Frankenstein* (1931), *Dracula* (1931) and many others of note. The exclusion of *Frankenstein*, particularly, suggests an early tendency not to take the horror film seriously. Only one horror film, *The Exorcist* (1973), has ever claimed any honors for itself. It was nominated for best picture by the Academy of Motion Picture Arts and Sciences (it lost the Oscar to *The Sting*), and the Golden Globe Award went to it for the Best Film, Drama, of the year.

Horror movies have come a long way from Méliès's first attempts in 1896. Great stars have emerged, such as Lon Chaney Sr, followed by Boris Karloff and Bela Lugosi. Then came Peter Cushing, Christopher Lee and Vincent Price, who inherited the mantle of a previous age. Cushing played the suave, no-nonsense type of mad scientist, whose sense of authority and competency never wavered. Lee was great as the vampire, the Frankenstein monster and the mummy. Price was the debonair crime investigator, the fiendish scientist and the crippled monster, and made it look easy, doing it with a sense of humor.

But now we're into blood and gore. Have modern horror films gone too far? Are they too gruesome, too realistic? They are certainly more ghoulish and ghastly than the films of the 1930s. But the same sort of charges were made against the horror films of the 1930s in their day. Have we simply become more hardened to death and violence, or is it that we have merely become more sophisticated about movie techniques? Many scenes that shocked and terrified film audiences of an earlier era look quite laughable today. We know that there is an actor under all that makeup. Audiences of the future may look at these piles of rotting corpses and not shudder but snicker, instantly recognizing them as the plastic and rubber models that they are.

This is a dilemma, but perhaps there is another way to go in the future. Perhaps the film-makers have not come up with all the different types of monsters possible. There is one kind of monster that may become the favorite of the future. It cannot be killed. It cannot be outwitted. It can only be unplugged.

PAGE 185: Blood and gore were the features of *Alien* (1979), which featured stomache-churning violence, slime and shocks.

RIGHT: Gore was the word to describe *Friday the 13th* (1980).

OPPOSITE: The photography in *Poltergeist* (1982) was mind-boggling.

BELOW: Father Karras (Jason Miller, left) and Father Merrin (Max von Sydow) in the midst of the exorcism in *The Exorcist* (1973).

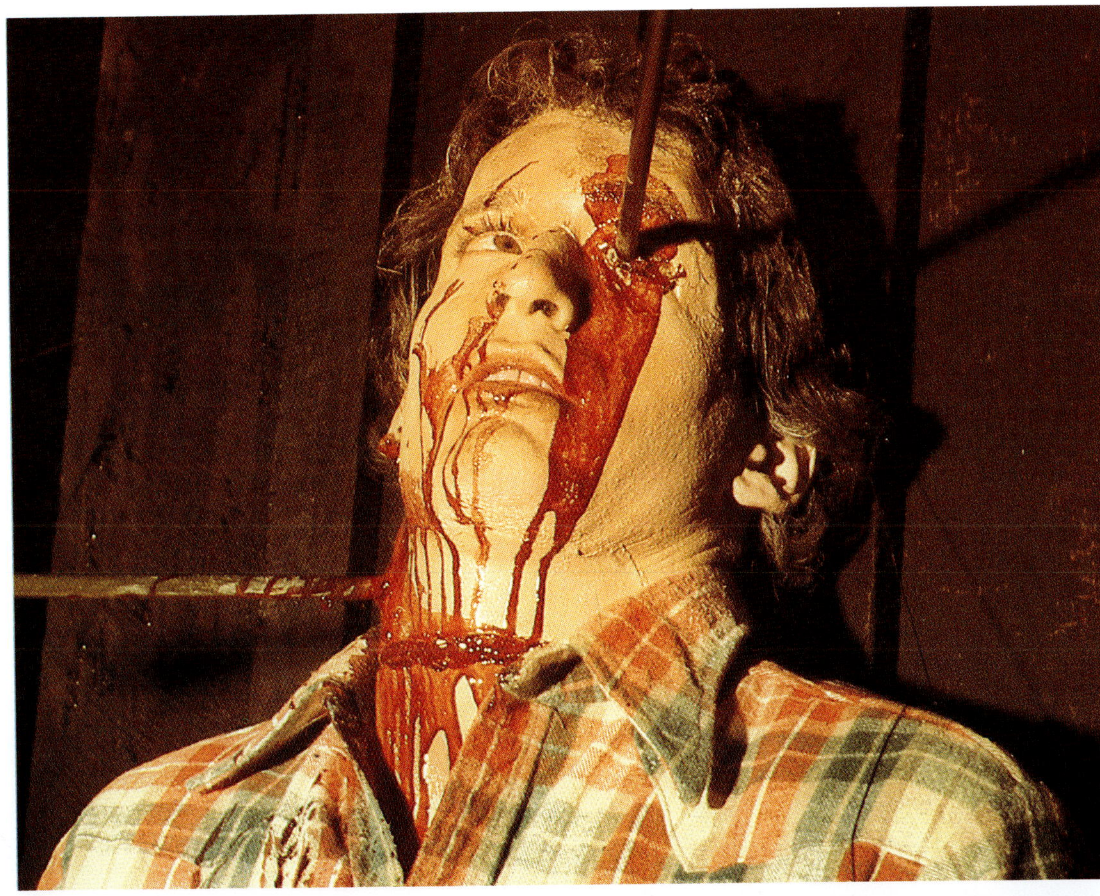

Stanley Kubrick introduced us to this monster in his 1968 film *2001: A Space Odyssey*. On the surface, this may have appeared to be a science-fiction movie, but it was a true monster picture, and the name of the monster was Hal.

The scene is aboard a space ship, perhaps on its way to another galaxy. A computer named Hal plans all the activities of the crew, whether they are awake or sleeping. The problem is that the computer has a mind of its own. Instead of looking out for the welfare of the crew and doing their bidding, it rebels and sets out to do away with its masters. What is this but the man-made monster of the horror films?

The computer is the golem, or the Frankenstein monster, projected into the future. It is more sophisticated than earlier monsters, and that makes it more dangerous. Indeed, it can outthink its own creators. It also is able to become emotional at the point when it is finally, after the astronauts have discovered its plan, unplugged. It even suffers from electrical deprivation.

What will they think up next?

ABOVE: Gary Lockwood (left) and Kier Dullea check out the mechanics of Hal, the computer, in happier times in *2001: A Space Odyssey* (1968).

OPPOSITE: The monster alien from *Alien* (1979).

INDEX

Acknowledgments

Photo Credits
Thomas C Aylesworth Collection: 4 (top left), 10, 11, 20, 22 (bottom), 26, 45, 47, 49 (bottom), 51 (top), 54 (bottom), 55 (top), 57, 58 (bottom), 59 (top), 68, 70, 72, 73 (bottom), 91 (top), 94, 103, 121 (bottom), 129 (bottom), 130 (top), 131 (bottom), 135 (top), 139 (left).
Bison Collection: 1, 4 (bottom left), 5 (top and bottom), 6-7, 19 (bottom), 21, 27, 31 (top), 32, 33 (center and bottom), 36, 37, 38, 49, 40, 41, 42 (bottom), 48, 49 (top), 50 (top), 51 (bottom), 52, 53, 54 (top), 55 (bottom), 56, 59 (bottom), 60 (top right and bottom), 61, 62, 63, 67, 69 (top), 71, 74, 75 (bottom), 76, 77, 78 (bottom), 79 (bottom), 80, 82, 83, 84-85, 86, 88-89, 90 (top), 92 (bottom), 96 (bottom), 97, 98, 99, 100, 104, 105, 108 (bottom), 109 (bottom), 110 (top), 111, 112, 113, 114, 115, 116, 118, 119 (bottom), 121 (top), 123, 124, 126, 127, 128, 130 (bottom), 131 (top), 132, 133, 134, 135 (bottom), 136, 137, 138, 139 (right), 140, 141, 143, 147, 148 (bottom), 149 (top), 150 (bottom), 152, 153, 155, 158 (top), 159, 161, 162, 163, 164, 165 (bottom), 166, 167 (bottom), 168, 169, 172, 173, 174, 176 (top), 179, 180 (top), 182 (bottom), 183, 187 (bottom), 188, 189.
Museum of Modern Art: 9, 14 (bottom), 17, 18, 19 (top), 22 (top), 24, 25, 28 (top and bottom), 30, 42 (top), 43, 65 (top), 73 (top), 75 (top), 78 (top), 79 (top), 81, 90 (bottom), 91 (bottom), 92 (top), 93, 95 (bottom), 119 (top), 125, 128 (bottom).
National Film Archives: 8 (top and bottom), 13, 23, 28 (center), 29, 31 (bottom), 33 (top), 46, 50 (bottom), 65 (bottom), 95 (top), 96 (top), 106 (top), 109 (top), 110 (bottom left and right), 120, 145 (bottom), 156 (bottom), 160 (top), 178.
Phototeque: 2-3, 12, 14 (top), 15, 58 (top), 60 (top left), 64, 69 (center and bottom), 87, 101, 106 (bottom), 107, 108 (top left and right), 117, 144, 145 (top), 146, 148 (top), 149 (bottom left and right), 150 (top), 151, 154, 156 (top), 157, 158 (bottom), 160 (bottom), 165 (top), 167 (top), 170-71, 175, 176 (bottom), 177, 180 (bottom), 181, 182 (top), 185, 186, 187 (top).